Parmenides & Translation

D. M. Spitzer

Parmenides & Translation

Figures of Motion, Figures of Being

PETER LANG

New York, Berlin, Bruxelles, Chennai, Lausanne, Oxford

Library of Congress Cataloging-in-Publication Data
Names: Spitzer, D. M., 1975- author
Title: Parmenides & translation : figures of motion, figures of being / D.M. Spitzer.
Other titles: Parmenides and translation
Description: New York : Peter Lang, 2025. | Includes bibliographical references and index.
Identifiers: LCCN 2025009152 (print) | LCCN 2025009153 (ebook) | ISBN 9781636677750 hardcover | ISBN 9781636677767 ebook | ISBN 9781636677774 epub
Subjects: LCSH: Parmenides. Nature | Parmenides–Translations–History and criticism | Philosophy, Ancient–Translating
Classification: LCC B235.P23 N38366 2025 (print) | LCC B235.P23 (ebook) | DDC 180–dc23/ eng/20250407
LC record available at https://lccn.loc.gov/2025009152
LC ebook record available at https://lccn.loc.gov/2025009153

Bibliographic Information published by the Deutsche Nationalbibliothek
The Deutsche Nationalbibliothek lists this publication in the Deutsche Nationalbibliografie; detailed bibliographic data is available in the internet at http://dnb.d-nb.de.

Cover Image: © Hunchbellgo, Atelier Platen
Cover design by Peter Lang Group AG

ISBN 978-1-63667-775-0 (Print)
E-ISBN 978-1-63667-776-7 (E-PDF)
E-ISBN 978-1-63667-777-4 (E-PUB)
DOI 10.3726/10.3726/b21440

© 2025 Peter Lang Group AG, Lausanne, Switzerland
Published by Peter Lang Publishing Inc., New York, USA

info@peterlang.com

All rights reserved.
All parts of this publication are protected by copyright. Any utilisation outside the strict limits of the copyright law, without the permission of the publisher, is forbidden and liable to prosecution. This applies in particular to reproductions, translations, microfilming, and storage and processing in electronic retrieval systems.

This publication has been peer reviewed.

www.peterlang.com

for Maya, Ani, Luna—enduring three long, tiresome years of unusual and probably mysterious circumstances and learning to thrive in your own ways—
&
for Sara Shiva Spitzer

Contents

Acknowledgements ix

Notes & Abbreviations xiii

Introduction 1

1 Philosophy as Translation: From Singing to Philosophy 15

2 Philosophy through Translation: A Weave of Voice & Text 61

3 Translating Philosophy: Figures of Motion, Figures of Being 89

4 Translation through Philosophy: Translating the Parmenidean Poem 105

5 Translation as Philosophy: Trans-philosophy Towards Possibilities 127

Bibliography 137

Index 151

Acknowledgements

Renewed zeal for this project developed as I prepared a working paper for discussion with the Philosophy in/on translation *Lesekreis*. To the co-organizers of this academic group focused on the manifold entanglements and shared histories of philosophy and translation, Alice Leal (University of the Witwatersrand), and Philip Wilson (University of East Anglia), I send warm gratitude for the opportunity to generate a paper around which critical attention was revolved during the December 8, 2022 session. As a forum for close attention to a diversity of approaches and subjects within the fecund research area of translation and philosophy, Alice and Philip's initiative to form and sustain the *Lesekreis* constitutes a serious contribution to the field beyond reckoning. Thanks as well to the group's members who attended and offered some thoughtful criticism and responses to the paper. Since that session the project for the Philosophy in/on Translation group has taken a different form as a journal article under the title "Trans-philosophy: Translating philosophy on & beyond the Boundaries," aspects of which have been incorporated into *Parmenides & Translation: Figures of Motion, Figures of Being*. All the work of crafting the paper and then revising it for publication has informed my approach to this book and has inspired the work on Parmenides by the sense of fellowship and a widening shared zone for inquiry in/on the confluence of translation and philosophy.

Profound thanks, too, to Paulo Oliveira (Universidade Estadual de Campinas, Universidade de São Paulo) and Mauricio Cardozo (Universidade Federal do Paraná), whose collegiality, friendship, and collaborations on two different projects—as contributors to *Philosophy's Treason: Studies in Philosophy and Translation* and as co-editor and contributor, respectively, to *Transfiction and Bordering Approaches to Theorizing Translation: Essays in Dialogue with the Work of Rosemary*

ACKNOWLEDGEMENTS

Arrojo—have regularly generated depth and a breadth of perspectives to my thinking about the wider topic of philosophy and translation.

Luminous thanks numberless as starlight to Jeffner Allen for consistent support for and confidence in the multifarious practice(s) at work in *Parmenides & Translation* in its first version as a doctoral dissertation produced at Binghamton University in the Department of Comparative Literature. To my committee members Anthony Preus, Rosemary Arrojo, Jeroen Gerrits, and Benjamin Paloff, I send lasting gratitude for their willingness to be involved with this project and their insights and guidance. Also, I extend this gratitude to Luiza Moreira, chair of the Department of Comparative Literature, for her thorough-going support and rich creativity in developing ways for my continued association with the department.

Sections of this work have appeared in different forms in a few places, all of which flow from my doctoral dissertation. An early version of chapter two was presented as "Figures of Being: The Song of Parmenides as Performance" at the 2016 Annual Meeting of the American Comparative Literature Association, Harvard University, March 19, 2016. Special thanks are due to Professor Tony Preus for generous conversation and shared readings of the poem during that spring and to Professor Haun Saussy for encouraging the production of an article-length paper in preparation for the ACLA seminar, "Adaptation as Archaeology and Critique," in which an abbreviated version was given. A subsequent and different version of that study appeared in the journal *Ancient Philosophy*, and I give many thanks to Ronald Polansky, the journal's editor, for his support and confidence in that paper. Aspects of the first chapter of my dissertation provided a framework for an article, under the title "Ghost in the *kerameikos*: Parmenides, Translation, and the Construction of Doctrine," published in *Labyrinth: An International Journal for Philosophy, Value Theory, and Cultural Hermeneutics*. I would like to extend grateful acknowledgements to Dr. Yvanka Raynova, editor of *Labyrinth*, for her appreciation and publication of this piece. Though thoroughly revised, reconsidered, and altered with new insights animated by comments from Peter Lang's reviewers, both versions (the dissertation chapter and the journal article) have been a scaffold for chapter one of *Parmenides & Translation*. Finally, as part of a collection called "Displacements: Poems of Trauma & Migration from Ancient Greek," a version of the opening nine lines of the translation that forms chapter three was published in the inaugural issue of *Ancient Exchanges*. To Adrienne K. Ho Rose, editor of *Ancient Exchanges*, I offer sincere thanks for publishing that selection and, more broadly, for creating and sustaining a venue for multiple approaches to translating ancient texts to thrive. Full entries for these publications appear in the bibliography.

Thanks also to the anonymous reviewers at Peter Lang Verlag, whose comments, in addition to inspiring a reconfiguration and enhancement of the first chapter, provoked many changes to the whole project. To Dr. Philip Dunshea, editor at Lang, I am deeply grateful for excellent support and guidance through the publication process with Lang and, moreover, for genuine confidence in this project.

Finally, thanks numberless as spring blossoms to Gowri Sankar and the production group at Peter Lang Verlag, whose magnificent work on the translation (chapter three) and its complex, difficult arrangements on the page has far exceeded my own expectations. Their care and attention has enabled those pages of this book to enact the Parmenidean poem's figures of motion and figures of being in translation.

Notes & Abbreviations

Notes

Unless otherwise noted, all translations, including those of secondary sources, are mine.

Because the majority of the dates given in this study refer to the period *before the common era*, the abbreviation b.c.e. is withheld. Instead, c.e. will abbreviate *common era* and will appear when needed.

Sources & Texts

For most early Greek thinking including so-called presokratika, editions are announced in the footnotes. For lyric and elegiac poetries, editions are given by editor's surname in the in-text citation.

The texts of the Milesians, Zenon, and Melissos, are primarily from editions of the sources preserving their sayings (e.g. Simplikios). These are coordinated with either the Diels and Kranz or Graham's numbering systems. Accordingly, two references appear for these thinkers in in-text citations: one to the ancient sources themselves, coordinated with a second to the numbering (not the page numbers) in Graham's edition, e.g. (Simpl. *in Phys.* 24.20-1=Graham 9).

Complete entries for these and all editions in use are presented in the bibliography.

Abbreviations

Abbreviations of ancient authors and texts conform to those laid out in *The Oxford Classical Dictionary*, 3rd rev. ed. (OCD^3), edited by Simon Hornblower and Anthony Spawforth, xxix-liv.

A few poets of the *Greek Anthology* cited frequently in this study are assigned abbreviations and are given in the following list, though they are not given abbreviations in OCD^3. These abbreviations appear in in-text citations throughout the book.

NOTES & ABBREVIATIONS

Table 1 Abbreviations of ancient sources & texts

Author	Author abbreviation	Text(s)	Text abbreviation
Agathemeros	Agath.		
Aristoteles	Arist.	*Metaphysics*	*Metaph.*
		Physics	*Ph.*
		Politics	*Pol.*
Diogenes Laertios	Diog. Laert.		
Empedokles	Emp.		
Eusebios	Eus.	*Praeparatio evangelica*	*Praep. evang.*
Herakleitos	Hera.		
Herodotos	Hdt.		
Hesiod	Hes.	*Theogony*	*Theog.*
Hippolytos	Hippol.	*Refutatio omnium haeresium*	*Haer.*
Homer	Hom.	*Iliad*	*Il.*
		Odyssey	*Od.*
Klemens (Clement of Alexandria)	Clem. Al.	*Stromateis*	*Strom.*
Melissos	Mel.		
Mimnermos	Mimn.		
Parmenides	Parm.		
Phokylides	Phokyl.		
Platon	Pl.	*Ion*	*Ion*
		Meno	*Meno*
		Parmenides	*Prm.*
		Phaidros	*Phdr.*
		Symposion	*Symp.*
		Theaitetos	*Tht.*
Plutarkhos	Plut.	*De Pythiae oraculis*	*De Pyth. or.*
		Moralia	*Mor.*
		Quomodo adulescens poetas audire debeat	*Quomodo adul.*
Proklos	Procl.	*In Platonis Cratylum commentarii*	*In Crat.*
		In Platonis Timaeum commentarii	*In Ti.*
Pseudo-Plutarkhos	Ps. Plut.	*Placita Philosophorum*	*Plac.*
Sextos Empirikos	Sext. Emp.		*Math.*
Simplikios	Simpl.	*In Aristotelis de Physica commentarii*	*in Phys.*
Xenophanes	Xenoph.		

Introduction

...ὁδοὶ μοῦναι (Parm. 2.2)[1]
—pathways only

Multiple pathways open for engaging the assemblage of dactylic hexameter lines attributed to a shadowy figure of the late sixth and early fifth centuries. *Parmenides & Translation* follows three intersecting ways of and for inquiry. Along one way, the investigation contours the movements of early Greek thinking from *singing*—a way of opening towards memory and others in a transformative experience—to *philosophy* and its translational engagement with earlier thinkers. What translational actions operate within and propel early Greek thinking as singing? In its later and more determinate stage in the Classical period, what translational mode does *philosophy* enact that reduces the sinuous movements and dense, resonant language(s) of archaic Greek thinking into statements of fixed doctrine? Another pathway follows the entanglements of oral and written dimensions of the Archaic Greek period: how do the conditions of oralcy interact with the written text to generate a tense weave of meanings that destabilizes doctrinal interpretations? Passing through and converging with these pathways, a third avenue for interpretation takes place as translation in a broad sense: as an activity that includes interpretation and recomposition (translating), as an indissoluble feature of the composition, and as a theme within the composition itself.

Parmenides & the Parmenidean Poem

One hundred forty-six or so lines of dactylic hexameter presented as twenty "fragments" form the remains of the poem attributed to a man named *Parmenides*. Even Diogenes Laertios, the third-century c.e. doxographer, has little to offer towards a biographical account of Parmenides, son of Pyres. Parmenides is said to have associated with the exiled Kolophonian thinker Xenophanes, but to have learned from a Pythagorean named Ameinias and, according to Theophrastos (ca. 370-288), from the Milesian Anaximandros. Possibly a lawgiver, Parmenides dwelled in the polis Hyele, better known by the later version

---

1 Except where noted, all references to the Parmenidean poem are to the text presented in David Gallop, ed. and trans. *Parmenides of Elea: Fragments: A Text and Translation with an Introduction* (Toronto: University of Toronto Press, 1984). N.b. I have replaced omega-iota [ωι] combinations printed in Gallop's edition with omega with iota-subscripts [ῳ].

of its name, Elea (Diog. Laert. IX.3.21-23). From a stone inscription discovered at Hyele in 1962, Parmenides has been identified as a healer-priest of Apollo [ΠΑ<ΡΜ>ΕΝΕΙΔΗΣΠΥΡΗΤΟΣ / ΟΥΛΙΑΔΕΣΦΥΣΙΚΟΣ].[2]

Parmenides & Translation operates in the gap between the person Parmenides and the assemblage of dactylic hexameters gathered under this name. Whoever the historical person named Parmenides may have been in the newly formed diasporic community of Hyele on the western shore of the Italian peninsula at some moment in the transition from the sixth to fifth centuries, no lines of textual transmission flow independently of later authors who paraphrase, summarize, and present select quotations from an otherwise absent source. Instead, as a character Parmenides emerges in the fourth-century dialogues of Platon and later as a source of a doctrine in Aristoteles' discourses; both these philosophers quote sparsely and give little attention to the language of what they do quote—a language that seeps into the historical record over many centuries. The text of the first major fragment, for instance, does not appear until the work of Sextos Empirikos (ca. second century c.e.), who reads its narrative allegorically as a movement away from sense towards reason. Similarly, the grand passage now known as fragment eight remains silent for over a thousand years after Parmenides unto the time of Simplikios (sixth century c.e.), finally emerging from its silence in the context of philosophic traditions developed well after the archaic Greek period. In an important sense, the composition has existed only as *translation*, as a text always without an original, as surviving in and as others' work and their interpretive horizons.

Passing through these appearances in the texts of later philosophers can be felt the interest in assigning views to an individual author. Aristoteles tends to eschew direct quotation of the earlier thinkers, including Parmenides, instead giving prosaic statements of doctrine abstracted from the texts and bound to an earlier thinker's name. In the dialogue *Parmenides*, Platon stages the alignment of author and text, though in a complex manner typical of Platonic writings. Where Parmenides might have been given the role of answering for the text attributed to him, Platon's dialogue instead ushers a proxy in the figure of Zenon and texts attributed to him, which are understood as advancing the same thing [ταὐτόν (Pl. *Prm.* 128a.6)] as the Parmenidean poem—and then Parmenides becomes involved in the dialogue with Sokrates set in motion by the writings of Zenon, effectively answering for another. The phrase and the

---

2 Paul Ebner, "L'errore di Alalia e la colonnizzazione di Velia nel response delfico," *Rassegna Storica Salernitana* 23, no. 1-4 (1962): fig. 6. The PM in chevrons are my additions; the surface of the stele in that place has been damaged.

scene forecast the theme of αὐτό as same-not-same through Sokrates' statement that both Parmenides and Zenon appear to say nothing of the same things [μηδὲν τῶν αὐτῶν], while saying nearly the same things [σχεδόν...ταὐτά (Pl. Prm. 128b.3-6)]. In the dramatic arrangement, the dialogue cleverly suggests that the call for someone to take responsibility for a text addresses itself beyond a single author and to a wider area, a community of readers-auditors ready to take up the thinking of another for themselves. After all, if he had a text of the poem attributed to Parmenides, Platon the literary artist likely would not have failed to notice that Θεά [Thea, Goddess], and not the κοῦρος [kouros, the young man who is narrator and traveler in the poem], speaks directly, with the kouros instructed to take into his care [κόμισαι] Thea's speech. The discourse seems to involve a kind of recollection (in the form of narration) so as to provoke returns to beginnings for thinking: the pulsing way of disclosure in its steady opening-closing movements [ἡμὲν ἀληθείης εὐπειθέος ἀτρεμὲς ἦτορ] and the ways of appearing in their multiplicity [ἠδὲ βροτῶν δόξας (Parm. 1.29-30)] and, perhaps most profoundly, the way(s) these two paths converge and how the poetry—far from posing an "obstacle to be removed"—generates further and significant insights on these paths and their convergence(s).[3] Such a return seems further to involve a directedness towards what is different and other: in the way along which the kouros is transported [φερόμην (Parm. 1.3-4)]—later described as far from ordinary paths (Parm. 1.27); in the Ἡλιάδες [Heliades Daughters of the divine Sun] and their guidance towards a mysterious gate full of αἰθήρ [aither, bright atmospheric element (Parm. 1.8-13)]; in the multifarious and multidimensional Thea and her opening statements on the suitability [θέμις τε δίκη τε χρεώ] of inquiring [πυθέσθαι] in the direction of totality, which is to say, in multiple directions (Parm. 1.28-32). In each case a radical openness and a way of being guided by others—or, the confluent turbine of selves-others in the task of thinking—fills the poem's whole atmosphere, both of which often resonate in Platonic dialogues.[4]

To keep visible the gap between a (putative) single identifiable author of the text and the text as a work in translation (in multiple senses), the phrase

---

3 Albert Keith Whitaker, *Plato's Parmenides* (Newburyport, MA: Focus, 1996), 8.
4 With their multiple speakers and ideas, the dialogues themselves obscure an easy alignment of author and view, perhaps by their very form opening the area between author and text for auditors-readers to inhabit the possibilities offered by the text. Just as the texts show multiple figures interacting, listening, speaking, and in this way illuminate the multi-directional paths and sources of thinking never fully isolable and identified with an individual, so they may be urging a similar range of sources for the texts as texts, widening beyond an attributable single author and that author's alleged view.

Parmenidean poem draws attention to the already-translated and translational character of the work,[5] its formation through and its staging of thinking's arrival and the mutual effort made to prepare for and welcome such an arrival. Just as the epic poems the *Iliad* and *Odyssey* and the hymns can meaningfully be understood as *Homeric* because they are shaped at least as much by tradition as by a single poet, the assemblage of texts attributed to Parmenides—ever-shaped by and passed through the hands of interpreters, translators, performers—can be meaningfully understood as *Parmenidean*. In both cases, nothing prior or independent of the traditions offers a comparison or foundation according to which the transmitted texts might be measured. Rather, they are as contour drawings whose lines themselves compose the shape they describe, a shape that emerges only in, through, and *as* the contour(-ing lines).[6] In the case of the Parmenidean poem, the selection and interpretation of the lines (the dactylic hexameters) *shape* the poem in a strong sense that they *compose* or *make* the poem.

This way of shaping, composing, making does not mean to imply that the passages quoted in later sources are in any sense forgeries invented by the later authors, but that the specific lines quoted occur in the form or shape of the interpretation developed by the author quoting them. When Sextos Empirikos, for instance, intends to illustrate a point about knowledge, he turns from Xenophanes, some of whose lines Sextos has quoted in the shape of a doxastic position [δοξαστήν (Sext. Emp. *Math.* VII.110)], to Parmenides. The passage Sextos adduces, comprising the first thirty lines of what is now the first fragment plus additional text from what are now considered other fragments,[7] contours an epistemic position [ἐπιστημονικόν (Sext. Emp. *Math.* VII.111)], but only after it has undergone what Cassin has called "radical translation."[8] In this translation, the lines from the Parmenidean poem take on new shapes as a tiered passage from sensory to intellective ways of knowing, culminating not only in what Sextos terms both the "intelligence [τὴν διάνοιαν] which holds safe the apprehension of things" and the "cognitive reason" [ἐπιστημονικὸν λόγον] distinct

---

5   The phrase *Parmenidean poem* is inspired by Valentine's use. Joanna Valentine, "The Archaeology of Parmenides: Philosophy, Poetry and Ritual in Fifth-Century Campania" (PhD. diss., University of Southern California, 2011), 7 et passim.
6   This figure of contouring draws on Sallis's thinking of *profiling* and *imaging* as the constitutive action of images' showing-concealing more primary than an image understood as a "quasi-thing." John Sallis, "Image and Phenomenon," *Research in Phenomenology* 5, no. 1 (1975): 74-5.
7   Sextos' quotation adds six lines and a single word from what are now the seventh and eighth fragments (Parm. 7.2-6; 8.1 + λείπεται from 8.2).
8   Barbara Cassin, *Parménide: Sur la nature ou sur l'étant: La langue de l'être?* (Paris: Éditions du Seuil, 1998), 15.

from sense and the measure [κανόνα] of truth (Sext. Emp. *Math.* VII.113-115),[9] but also in the establishment of Parmenides as both the "first true philosopher" and the "first rationalist."[10]

Sextos' view onto the poem comes to pass through the aperture of schools and a robust history of philosophy as a discipline that antedates the late archaic Greek thinkers, so that already in the ancient world a "misfit" has developed between the practice(s) of philosophy and the Parmenidean poem.[11] A composition of dactylic hexameters from the late sixth or early fifth century, the Parmenidean poem surfaces during a period when philosophy as an area is at most still forming, though not yet forming under the name *philosophy*. Neither Parmenides nor the contemporary archaic Greek thinkers identify themselves as philosophers or what they do as philosophy, though a narrative reported long after the Greek Archaic period by Cicero (106-43) associates the term with Pythagoras. In response to the Phliasian ruler Leon as to what art he practices, Pythagoras states that he knows no art, but that he is a *philosopher*, which he then characterizes by way of a simile that links life to attending a festival: some pursue renown, some riches, while others—the best sort—observe with careful attention the nature of things [*rerum naturam studiose intuerentur* (Cic. *Tusc.* V.9)]. In another version of the narrative Diogenes Laertios attributes to Sosikrates (ca. second century), Pythagoras voices a belonging of philosophers to ἀλήθεια [typically translated: truth (Diog. Laert. VIII.1.8)], a belonging that, together with the festival simile and the philosophers-as-witnesses, characterizes the practice of philosophy as a discernment of meanings, which overlaps, on Burch's reading, with the activity of poets[12]—and translators, one might add. The term itself surfaces in a Herakleitean phrase declaring that philosophers [φιλοσόφους] are inquirers of a great many areas [μάλα πολλῶν ἵστορας (Hera. 35)].[13] Since elsewhere in Herakleitean thinking the practice of inquiry [ἱστορία] bears a rather negative

---

9 Translation is from R. G. Bury, trans. *Sextus Empiricus*, vol. 2, *Against the Logicians* (Cambridge: Harvard University Press, 1935), 61, 63, respectively.
10 Cassin, *Parménide: Sur la nature ou sur l'étant*, 17.
11 In terms of literacy and its assumptions, Wilkinson brings attention to the "misfit" of contemporary and ancient practices and ideas about what constitutes philosophy. Lisa Atwood Wilkinson, *Parmenides and To Eon: Reconsidering Muthos and Logos* (New York: Continuum, 2009), 4.
12 Robert Burch, "Thinking Between Philosophy and Poetry," general introduction to *Between Philosophy and Poetry: Writing, Rhythm, History*, eds. Robert Burch and Massimo Verdicchio (New York: Continuum, 2002), 3-4.
13 All texts of Herakleitean thinking are from T. M. Robinson, ed. and trans. *Heraclitus: Fragments: A Text and Translation with a Commentary* (Toronto: University of Toronto Press, 1987).

valence (Hera. 129), and Pythagoras, along with Xenophanes, elicits scorn for the *polymathia* that seems to flow from inquiry but not to result in attentive-awareness [νόον (Hera. 40)], it may be that Herakleitos, rather than identifying his activities with the ranging inquiries gathered in the term philosophy, intends to open a distance between his own tasks and the practice of philosophy.

The term *philosopher* may occur in early Greek literature, but the sources are obscured by their historical positions *after* the term had crystallized. For the most part, *philosophy* is applied retrospectively, and rarely in the Archaic and early Classical periods, to the early Greek thinkers and the "dense and brilliant tableaux of investigations, debates, and practical norms" that made up their activities.[14] Whatever the range of such activities includes, in the case of the Parmenidean poem and its rich tapestry of image, scene, character, not to mention the performance elements that typically lie dormant when the poem is interpreted as merely a vehicle for logical reasoning, *philosophy* only suitably designates the poem if the term remains open to important dimensions beyond this or any disciplinary enclosure—open, that is, to being ever-more than itself, ever in the plural. Moreover, Parmenidean and other early Greek thinking might summon a movement away even from coordinating multiple disciplines—philosophy, poetry, philology—through interdisciplinarity and towards something else, some approach(-es) that take seriously the bond joining philosophy and translation, something that might be termed *trans-philosophy*, a movement through and across a range of disciplines that, in such motion, transforms disciplines and their subjects in multiple ways.[15] The inventive spirit of philosophy as "a fundamentally *creative endeavor*" and as "*an expressive, evocative, imaginative, and visionary art,*"[16] its capacity to open itself and enact hospitable ways of being towards the different, calls for both an alertness to the ways the Parmenidean poem does more than advancing arguments and delivering doctrines and a pursuit of increasingly expansive ways to access and engage with the abundance of early Greek thinking. Even at its putative beginning, philosophy not only "exceeds the boundaries of what is recognized as philosophy,"[17] but also

---

14 Christopher Moore, "Anaxagoras, Socrates, and the history of 'philosophy,'" *CHS Research Bulletin* 4, no. 2 (2016): 1§1. http://nrs.harvard.edu/urn-3:hlnc.essay:MooreC.Anaxagoras_Socrates_and_the_History_of_Philosophy.2016.
15 See Spitzer, "Trans-philosophy Translating philosophy on & beyond the boundaries," *The Journal of Speculative Philosophy* 37, no. 3 (2023): 574-5.
16 John J. Stuhr, "Lost, Looking Around, and Looking Ahead," *The Journal of Speculative Philosophy* 32, no. 1 (2018): 41. Emphasis is in the original.
17 Robert Bernasconi, "Almost Always More Than Philosophy Proper," *Research in Phenomenology* 30, no. 1 (2000): 5.

performs a way of thinking that discloses moments of boundaries self-opening, e-merging, shimmering.[18]

The phrase *Parmenidean poem* works as a reminder of the always-in-translation character of the text. Further, the phrase intends to prompt an effort to suspend some critical-interpretive presuppositions borne by the name itself, *Parmenides*, and its long-standing location within a discipline of philosophy in order to make room for a rethinking of the text along other pathways. Referring to the poem throughout this book as both the *Parmenidean poem* and the *Parmenidean Song of Being* seeks to call attention to the expansiveness of the poem, its span beyond the grasp of an author as its "symbolic" aspect opens a multiplicity of interpretive possibilities.[19] Already by the time of its earliest reception the poem undergoes *translation* in an ample sense: inventive re-creation by way of close engagement, such as that by Zenon and Melissos, identified in the diadokhic tradition as pupils of Parmenides (Diog. Laert. IX.5.25; IX.4.24, respectively). Similarly, the opening scene of the poem itself discloses thinking as a *reception*, an *interaction*, and an activity of *listening* in the grasp of the foreign (Parm. 1.22-23, 2.1)—said otherwise, as *translation*.

Translation

Pathways into the Parmenidean poem open through and as translation.[20] Throughout, the study illustrates the cycle along which turns the complementary and ever-joined pair of philosophy and translation, showing both "that translation is inherently philosophical," as Foran has put it, "and that philosophy

---

18 This term, active throughout *Parmenides & Translation*, works from Maly's articulations. Kenneth Maly, "Echoes at the Edge: Shimmering Images in *Delimitations*," in *The Path of Archaic Thinking: Unfolding the Work of John Sallis*, ed. Kenneth Maly (Albany: SUNY Press, 1995), 123-4.

19 Where Mackenzie stresses the authorial intent of Parmenides and other early Greek thinkers, the important distinction between symbolic and allegorical releases the poem from an authorial grasp. Further, the poem's imagery seems to recommend thinking as something more like striving-reception than as the deliberate intentions of a single author. Tom Mackenzie, *Poetry and Poetics in the Presocratic Philosophers: Reading Xenophanes, Parmenides and Empedocles as Literature* (Cambridge: Cambridge University Press, 2021), 11-15, 97-8.

20 For a broader discussion of the ways translation is a condition for not just the Parmenidean poem or early Greek thinking, but the study of and work on ancient philosophy and literatures more generally, see Spitzer, "SAGP: Studies and Society," in *Studies in Ancient Greek Philosophy in Honor of Professor Anthony Preus*, ed. D. M. Spitzer (New York: Routledge, 2023), 8-10.

not only demands, but also itself engages in, a type of translation."[21] In light of the inseparability of translation and critical engagement with the Parmenidean poem, throughout this study translation itself is thematized and forms the inquiry's main approach. Drawing on resources from the trans-disciplinary field of translation studies to engage with philosophic and literary texts from the ancient and modern periods, *Parmenides & Translation* develops a history of philosophy and translation that both characterizes early philosophical activity and has transformed a narrative poem in dactylic hexameter into a vehicle for a doctrine of being. Approaching the poem through and as translation raises into view some ways in which the textualization of the poem—its reception as primarily a text of philosophy to be read—reinforces the doctrinal character of the poem established by the early translational engagements with it.

Translation already conditions any reception of the poem, in several senses: in the ample sense through which the opening chapter develops, translation names the historical processes of interpretation, reception, and emplacement within disciplinary boundaries (in this case, philosophy); in the more conventional sense of interlingual translation through which access to the poem always begins (because ancient Greek requires formal instruction based on translation *into* contemporary languages); in the related sense of translation as conjoined with interpretation, so that all editions, presentations, and interlingual translations of the poem already bear the stamp of the editor-translator's perspective. From this wide span of translation *Parmenides & Translation* opens a range of possibilities encompassed in a threefold directory:

- *reception*, understood as taking-up of thinking and a giving voice to experience, where transformations in the encounters of early Greek thinking develops into the ascription of doctrine by later Greeks and the subsequent history of philosophy
- *adaptation* from an orally performed poem to a primarily written text and presentation in such a way that the oral dynamics are silenced
- *alteration* of language(s), in the forms of inter- and intralinguistic activities (even within a single text)

This broad schema of translation bestows the guiding trope and organizing arrangement for *Parmenides & Translation*. Accordingly, translation works in various ways to interpret the Parmenidean poem and other texts.

---

21 Lisa Foran, "What is the Relation between Translation and Philosophy?," introduction to *Translation and Philosophy*, ed. Lisa Foran (Bern: Peter Lang, 2012), 11.

Translational Actions & Translative Gestures In the first chapter attention to translation directs the inquiry towards an articulation of a history of early Greek thinking in terms of *translational actions* and *translative gestures*.[22] Translational actions include the three-part schema of translation articulated by Jakobson (intralingual, interlingual, intersemiotic),[23] but also processes like adaptation and interpretation. In the Parmenidean poem as well as texts of Zenoan and Melissoan thinking, translational actions come to light as intralingual translations (for instance, see below, pp. 48-50, on the shiftings between forms of εἶναι and πελ- in the Parmenidean poem) and as instances of restatement and repetition towards differentiation (as in the links joining ἀνάγκη-αὐτό-ἐόν across so-called Eleatic thinking, below pp. 33-35). Among thinkers from the Milesians to Zenon and Melissos, translational actions disclose the belonging-together of thinking and translation, ways in which experience and articulation take place as translational. Through the engagements with early Greek thinking that seek to locate the Parmenidean poem and other early Greek thinking into the disciplinary range of philosophy, translational actions (initially intralingual in texts of Platon and Aristoteles) increasingly take place as interpretations that transform a narrative poem in dactylic hexameter into a vehicle for a doctrine of being, the origin and emblem of metaphysics, a doctrine clothed in a disposable poetic garment or, as Plutarkhos (ca. 50-120 c.e.) phrased it, as a vehicle [ὄχημα] adopted so as to flee from pedestrian, ordinary language [πεζόν (Plut. *Quomodo adul.* 16c-d=DK 28 A15)].

As a complementary interpretive aperture, *translative gestures* bring forward dimensions of texts that point in the direction of translation in its broad scope. In a way, translative gestures take their bearings from the critical practice known as *transfiction*. Looking to fictional scenes, passages, and texts in which translation figures explicitly, centrally or peripherally, transfiction identifies and articulates insights or assumptions concerning translation, translators, and translated works. As transfiction locates diverse sites for an expansion and elaboration of theoretical discourse on translation "beyond," as Arrojo has put it, "the limits of what we conventionally call theory or philosophy," boundaries between fiction and

---

22 These terms are articulated and put to use in Spitzer, "Past the Fire's Edge: Figures of Translation from Herodotos 1.86," *Translation Review* 99, no. 1 (2017): 15-25, and in "Detours of Babel," in *Transfiction and Bordering Approaches to Theorizing Translation: Essays in Dialogue with the Work of Rosemary Arrojo*, ed. D. M. Spitzer and Paulo Oliveira (New York: Routledge, 2023), 79-93.

23 Roman Jakobson, "On Linguistic Aspects of Translation," in *The Translation Studies Reader*, 3rd ed., ed. Lawrence Venuti (New York: Routledge, 2012), 127.

non-fiction, between literature and theory, fray.[24] *Parmenides & Translation* centers on a poem that, although retrospectively positioned within the field of philosophy, antedates such boundaries and limits while intimately and thoroughly concerning itself with boundaries and limits: the Parmenidean poem thematizes boundaries and limits, both as sites of passing-through and transgressing (*trans-lation*)—as in the opening scene's energetic movement towards and through the gates of the paths of Night and Day (Parm. 1.1-21)—and as discursively established in-as ontological strictures (e.g. Parm. 7.2; 8.14-15). Given the poem's narrative stress on transgressing and passing-through, importantly made explicit in the final statement of Thea's opening address (Parm. 1.31-2),[25] such limitations double as invitations or provocations to think (translatively, translationally) *through* and *across* those limits.[26] Movement and travel operate as translative gestures, evoking the theme of translation in its broad sense of transformation. Similarly, scenes of transformation, alteration, relocation, when unfolded within an atmosphere of translation, gather within the unclosed circumference of translative gestures. In Empedoklean thinking thematization of transformation as describing the ownmost motions of thinking a living totality manifests as translative gestures so thoroughly that "in a sense, Empedokles names and is a philosophy of translation."[27]

Translating The subtitle of this book comes from the new translation of the Parmenidean poem that forms the third chapter: *Figures of Motion, Figures of Being*. This translation attempts to unmoor the thinking from conventional interpretive bonds. In so doing, the translation offers possibilities, inchoate lines of thinking intimated as directions for inquiry, intent on setting the text in motion. Most vividly on the page, this orientation manifests as a dynamic interplay of text and white-space that traces diverse and multiple figures as the poem, as its very speaking, its translating language. In the later movements of the poem as *Figures of Motion* (the sections translating fragments 9-19), the figures settle into a regularity that nevertheless sustains the dynamics of text—blank, is—is-not, presence—absence, and as the Parmenidean poem offers it, light—night. Yet,

---

24 Rosemary Arrojo, "The Power of Fiction as Theory: Some exemplary lessons on translation from Borges' stories," in *Transfiction: research into the realities of translation fiction*, ed. Klaus Kaindl and Karlheinz Spitzl (Amsterdam: John Benjamins, 2014), 46.
25 See below, pp. 79-80 and 114-18, for further discussion of this moment in the poem.
26 Wilkinson gives attention to this doubled injunction-provocation. Wilkinson, *Parmenides and To Eon*, 100-3.
27 Spitzer, "Translator's Note" to "Displacements: Poems of Trauma & Migration from Ancient Greek," *Ancient Exchanges* 1, no. 1 (2020), https://exchanges.uiowa.edu/ancient/issues/departures/displacements/.

the very regularity puts pressure on the reader's involvements in the poem, in the work of meaning-making, the translating:

now then	*radiance*	*& night*
totality		*names*
those	*other*	*powers*
woven		*many others*
everything	*full*	*singular being*
is		*together*
of radiance	*of invisible*	*darkness*
together		*in each*

(Parm. 9.1-3)

The translation's figures of motion open multiple possibilities for reading the text, where vertical and horizontal arrangements confronts readers with their choices to determine meanings or let them drift and hover. To read those lines in any one direction is not to foreclose all others, but to turn in a direction that momentarily precludes turning in another while sustaining the other directions for later and other turnings; but it is also to commit (at least on each reading) to a specific sequence of interactions and not another, a sequence that will itself be an opportunity for meaning.

In harmony with Lombardo's translational practice with the Parmenidean poem, this translation seeks to "radicalize" the text towards the reverberations between text and translator that animate the translation.[28] Through an experience of these reverberations translation wrights-writes an-other poem, a poem of the moment of its composition in the turbine, non-linear temporal churn and helical circularity. If the translation of *Figures of Motion* seems anachronistic, it is no more so than any other translation, nor again of logical analysis or any other interpretive approach: further, all engagements with the ancient poem conjoin temporality, disrupt the culturally specific linearity of time that governs the thought of anachronism. The *radicalization* at work in *Figures of Motion, Figures of Being* assumes a different complexion in the fourth chapter's poetics of translation organized in three dimensions of translating: *archaeologics, daimonologics, erotics*. Of these, archaeologics evokes another sense of *radicalization*, activating

---

28 Stanley Lombardo, *Parmenides and Empedocles: The Fragments in Verse Translation* (San Francisco: Grey Fox Press, 1982), 2.

linguistic *radices* not as roots, but as *rhizomes*—recalling Empedoklean thinking once more.

Singing

Parmenides & Translation emerges from a commitment to sustaining both the oral and the written aspects of the poem, approaching them as an intricately woven fabric of meanings in tension. On this line of inquiry, Wilkinson's study of the Parmenidean poem has opened a horizon of interpretive possibilities by close attention to the ways epic-language works in archaic Greek culture and attending to the reconfiguration of the enmeshment of *logos* and *mythos* in an archaic experience of non-representational language as not about events, but as event(s), happening(s).[29] Because much interpretation of the poem attributed to Parmenides advances along just one thread (the textual), the vivid interaction of oralcy with written text does not typically surface. As a weave of oral and written dimensions, tensions build within whatever statements or declarations the poem's speaking character, Thea, makes as both stabilized on the page, reinforced by the writing itself, and steadily passing in the motion(s) of the poem. Throughout the book, the term *singing* describes (among other things) the latter dimension: the moving of language in the cadences of the poem and in the passing motion(s) of the performance. Such moving, when raised into awareness, adds meanings that do not seem to reinforce the poem's statements, but instead energize it with the experience of change, origination, cessation—all of which the poem has been understood to disavow, at least in connection with τὸ ἐόν [typically translated: *being*].

Even if the Parmenidean poem has always existed as a written text, that text promotes and features oralcy and, what is more, that text has prompted oral performance in multiple ways. Oral performance need not imply some kind of ritualized chant or magical speech sounded in a remote past (though it does not preclude these), nor does it only encompass performance contexts from a dimly understood Greek Archaic age at the transition of oralcy towards literacy. The range of oralcy and oral performance also includes the reading and study of the text *as a text*. Reading aloud in an educational setting forms part of the work of interpretation and engagement, reading a conference paper treating the poem, reading as preparation for a translation,[30] all belong to the region of literacy, such that the two entwine, are woven. Writing and texts form part

---

29 Wilkinson, *Parmenides and* To Eon, 81-3.
30 Lucio Angelo Privitello, "Approaching the Parmenidean Sublime—Part II," *Epoché* 25, no. 1 (2020): 103.

of a weave through which oralcy runs and from which it cannot be removed without altering the entire fabric. Put differently from within the network of figures animating the poem, the two form a circle, ever-turning along the shared and differentiated arc (Parm. 5).

Singing also names a mode of thinking active throughout early Greek thinking, the region spanning Homeric and Hesiodic poetries to Zenon and Melissos and the area investigated in the first chapter. An opening of awareness and intention in the direction of Memory-Mousa(i), singing takes place as an experience of and active engagement with the flow of thinking that courses already in the language and imaginary termed in *Parmenides & Translation* the *already-there*. This experience and engagement with the already-there, a region or horizontal expanse in- and from-which thinking moves, unfolds as a translational action.

*

* *

Because the Parmenidean poem predates the formation of philosophy as a distinct practice and area of inquiry, might interpretation gain from variegated ways of thinking and writing about the texts of early Greek thinking? For *Parmenides & Translation*, the way of writing intends to evoke some of the Parmenidean poem's poetic dimensions inseparable and pulsing with meanings—the richness of imagery, the juxtapositions of language in taut or evocative phrases, the occasionally strained wording as language presses for fresh terms and phrases to generate and re-activate meanings dormant or previously unsounded. One of the more vivid examples of this strain sounds in the opening chapter through the motifs of elements and singing. This literary character may strike some readers as inappropriate to a book engaged with ancient philosophy, yet philosophy's inextricable bind with literature and, moreover, the inalienable literariness of its canon—from the early Greeks and Plato, through Lucretius, Augustine, Descartes,[31] Nietzsche, Kierkegaard, to Heidegger, Deleuze and Guattari, Glissant, Lugones, Anzaldúa, to name only a few—recommends an openness towards and willingness to engage with diverse approaches, none of which has a claim to the proper mode, or a pure, neutral, straightforwardly *philosophic* mode.

---

31 René Descartes, rationalist, scientist, may seem to be out of place in such a list, but see Kyoo Lee's insightful reading of Descartes by way of four figures out of *Meditations*. Kyoo Lee, *Reading Descartes Otherwise: Blind, Mad, Dreamy, and Bad* (New York: Fordham University Press, 2012).

If the phrasings and insights in *Parmenides & Translation* work at times more along lines of suggestion and gesture than argumentation and demonstration, it is in part because the atmosphere of the Parmenidean poem itself works in just such a way, as if urging a way of speaking and thinking that moves—at times rapidly, at times gradually—according to the pliability and suppleness of images: forming into articulation, shimmering under scrutiny, permeable at the edges and boundaries. Attempting to hear the Parmenidean poem involves following the pathways indicated by Thea, the way of figures, images, of many signs [σήματ…πολλὰ μάλ᾽ (Parm. 8.2-3)]. The shadow-casting composition of narration (memory) and poetry—the artificiality of this mode of speaking, its *madness* glistening aura-like as the very surface of the poem, which has meaning-bearing capacities and roles not merely according to the opposition of appearance and reality[32]—shimmers through everything spoken by Thea.

Straining to find a place within the range and zone of—and in excess of—what is now considered *poetry* within which the Parmenidean poem speaks works to activate some of the tensions and meaning-provoking dimensions of poetry, while it also opens up another area for the poem to sound, not altogether apart from the region of logical argumentation, but in a way that keeps open possibilities for interpretation that exceed that region. If the poem is not altogether poetry, it would also be fair to say that the poem likewise is not altogether philosophy, if by philosophy is meant a primary concern for argumentation and demonstration. Since much of the poem's reception has involved translating the poetry of the Parmenidean poem to prosaic statements, assertions, or doctrines in an attempt to clear aside the poetic aspects that obstruct the view onto clear and distinct propositions, *Parmenides & Translation* may lean, as a counter-balance, towards the side of the gestural, the figural—which is to say, the poetic that invokes and reverberates with the voice of the foreign.[33] This would be to let the tremors in the poem resound and (re-)shape themselves once again into ever-renewing figures of motion, figures of being that open a unity (such as philosophy when thought as a stable and monolithic practice) into the multiplicity teeming within and animating its movements, its figures of translation.

---

32 Spitzer, "Trans-philosophy," 576-7 and n. 22.
33 As in Heidegger's thought that poetic language infuses the familiar with foreign (*das Fremde*). Martin Heidegger, "…Dichterisch wohnet der Mensch…," in *Vorträge und Aufsätze* (Stuttgart: Klett-Cotta, 1954), 194.

CHAPTER 1

Philosophy as Translation

From Singing to Philosophy

> εἰ δ' ἄγ' ἐγὼν ἐρέω, κόμισαι δὲ σὺ μῦθον ἀκούσας (Parm. 2.1-2)
> Come, I will speak, and you, hearkening
> to a traditionally arranged
> speech, gather it into your care[34]

Two paths open for the translation—the transmission, the transportation, the tradition—of the Parmenidean poem through the gates of the twilight land, the west. Along the first sounds the voice in song, in singing, and this is the path of water and devouring fire, of elemental translation. This pathway sings in the dactylic hexameter of an already ancient tradition by the sixth century, binds thinking to the meaning-rich patterned motions of rhythmic speech. The transition from one to the other pathway spreads through the prose of Zenon and Melissos, a prose that, like Milesian thinking, in its differing-through-translation, joins itself to some of the energies and resonances of the hexameter tradition, the way of singing. A second way unfurls as a mode of abstraction—of pulling-apart—what in the first path, the pathway of singing, had been bound, fused, entwined as notes of a harmony. Creating a seam along the poetic and philosophic, the second path severs the two and concentrates attention on the latter as constituted by stable, fixed ideas gathered from rational argumentation, in competition with one another, and attributable to individual named thinkers.[35] The way of the second path already takes place as a translational task of philosophy, perhaps its most characteristic task: severing form and content, promoting content, asserting this very separability and an associated availability of a purely intellectual content to a range of material expressions or vehicles aimed at concise articulation. For the Parmenidean poem, this second pathway results in the construction of a doctrine independent of the sinuous language of hexameter thinking and its voice: Thea.

---

34 This translation first appeared in Spitzer, "SAGP: Studies and Society," 12.
35 Drawing on Wians's initial differentiation of *logos* from *muthos*. William Wians, "From *Logos* and *Muthos* to…," introduction to *Logoi and Muthoi: Further Essays in Greek Philosophy and Literature*, ed. William Robert Wians (Albany: SUNY Press, 2019), 11.

CHAPTER 1

Water to Fire

One pathway begins a song of water on the scudding tide of dactylic hexameters, ceaselessly translating. Possibly, Thales of Miletos voiced the song of beginning in-as-from water in the patterned speech of Homeric meter (Plut. *De Pyth. or.* 402f; Diog. Laert. I.1.34-5). Thales' Milesian associates, however, do not seem to take up the hexameter song, turning instead to a mode of speaking and thinking that embeds images and resonances of the ancient tradition of hexameter singing into the unmetered speech of prose. In the reckoning of Simplikios, Anaximandrean thinking occurred in "rather poetic terms" [ποιητικωτέροις οὕτως ὀνόμασιν (Simpl. *in Phys.* 24.20-1=Graham 9)], while Anaximenean thinking followed this line in figures and similes, which is to say, poetic features: earth is shaped like a table [τραπεζοειδῆ (Ps. Plut. *Plac.* III.10.3=Graham 14)]; earth and clouds assume their shapes by a process like felting [πιλουμένου (Euseb. *Praep. evang.* I.8.3=Graham 11); κατὰ τὴν πίλησιν (Hippol. *Haer.* I.7=Graham 12)]. Simile-rich poetic speech already translates in the jointures disclosed through its terms and its linkages that span and preserve difference in spanning.

New meanings emerge from the proximate-distancing translational action of simile, as the first simile of the *Iliad* joins in its fleet passing the luminous deity Apollo with a seeming opposite, the ancient and profound Night. Having been summoned through the prayer of Khryse, the god descends:

> ...Luminous Apollo [Φοῖβος Ἀπόλλων] heard the other,
> and, his heart enraged, down he strode keeping his bow
>   and quiver on his shoulders,
> along the peaks of Olympos,
> and the arrows rattled on his shoulders
> from his fury-rush, *and he approached like Night*.
> Far from the ships sat he, and his arrow flew,
> while from the silver bow
>   a dread noise rose (Hom. *Il.* I.43-9)

The bright youth of Zeus' son and the solemn maturity of great Night born of Khaos (Hes. *Theog.* 123), light and darkness converge in the simile, bestowing an image of φύσις [upsurge and withdrawal; typically translated *nature*][36] as both irreducibly plural and dissolving presumed oppositionality and static identities. Translating, similes let differences pulse and move in their multiple directions,

---

36 Krell suggests "upsurge," in concert with Heidegger, for translating φύσις. "Upsurge" itself translates Heidegger's translation of φύσις as "Aufgehen und Sichverbergen." David Farrell Krell, "Nietzsche Hölderlin Empedocles," *Graduate Faculty Philosophy Journal* 15, no. 2 (1991): 44; Heidegger, "ALETHEIA (Heraklit, Fragment 16)," in *Vorträge und Aufsätze*, 263.

touching and entwining but not resolving one into another, rendering transformations in their continual interplay.

Translation, in taking up and reconfiguring the poetic resources of traditional poetries, is intimately involved with the rise of philosophy among the eastern Greeks. Diogenes Laertios reports that Thales' ancestry lay in the Phoinikian city of Tyre and the royal house of Kadmos and Agenor (Diog. Laert. I.1.22=Graham 1); according to West, the name of Thales' father, Examyes, "is certainly Anatolian, perhaps Carian."[37] While he may have been born in Miletos, other accounts suggest he traveled to the Ionian city alongside a companion who had been exiled from Phoinikia, or that he made his way there after practicing philosophy in Egypt (Ps. Plut. *Plac*. I.3.1=Graham 11]). Were the Milesian thinkers themselves translators in the conventional sense, bi- or multilingual migrants infusing Greek language with the images, if not the terms, they had learned from Egyptians, Mesopotamians, Persians? In the case of Thales, if his parents were of Karian or Phoinikian and Greek backgrounds, bilingualism seems likely, suggestive of the possibility that philosophy began to speak Greek in a "translated voice," a "voice full, perhaps, of the language(s) of Egypt, Phoenicia, and Mesopotamia," a voice voicing Greek differently "by translating from other cultures."[38] The more Anaximandros is linked to writing—Kahn views his *writing* as inaugurating the history of Greek philosophy[39]—the more he may also be imagined in the learning centers posited by Burkert where opening passages of "classical eastern literature" are likely candidates for practice texts used to learn the emerging technology of writing.[40] Even if, in the case of Anaximandrean cosmology and its wagon-wheel bands of celestial fire (Ps. Plut. *Plac*. II.20=Graham 22-5), direct knowledge of a specific Akkadian-Babylonian text that advances remarkably similar views is unlikely and without evidence, the associations of the Anaximandrean scheme with "the basic conceptions expressed in the Assyrian text" remain to Marciano "undeniable."[41] The Anaximenean image of the constellations as resembling

---

[37] M. L. West, *Early Greek Philosophy and the Orient* (Oxford: Oxford University Press, 1971), 214.

[38] Spitzer, introduction to *Philosophy's Treason: Studies in Philosophy and Translation*, ed. D. M. Spitzer (Wilmington: Vernon Press, 2020), v.

[39] Charles H. Kahn, *Anaximander and the Origins of Greek Cosmology* (Indianapolis: Hackett, 1985), 7.

[40] Walter Burkert, *The Orientalizing Revolution: Near Eastern Influence in the Early Archaic Age*, trans. Margaret E. Pinder and Walter Burkert (Cambridge: Harvard University Press, 1992), 95.

[41] M. Laura Gemelli Marciano, "East and West," in *Ancient Philosophy: Textual Pathways and Historical Explorations*, ed. Lorenzo Perilli and Daniela P. Taormina (London: Routledge, 2018), 19-20.

CHAPTER 1

drawings of living things [ὥσπερ ζῳγραφήματα (Ps. Plut. *Plac.* II.14=Graham 17)] sounds to Burkert almost "like a translation of the Assyrian text" in which "Enlil 'designed' or 'drew' the constellations on the heaven of Iaspis."[42] Responding to and reimagining the multitude of images and ideas that forms a multicultural tapestry in archaic Miletos, translation of this sort has formed, as Rée has disclosed, a constitutive dimension of the European philosophic tradition,[43] and may be discerned also at its self-narrated beginnings. Enfolding, dynamically open and responsive to ideas and images alive in the (trans-)cultural estuary of Miletos and the eastern Aegean of the Archaic period, Milesian thinking develops translationally, as translation in the richer and broader sense of thinking and understanding as involved meaningfully in the matrix of *already-there* in which thinking can never be fully detached: an interpretational involvement in meaning-making, a being-in-the-world.

Milesian translational actions—possibly interlingual, intralingual, and transmodal (if not in the case of Thales, then in the prose-shaped inquiries of Anaximandros and Anaximenes)[44]— occur not as a repetition of the same, what Sallis has termed the "classical determination of translation" according to which a translator circulates from a word to a (detachable) meaning and then to a term in another language that corresponds to the stable meaning, with the result that translation occurs as a repetition, circulation, a "restitution of meaning."[45] Nor does Milesian thinking operate (only) as a dialectical unfolding of an under-developed thought—as, for instance, the persistent notion that Thalean considerations bring into sharper focus a most ancient but inchoate sense found in Homer that water constitutes a source and principle [ἀρχή] of totality (Arist. *Metaph.* 983b.27-984a.5). Rather, the translational actions operative in Milesian and other archaic Greek thinking unfurl as a translating of the translator who moves (and *is moved*) in the direction of the call of an-other, a sense of foreignness in the familiar that moves thinking towards a rupture in

---

42 Burkert, "Prehistory of Presocratic Philosophy in an Orientalizing Context," in *The Oxford Handbook of Presocratic Philosophy*, ed. Patricia Curd and Daniel W. Graham (Oxford: Oxford University Press, 2008 [online 2009]), 72.
43 Jonathan Rée, "The Translation of Philosophy," *New Literary History*, vol. 32 (2001): 230-8.
44 *Intralingual*: Greek to Greek. *Transmodal*: recall that Thales was credited with certain field work, such as taking measurements and articulating geometry that likely would have involved extra-lingual and diagrammatic features; that Anaximandros established a *gnomon* at Sparta (Diog. Laert. II.1=Graham 1), and that he produced a map of the inhabited world [τὴν οἰκουμένην (Agath. I.1=Graham 6)].
45 John Sallis, *On Translation* (Indianapolis: Indiana University Press, 2002), 63-4.

that very familiarity towards an experience like non-experience [ἄπειρον—ἀ-πειράω][46]—that is, no longer moored by the habitual pathways and words of ordinary experience, so that a need emerges for different and fresh ways of saying. Such ways of saying-anew translate thinking as thinking has been translated; they transport speaker and hearer along the passage of thinking's transformation.[47] Translation activates a return to beginning(s) and a re-beginning through which (re-)sounds an experience of thinking, rather than its echoes or re-statements in the form of repetition of the same or the taking up the established doctrine of a predecessor as a starting point. As Nietzsche writes about the relation joining Xenophanes and Parmenides, each thinker would have needed to translate the other's thinking into their own language [*in seine eigne Sprache übertragen*] just to understand it, and that translation would have lost the specificity determinative of the other's thinking.[48] Translation would then have worked as a catalyst, a (re-)beginning instead of a finalization. Where something like repetition occurs, it takes place as a translational double movement marked by variation and differing in-as each attempt: the entanglements of the translator with the translating language and the irreducible movements of the translated language within itself. Such translation takes place by way of repetition *and* variation, placement *and* displacement, a movement described by Maly as "tautological," a re-turn along the circle of the same in its differing from itself, a repetition that summons a "second, fresh look at the same," what comes to thinking.[49]

Not only do the Milesian translations unfurl elements of the earlier hexameter tradition—including, perhaps, the hexameter itself—they also elaborate, translate, hexameter's vision of thinking as a dynamic of confluences. In the Homeric poems and in the Hesiodic *Theogony*, as well as other early Greek hexameter thinking, thinking's initiation in and through memory takes place as a turning-towards-another, and of a being-turned-towards-another. Invoking Mousa(i), Homeric hexameter thinking summons *and* heeds a summons from another, opening awareness to a multimodal and multicentered fluid source: Memory, Μνημοσύνη. Turning to the divinity(-ies), Mousa(i), means turning

---

46 Spitzer, "Images in Archaic Thinking," *Epoché: A Journal for the History of Philosophy* 26, no. 1 (fall, 2021): 12.
47 Heidegger, *Parmenides*, trans. André Schuwer and Richard Rojcewicz (Bloomington: Indiana University Press, 1992), 11-13. This reading of Heidegger is informed by Kenneth Maly's work in "Parmenides: Circle of Disclosure, Circle of Possibility," *Heidegger Studies* 1 (1985): 16-17.
48 Nietzsche, *Die Philosophie im tragischen Zeitalter der Griechen*, in *Die Geburt der Tragödie und weitere Schriften zur griechischen Literatur und Philosophie*, ed. Bernhard Greiner (Berlin: Alfred Kröner Verlag, 2014), 191.
49 Maly, "Parmenides: Circle of Disclosure, Circle of Possibility," 14.

towards the voice of Memory that speaks beyond the speaker, the thinker, a source teeming in the span of multiplicity that (at least) blurs a notion and sense of agency.[50] Re-turning to Mousa(i) in *Iliad* Book II, Homeric thinking opens itself to the overflow and surge of memory as awareness and being-with, as an act of hearkening and voicing:

> Now tell me, Mousai who dwell on Olympia—
> since you are divine, and you are present, and you see
>   totality-in-motion [πάντα]
> yet we hear glory-of-radiance [κλέος][51]
>   and do not see (Hom. *Il.* II.484-6)

Mousai unclose thinking, opening it to the vast richness of a meaningful and extensive world overflowing putative borders of thinkers and identities. The one who calls the Mousai sings that he would be unable, even with ten tongues and mouths, even with a tireless voice and a heart of bronze, to open speech [μυθήσομαι] in the direction of numerous others without the Mousai and their opening of memory [μνησαίαθ' (Hom. *Il.* II.487-92)]. In order to open in this way, the one who calls and hearkens to an other enacts thinking as "une tâche d'écoute" [a task of listening], though a listening like reading that takes place not as mere echo or received voice, but as thinking's differing.[52]

The fullness of memory-Memory extends, overflows, bears totality in its currents and tides, and permeates, ever-exceeding boundaries. Lombardo's translation of the *Odyssey*'s invocation calls attention to the meaning of Mousa(i) as memory: "Speak, Memory."[53] Mousa(i) stands at the threshold of, and opens the way for, thinking that ever-exceeds a thinker, moves otherwise than within a circle of subjectivity or a self-enclosed *res cogitans*, moves instead as an already-translated openness full of others: as Foran writes, there exists "no untranslated self or Other, that has not in some way been informed and enriched by

---

50 Wilkinson, *Parmenides and* To Eon, 68.
51 κλέος and light in a sense translate one another or, rather, κλέος names illuminated beings and deeds. Herodotos brings to light in a gesture of showing [ἀπόδεξις] the wonders and deeds of Greeks and others in order to prevent them from eclipse, from the non-light, the darkness of ἐξίτηλα [faded] and ἀκλεᾶ [unilluminated (Hdt. 1.proemium)].
52 Günter Figal, "Tautophasis: Heidegger et Parménide," trans. [into French] Anne Merker, *Les Cahiers philosophiques de Strasbourg*, no. 36 (2014): 45-6. Figal is describing Heidegger's thinking of thinking's task in engagement with Parmenidean thinking.
53 Stanley Lombardo, trans., *Homer: Odyssey* (Indianapolis: Hackett, 2000), 1.

many Others."⁵⁴ The folded, multiply-contoured region of memory—Memory, Mnemosyne [Μνημοσύνη]—en- and un-folds the temporal spanning of human being that exceeds each human being, reaching into the folded expanse of beings whose presence [τά τ' ἐόντα] en- and un-folds towards-beings-yet-to-come [τά τ' ἐσσόμενα] and beings-before-us-in-the-past [πρό τ' ἐόντα (Hes. *Theog.* 38)]. Mousa(i) can disclose for human beings the foldedness of time present (a translational action),⁵⁵ its fabric ever en- and un-folding past and future, a sense ordinarily concealed from human beings: *Theogony* voices this in the articulated difference of temporality between the song Hesiod can sing by the bestowal of Mousa(i) and that sung by Mousa(i) (Hes. *Theog.* 32, 38, respectively). The full range that gathers both and spans the difference between the two describes the region of Mnemosyne, the (en-)twined weave of memory and forgetting, another name for which might be: ἀλήθεια [opening-closing movement of dis-closure].⁵⁶ Accordingly, the song of Mousa(i), shaped out of the dynamically expansive horizonal zone of Mnemosyne, entwines ψεύδεα [concealments-that-appear-as-such]⁵⁷ and ἀληθέα [disclosures (Hes. *Theog.* 27-8)], discloses the ceaseless turnings out from darkness into a luminous and ever-shadowing, ever-shadowed presence. Such a region continually outspans itself and each manifestation and being even as it gains itself only by human beings in thoughtful awareness, in thinking, in singing, according to a "reciprocal co-belonging" structured as "participant-recipient" mutuality,⁵⁸ a cycle of hearkening and speaking.

54 Foran, "Translation as a Path to the Other: Derrida and Ricouer," in Foran, *Translation and Philosophy*, 80.
55 Berman includes "un *dépliement* de ce qui, dans l'original, est 'plié'" [the unfolding of what is folded in the original] as characteristic of the third of the deforming tendencies of translation. Antoine Berman, "La traduction comme épreuve de l'étranger," in *Traduction: textualité Text: translatability* (Toronto: Les Éditions Trintexte, 1986), 73.
56 Heidegger brings out the motions of this word as presencing and presence and the twofold of concealing and unconcealing that together animate ἀλήθεια. Heidegger, "ALETHEIA," 254. Heidegger's discussion in his lectures on Parmenides develop a fourfold directive for translating (thinking) ἀλήθεια: the first thinks the root of λήθη as concealment; the second, meditates on the privational character of ἀ-; the third requires much effort as it thinks the history and transformation of the oppositional character of ἀλήθεια; the fourth attends to the light, lightening, and open clearing of and as a fundamental human reciprocity with Being and beings. Heidegger, *Parmenides*, trans. Schuwer and Rojcewicz, 15-16, 26, 146, respectively, as exemplary statements of Heidegger's thorough investigations.
57 Building here on Heidegger's reading of ψεύδεα that take place as "always already an unveiling and showing and bringing-to-shimmering [*Zum-erscheinen-bringen*]." Heidegger, *Parmenides* (Frankfurt am Main: Vittorio Klostermann, 1982), 45.
58 Niall Keane, "The Silence of the Origin: Philosophy in Transition and the Essence of Thinking," *Research in Phenomenology* 43, no. 1 (2013): 32-3.

Memory extends as the multiplicitous, polyvalent totality, an always-already active region of meanings disclosed—but also en-closed—for human beings by way of Mousa(i). Thinking takes place as a remaining open to the bestowals of the multiplicity named by Mousa(i) and leading back to the doubling, comet-tail auras of sources in Mnemosyne and Zeus: from Mnemosyne as source teems an expansive openness delivered of the joining of earth and sky—Gaia and Ouranos (Hes. *Theog.* 132-6), which itself trails back into the happening [αὐτὰρ ἔπειτα] of Gaia and the primordial opening-closing of Khaos (Hes. *Theog.* 116-17). To that event Mimnermian thinking—as reported (translated) by Pausanias—links Mousa(i) more directly, speaking their origin as plural, with more ancient Mousa(i) [τὰς ἀρχαιοτέρας Μούσας] descended from the union of Gaia and Ouranos and younger Mousa(i) from Zeus, as well as possibly developed from Gaia herself (Mimn. 13 Gerber). From Zeus as source flows the entwined lightening-darkening of the lightning, a light momentany that reaches and shows the edges of surrounding darkness, as well as the overcoming of sheer, brute, annihilative darkness of a yet-unmarked or unarticulated temporality of presence as (violent) containment figured in the brutality of Kronos (Hes. *Theog.* 459-500).[59] The multiplicitous sources of Mousa(i) open for human beings a dynamic, temporally-expansive, and en-twined, enfolded region. Solon's replete invocation gestures to the multiplicity exceeding the singer or thinker from which thinking flows:

> Of Mnemosyne and of Zeus Olympian, shimmering
>   ensembles [ἀγλαὰ τέκνα],
> Mousai Pierian, hearken unto my beseeching:
> bestow unto me good fortune from the blessed divinities
> and ever-good significance from all human beings (Solon 13.1-2 Gerber)

Through a circuitry of listening-voicing-hearkening, thinking unfurls as a re-sounding of such bestowals trailing off into comet-tail auras of these multiplicitous

---

59 The close association between Kronos [Κρόνος] and Khronos [Χρόνος] surfaces in Proklos' comment that "Orpheus called the first cause of all things Khronos [Χρόνος], nearly a homonym with Kronos [Κρόνος]" (Procl. *In Crat.* 64 Boissonade=LM T17 [in Cosmological Speculations]). André Laks and Glenn W. Most, eds. *Early Greek Philosophy*, vol. II, part 1, *Beginnings and Early Ionian Thinkers* (Cambridge, Mass: Harvard University Press, 2016), 78. Kirk and Raven, about Pherekydes, write: "The connexion of Kronos with Chronos was certainly made by later Orphics…but according to Plutarch (*Is. Osir.* 32) this was a common Greek identification." G. S. Kirk and J. E. Raven, *The Presocratic Philosophers: A Critical History with a Selection of Texts* (Cambridge: Cambridge University Press, 1957), 56-7 and n. 1.

sources, a recovery and revoicing of their entwined opening and closing as darkening-lightening, as ἀλήθεια.

On just this moment of hexameter thinking, the Milesian circle translates variously, richly, voicing an experience of the living world in its overflowing currents. Thalean, Anaximandrean, and Anaximenean thinkings translate Mousa(i) and Memory, re-thinking the expansive variegated flow, an articulated contiguity defying unity and plurality and complicating identity as the song of singing spills from elsewhere and otherwise through the voice, bearing source(s), singer(s), hearer(s). Remaining open to the happening of singing, the early Milesians enact what Kirkland reads as the task of philosophy Nietzsche articulates in his study of the early Greeks, a "personal attunement" that enables "the always prior sounding of the world" to "resound" or "echo,"[60] first through or within the thinker and then—in a translational moment—from this primordial experience into, as Nietzsche writes, "a stammering medium, at bottom [*im Grunde*] a metaphoric, entirely faithless translation [*Übertragung*] in a different sphere and language."[61] With different emphases, Thalean ὕδωρ and its teeming opacities, Anaximandrean ἄπειρον as naming the open-horizon and open-expanse, Anaximenean ἀήρ as the enclosing—un-enclosing surplus, each translates this experience (what the epic poets seem to have voiced as Mousa[i] as Memory) of the surrounding-permeating texture of being-in-the-world, conjoined, in-relation, and enmeshed.

Re-turning to memory, Xenophanean singing takes up the atmospheric fluidities of thinking: Mnemosyne and well-crafted song [τόνος][62] about excellence bestow on the singer an ability to bring to light [ἀναφαίνῃ] noble things (Xenoph. 1.19-20).[63] With meanings [δόκος][64] suffusing totality (Xenoph. 34.4), Memory spans beyond any individual singer or thinker and channels the flow of meanings into song and its special arrangement (in this case, hexameter). Translating

---

60 Sean D. Kirkland, "Nietzsche and Drawing Near to the Personalities of the Pre-Platonic Greeks," *Continental Philosophy Review* 44, no. 4 (2011): 426.
61 Nietzsche, *Die Philosophie im tragischen Zeitalter der Griechen*, 168.
62 The phrase "well-crafted song" translates the term τόνος. Such a translation attempts to register both the effort involved in doing this work of praise and the form (hexameter or elegaic meter based in hexameter) that grants the praise its special character. For τόνος as form, see Herodotos' narration of the famous Pythian utterance articulating the scope of oracular knowledge said to be ἐν ἑχαμέτρῳ τόνῳ [in hexameter form (Hdt. I.47.2-3)].
63 All references to Xenophanean thinking in this chapter are to the text given in J. H. Lesher, ed. & trans. *Xenophanes of Colophon: Fragments: A Text and Translation and Introduction* (Toronto: University of Toronto Press, 1992).
64 For δόξα/δοκέω/δοκοῦντα as *meanings* in early Greek thinking, see Spitzer, "Trans-philosophy," 577-9.

CHAPTER 1

from the earlier poetries and Milesians, Xenophanean thinking voices the meaningfulness of world—the world as meaningfulness—as the fluid, circulating atmosphere where human open-awareness and thinking sound and resound.

Following the arc of the sun, its blaze of fire on the horizon in its descent into the halls of Night, Xenophanean thinking transports (translates) hexameter singing from Kolophon on the Aegean's eastern rim, through the foundation of Hyele in southwestern Italy where dwelled Parmenides, and then to Zankle and Katane on Sicily (Diog. Laert. IX.2.18). The light blazes on the surface of ancient waters, site of translation:

> earth and water all
> things are
>   rising and upsurge [φύονται] (Xenoph. 29)

In a translative gesture, translation figures as the elemental transformation that describes the upsurge of what comes to light [φύσις, φύονται]. The Xenophanean translation activates and preserves in its singing a resistance to the singular: earth *and* water *and* all things conjoin in the ceaseless movements of tidal pulses that sound in the patterned rise and fall of hexameter.[65] Such resistance shapes the vision of divinity, too, as the statement on totality would encompass the apparently unitary deity of Xenophanean thinking (Xenoph. 23-6). Furthermore, the seemingly unitary god drifts within a manifold region emphatically moved by difference: οὔτι...ὁμοίϊος...οὔτε [not...similar...not (Xenoph. 23.2)].[66] The whole acts in difference with itself, a folding and reflexion of whole into and on its own differentiated condition that speaks ever of embodiment and being-in-the-world, where the entanglement of οὖλος [whole] with the differentiated world of sensuous being speaks the language of bodily sense ὁρᾷ...νοεῖ...ἀκούει [sees...opens

---

65 Hexameter itself performs resistance to the singular in its dactylic base (— ˘ ˘) only reducing to the dyad in the fluidity of spondee (— —), which always flows into the following long syllable of the next foot. So too does hexameter thinking resist simple reduction to doctrine and consistency: cf. Xenoph. 27, posing earth alone as source and terminus.
66 The sense of being *within the manifold* is spoken in the first line's preposition and plural substantives ἐν τε θεοῖσι καὶ ἀνθρώποισι, among both divinities and human beings.

awareness towards[67]...listens] that always takes its bearing from encountering others and whose constitution is to perceive *something* (Xenoph. 24).[68]

As if staging this inextricable enmeshment of beings as already-there in a location and situation rich with meaningfulness, the Parmenidean poem opens this zone as a scene for the narrative it unfolds. Hesiod sings *Theogony* from the Mousai, while the Homeric *Iliad* and *Odyssey* both summon the divine presence at the outset of their songs, putting on display a translational action—the passage from the ordinary concealedness of (historical) memory to the living field of (trans-)historical memory (Mnemosyne, Memory) as source. Voicing the narrative, the human singer-poet is encircled and enfolded in the speech of hexameter tradition, its widening and disclosing of the memory saturating, but undisclosed in, quotidian ways of speaking and being. Translating Mousa(i) and Memory and the always-already active region of meanings they embody and to which they grant access, the Parmenidean poem opens *in medias res*—"The mares that are bearing me as far as engaged-being-in-the-world [θυμός] might reach / were sending me" (Parm. 1.1-2)—foregrounding from the outset this already-there emplacement of multiple living bodies in action. The poem offers a scene of strenuous motion towards a female-feminine divinity who offers instruction to be imparted through and with care [κόμισαι (Parm. 2.1-2)], a care that speaks both of alertness to one's own involvements and a poetic holding silent that preserves distance(s) and differing.[69] Might this divinity, Thea, harbor Mousa(i) and Mnemosyne within the ample manifold of her identity?[70] For the traditional translational action as invocation, the opening narrative of the Parmenidean poem gives a translation towards an active striving, a sigetic and intentional movement towards a source of speech and, as Wilkinson has suggested, perhaps towards *reverence* for that source;[71] the silence of the kouros recommends this, as does the statement in Diogenes' biographical notes on Parmenides that he was

---

67 "Open-awareness" and "openings" both voice the action of νοεῖν, registered here in the substantive νόημα, articulated by Gadamer as "die reine Offenheit für alles" [the pure openness for everything]. Hans-Georg Gadamer, *Der Anfang der Philosophie*, trans. Joachim Schulte (Stuttgart: Reclam, 1996), 143. On translating νοῦς-νοεῖν terms in this way, see also, Spitzer, "Trans-philosophy," 571-3.

68 As in Heidegger's articulation of perception as "always already immediately dwelling among things." Heidegger, *Basic Problems of Phenomenology*, trans. Albert Hofstadter (Indianapolis: University of Indiana Press, 1982), 66.

69 Keane describes something like this as a poet's task in "sigetic listening." Keane, "The Silence of the Origin," 40.

70 On this suggestion and its situation in various traditions, see Giovanni Pugliese Carratelli, "La Θεά di Parmenide," *La parole del passato* 43 (1988): 339-45.

71 Wilkinson, *Parmenides and* To Eon, 117.

turned in the direction of stillness [εἰς ἡσυχίαν προετράπη] by way of Pythagorean teachings (Diog. Laert. IX.3.21).⁷² Further, the image of the chariot itself works as a translative gesture, activating at once the movement of passage, transition, and engagement(s) with foreignness as the chariot-rider encounters a variety of beings and places along a route "beyond the path of human beings" (Parm. 1.27).

At the western settlement of Hyele, Parmenidean thinking translates elementally, sings the turnings of fire through shadow and light that constitute all things (Parm. 8.56-9; 9), perhaps engaging with the hexameter thinking of Xenophanes, perhaps hearing Milesian thinking from Anaximandros (Diog. Laert. IX.3.21). Translating in any case perhaps Anaximandrean ἄπειρον or Xenophanean γῆ [typically translated: earth] and ὕδωρ [typically translated: water],⁷³ Parmenidean thinking voices dark night and shimmering fire, their paired luminosities and polyphonies. As with Xenophanean thinking, the Parmenidean poem elaborates a twofold that courses through the thinking, entwined in the way meanings or appearings weave and exceed a thought towards any singular or unitary totality [διὰ παντὸς πάντα περῶντα-περ ὄντα⁷⁴ (Parm. 1.31-2)]: it makes itself visible explicitly in the wheels of the chariot (Parm. 1.7-8), in the figures of Night and Day (Parm. 1.11), the two ways Thea describes (e.g. Parm. 2), the forms for mortal thinking (Parm. 8.53; 9), the twofold of male and female (Parm. 12.4-6; 17; 18), and implicitly in the gates of the paths of Night and Day and the doors filling them (Parm. 1.11; 13), as well as the movement of disclosure enacted by the Heliades and Dike (Parm. 1.10, 17-18). Yet, even as the twofold surfaces thematically throughout Parmenidean thinking, the poem lets multiplicity course within the twofold, a reminder of the expanse ever-beyond the enclosures of any pair of strictly or metaphysically determined oppositions, as Thea brings into hearing as the deceitful arrangement of mortal discourse [κόσμον ἀπατηλόν Parm. 8.52)].⁷⁵ Such expansive multiplicity (re-)sounds in the unspecified number of Heliades (Parm. 1.9), and the indefinitely multiple pathways [κελεύθων] that reach the gates of Night and Day (Parm. 1.11), as well as the possibility of multiple pathways beyond the two Thea articulates—a possibility Thea raises through the apparent prohibition on both ways she discloses (Parm. 2; 6). Like earlier Greek thinking, the Parmenidean poem disrupts a drive towards unity.

---

72 The passive construction in Diogenes' narrative echoes the passivity narrating-voyager-kouros' standing as object of the horses' movement in the Parmenidean poem (Parm. 1.1).
73 On the multiplicity of Thalean ὕδωρ, see Spitzer, "Divining: ΥΔΩΡ, Opacity, and Thalean Considerations," *Research in Phenomenology* 51, no. 3 (2021): 426-47.
74 For discussion of this term and other readings of the text, see below (pp. 79-80 with notes).
75 See Spitzer, "Being-in-touch: Touch, Contact, and Bodies in the Poem of Parmenides," *Epoché: A Journal for the History of Philosophy* 29, no. 1 (2024): 11-12.

Translating the resistance to unity sustained by and in hexameter thinking, the Parmenidean poem activates multiple emphases on difference and likeness by way of the erotics of simile. Similaic thinking appears throughout the poem:

- the repetition and constitutive differentiation of συνεχές [with-holding] and ξυνεχές [with-holding (Parm. 8.6, 25)]
- the disclosure that all is similar [ἐπεὶ πᾶν ἐστιν ὁμοῖον (Parm. 8.22)]
- the simile εὐκύκλου σφαίρης ἐναλίγκιον [like the heft of a well-turned ball (Parm. 8.43)]
- the extension of the simile μεσσόθεν ἰσοπαλὲς πάντῃ [from the center in every direction (Parm. 8.44)]

More subtly, similaic thinking also makes itself felt in the pulse of repetition disclosed by Cassin in τὸ αὐτό, typically translated *the same*, where the expression quietly says: τὸ αὖ τό, *le re-le* [the once-again-the] or *ce re-ce* [this once-more-this], indicating "succession, repetition, opposition" as the living cadence of identity.[76] The same itself and identities themselves exceed themselves in repetitions of self-similarity, ever adrift in the tide of the similaic. An erotics of similaic thinking passes through the poem and comes to speech in the dual figure of Ἔρος [*Eros*] and δαίμων [*daimon*] that steer(s) the turnings of fire and night and the erotic configurations [κράσις, mixing] of bodies in their upsurge (Parm. 13; 12.3; 17, respectively). Thinking and open-awareness to elemental translation translate fire and dark night:

all—being, full
of same
light and silent dark
of night (Parm. 9.3)

and in all and in every: being is fullness [πλέον], openings [νόημα] (Parm. 17.4)

Voicing the foreignness and opacities of thinking and thought (as the light and night haunting everything), elemental translation works the action of the *daimon*, the erotic joining that keeps distances open for possibilities.

Along this path from the eastern Aegean to Hyele on the western Italian coast, singing bursts into light and life then fades to darkness, moving as fire and shadow. Coasting southward, hexameter thinking flows and skims the

---

76 Cassin, *Parménide: Sur la nature ou sur l'étant*, 42.

CHAPTER 1

Tyrrhenian sea to Akragas on Sicily. Mousa(i), in the Empedoklean poem(s), gleams [λευκώλενε] with the radiant heritage of abundant Memory [πολυμνήστη] and delivers singing from the sheltering, silent reverence [εὐσέβεια]. Mousa(i) delivers or sends [πέμπε] a thinking that takes place as well-suited [θέμις] to the hearkening [ἀκούειν] of ephemeral human being (Emp. 9/3.3-5).[77] Linked to the Heliades of the Parmenidean poem through the action of driving or leading a chariot [ἅρμα (Parm. 1.4-5, 20-21; Emp. 9/3.5)], the Empedoklean Mousa(i) moves as a figure of translation, a translative gesture: in both poems, the movement of Mousa(i) and Heliades progresses in the direction of speaking from a prior silent attentiveness like the faithless translation described by Nietzsche. Empedoklean thinking beseeches Mousa(i) for just this translation, a *passage-through* her consideration [διὰ φροντίδος ἐλθεῖν] of human concerns [ἡμετέρας μελέτας (Emp. 10/131.2)], where Mousa(i) forms a channel through which opens human awareness in its concernful in-the-worldness, its always-already involvements. To effect this translation, thinking summons Mousa(i) to a return-to-presence [νῦν αὖτε παρίστασο] as a specified embodiment—Kalliopeia—in order for thinking to let right speech come to light [ἀγαθὸν λόγον ἐμφαίνοντι (Emp. 10/131.3-4)]. A thoughtful attunement with and through speaking-as-Mousa(i) grants the possibility for a re-sounding of the already-active totality of meaning in which thinking already un-/re-folds itself, a kind of doubling or folded speaking, twice-spoken [δίς], radiant [καλόν], pressing [ὁ δεῖ (Emp. 29/25)].

In Empedoklean thinking, the already-there emerges shimmering and active in its multiplicities. Rhizomes [ῥιζώματα] come forward initially as a fourfold of specific divinities Zeus, Hera, Aidoneus, and Nestis (Emp. 12/6), specificities that resist simple, transparent, certain translation into the so-called elements: Hippolytos (second-third centuries c.e.) interprets Zeus as translating fire, Hera as earth, Aidoneus as air [ἀήρ], and Nestis as water (Hippol. *Haer.* VII.29=Graham 27), while the tradition flowing perhaps from Theophrastos (fourth-third centuries) holds that Zeus translates radiant air [αἰθήρ], Hera air [ἀήρ], Aidoneus translates earth, and Nestis water (Ps. Plut. *Plac.* I.3=Graham 26). Generating further resistance to a simple formulation according to which each element translates without any friction or remainder, another voicing of specificities announces earth, foam-crested sea [πόντος πολυκύμων], moist ἀήρ, and Titan αἰθήρ enclosing totality (Emp. 39/28).[78] Like specifying Mousa(i) as

---

[77] References are to the texts of Empedoklean thinking in Brad Inwood, ed. and trans. *The Poem of Empedocles: A Text and Translation with an Introduction*, rev. ed. (Toronto: University of Toronto Press, 2001).

[78] Alternatively, see Shaw's interpretation that raises the possibility of ἀήρ as an aspect of "the description of water as sea, waves, and moist air or mist" [ἀήρ], allowing sun [ἥλιος]

Kalliopeia, this identification locates dynamic rhizomatism concretely, not as abstract *elements* but as active ever-in-bodies and in-place, bodies that themselves embody multiplicity (Emp. 28/26.1-2) and resist a (translational) reduction to a simple unity. Whatever comes to be an apparent unity exists as a multiplicity, as embodied differing gathered in passing, as the temporary and already dissolving result of the joining [συμφύντα] and parting [διαφύντος] of the fourfold rhizomes (Emp. 28/26.10).

Empedoklean thinking translates rhizomes into the work of translation, reflexing elemental translation onto itself and spreading it into more numerous energies:

twofold will speak—once augmented one
                to be one alone out from manyness
    once more   surged apart [διέφυ] to be manifold out
                from one
fire and water and earth and *aith-aer*[79] uppermost
                and unfilled
clash [νεῖκος] ruinous schism [δίχα] of all
                similarity everywhere
and sex [φιλότης] in everything similarity reaches and spans (Emp. 25/17.16-20)

Rhizomes themselves undergo elemental translation in the sway from unity to manifold according to the translative-translational forces of νεῖκος [clash] and φιλότης [sex]. Such sway happens as two-folded [δοιή], each fold folded once again, a doubled-movement as emerging [γένεσις] and elapsing or self-abandon [ἀπόλειψις (17.3)]. Each moment of this double-folding resists simple, fixed, unitary identifications, opens rhizomes, as well as the translative-translational forces, in their multiplicities. Quickened from varied starts in multiple directions and nodes of relation, entanglements, anywhere along their filaments rhizomes "can be connected to anything other, and must be."[80] With each figuring the

---

    to occupy a position in a fourfold. The fourfold becomes, on Shaw's insightful reading, Zeus and Hera joined in brightness and rarity as πῦρ and αἰθήρ (respectively), and Hades and Nestis—a divinity whose associations with Persephone Shaw outlines—as γῆ and ὕδωρ (respectively). Michael M. Shaw, "Aither and the Four Roots in Empedocles," *Research in Phenomenology* 44, no. 2 (2014): 174-5 with notes, 179-82.

79 This term activates the ambiguities of translation-as-transmission: Simplikios gives the fourfold as πῦρ καὶ ὕδωρ καὶ γαῖα καὶ ἠέρος ἄπλετον ὕψος (Simpl. *in Phys.* 26.2), while Plutarkhos, quoting only this line as part of a scene he is developing, lists the fourfold as πῦρ καὶ ὕδωρ καὶ γαῖα καὶ αἰθέρος ἤπιον ὕψος (Plut. *Mor.* 63d).

80 Gilles Deleuze and Félix Guatari. "Introduction: Rhizome," in *A Thousand Plateaus: Capitalism and Schizophrenia*, trans. Brian Massumi (Minneapolis: University of Minnesota Press, 1987), 7.

other and full of otherness, in the multiplicity of rhizomes each manifestation turns from, resists, complexifies translation and surges as untranslatable—not a fixed terminus, but rather the energies that provoke continual translations.[81] Translation becomes a tracing, a momentary naming that voices and shapes, focalizes meanings in their rising and falling and in their various and variable relations. νεῖκος translates itself as the work of φιλότης transforming rhizomes through diverse moments of joined-in-difference (Arist. *Metaph.* 985a.24-29), where naming one moment of the cycle according to one of these names focuses and discloses some of the active dimensions that turn through and as shifting and polyvalent multiplicities.

Already enacting translation, speaking emerges from manifold or twofold as re-sounding in the circuitry of Mousa(i), listening and letting what-is come to suitably-arranged speech [μῦθος (Emp. 25/17.14)]. The Empedoklean saying on the doubling of speaking and the fourfold of multiplicities enacts the doubling, folding movements of speaking by way of its re-sounding of the directive for this very saying, as the opening two lines repeat the initial two lines of the entire speech:

δίπλ' ἐρέω· τοτὲ μὲν γὰρ ἓν ηὐξήθη μόνον εἶναι
ἐκ πλεόνων, τοτὲ δ' αὖ διέφυ πλέον' ἐξ ἑνὸς εἶναι

(Emp. 25/17.1-2, 16-17)

    double I yearn to speak—once enhanced one
        alone   being: from manyness
      once more   being: through
                        upsurge out
                        from one manifold

As Decker has highlighted, this way of speaking, through its disruption of habitual, oppositionally- or dualistically-patterned thought, reorients thinking towards "an awareness of multiplicity and paradox."[82] Along similar lines, Empedoklean thinking activates untranslatability as on-going translation; in its ceaseless movements, totality works *in translation* or, better, *as translating*, so that beings and thinking shimmer, pulse with the fluid energies of transformation.

---

81 Cassin, "Translation as Paradigm for Human Sciences," *The Journal of Speculative Philosophy* 30, no. 3 (2016): 243.
82 Jessica Elbert Decker, "I Will Tell a Double Tale: Double-speak in the ancient Poetic Tradition," *Epoché* 25, no. 2 (2021): 238.

Beings do not settle into *being* as the repetition of the same, but roam and tremble in their transformations (Emp. 25/17.11-13) in the manner of untranslatables: their very sameness pulses as an equivalence of foreignness through continual and multiple translations.[83] In waves numerous and glistening, elemental translation fluidly locates itself everywhere but always on the condition of similarity and its erotics that sustains difference:

> there all things never relent their thorough differings [διαλλάσσοντα] (Emp. 25/17.12)

Singing continues in the manner of a κύκλον [cycle (Emp. 25/17.13)], propelled by the motions of a ἑλισσομένην [helixing (Emp. 25/17.25)] and a δίνη [churn (Emp. 35.4)] that keeps active the movements across differentiation.

In its western movement, singing declines. The translation of singing ends in flame and shadow. From Xenophanes to Parmenides, from Parmenides to Empedokles, singing moves in dactylic hexameters—though already the smoke thickens and obscures the path.[84] On Sicily, the western island and its mountain of fire, Empedokles offers himself, the bodied voice of song, to the god of fire Hephaistos. Diogenes Laertius gives several accounts of the death of Empedokles. According to one, by elemental translation Empedokles departs:

> into the craters of the fire he leapt, turning
> in dance [ἐναλέσθαι],[85] and
> disappeared [ἀφανισθῆναι] (Diog. Laert. VIII.2.69)

Fire, agent and sign of elemental translation, marks the site of Empedokles' translation in another account, as from the place of burnt sacrifice the singer undergoes transformation to a divinity, drawn into the pageantry of celestial fires (Diog. Laert. VIII.2.68). Fire translates the mortal singer into a divinity and figures, too, the rich diversity appropriate to this mode of thinking-as-singing and its extinguishment, consonant with Diogenes' report of several accounts of Empedokles' death.

---

83 Drawing on Sabina Folnovic Jaitner, "Philosophical untranslatables and the concept of equivalence," in Spitzer, *Philosophy's Treason*, 81-6.

84 Diogenes presents various genealogies for Empedokles: that he modeled his songs on those of Parmenides or those of Xenophanes; that he was, together with Zenon, a student of Parmenides or a student of Pythagoras or of a Pythagorean (Diog. Laert. VIII.2.54-6).

85 This translation activates the resonance of dancing in Diogenes' verb ἐναλέσθαι, and of the shadow of ἀλλ- (other in the verbal stem: ἐν-αλλ-. The root -αλλ- cycles and resounds strongly through variation and repetition in Empedokles (e.g. Emp. 25/17).

CHAPTER 1

Singing follows the path of fire, reduces itself to ash and its legend. Rising in the Homeric epics and Hesiodic *Theogony*, coursing through other early hexameter thinking, philosophy's traditional narrative begins with Thalean considerations that *might* have voiced themselves in hexameter. Translated in other early Milesians, hexameter thinking smolders, its embers glowing in the simile-and-image-rich sayings of Anaximandrean and Anaximenean thinking before flaring once more in the Xenophanean thinking that voyages from the eastern Aegean to the western Italian coast and Sicily. A transitional moment, a kind of return to the Milesian way of a prose charged with the energies of the hexameter thinking, rises in Zenoan and Melissoan thinking—a fire burnt yet bright with shimmering embers. Throughout runs a translational and translative protocol of *re-turning* to beginnings for thinking, advancing as differing and multiplicity.

The flames of thinking as song quiet to smoldering embers and ash, leaving their trace in the transitional moment of a prose dense and resonant. In the wake of the Parmenidean poem, Zenoan and Melissoan thinking translate singing to prosaic inquiry, no longer skimming the rhythmic heave of a sea dark as wine but pulsing nonetheless with its own strides and cadences. In this translational movement, the two resemble the earliest moments of philosophy among the Greeks: taking-up in the Hyelean and Milesian traditions involves transformation—otherwise said: *translation*—from poetry to prose that relinquishes the regularity of hexameters, a shift that may itself resonate meaningfully. Where hexameter thinking bears along with it the grand totality of meanings from the epic tradition, thinking in prose opens a distance (but not a detachment) from that totality. Similarly, a distance from divinity-as-source and the divine sanction or authority of hexameter unfolds in prose thinking.

No longer divine, in Zenon the thinking once sung assumes a complexion of human mortality. In place of Memory in Xenophanes, Thea of the Parmenidean song, the Mousa of Empedokles, Akhilleus, in whom dwells a genetics of divinity wrenched by the ankle down into the mortal realm, moves as a figure in Zenoan thinking.[86] Not seeking merely a firmer establishment of settled principles, Zenon and Melissos unsettle thinking, translate the hexameter and take

---

86 Even where absent, Akhilleus' presence is felt. For instance, in the third paradox the "flying arrow" reverberates with the fall of Akhilleus by arrow to the heel. See Burgess' investigation on the traditions surrounding Akhilleus, his baptism for translation to immortality and, especially here, his death by an arrow wound to the ankle, which Burgess finds to have been "present in the Archaic Age and perhaps originated in pre-Homeric tradition." Jonathan Burgess, "Achilles' Heel: The Death of Achilles in Ancient Myth," *Classical Antiquity* 14, no. 2 (October, 1995): 225.

place as a (re-)beginning within the region where the singing of Xenophanes, Parmenides, and Empedokles (re-)sounded. Like Anaximandrean thinking in relation to Thalean, in which the radiant term ἄπειρον [typically translated: boundless] unsettles and releases beings from even the most supple and polyvalent determination as Thalean ὕδωρ [typically translated: water], Zenoan thinking advances from a kind of negativity. Reversing polarity, Zenoan thinking seems to follow a way along which multiplicity is cancelled or annulled, contouring the Parmenidean description of τὸ ἐόν as an inseparable [οὐδὲ διαιρετόν] totality bound within itself by and as similarity (Parm. 8.22), not severed from itself (Parm. 4), yet folded and contiguous (Parm. 8.24-5), restlessly differentiating itself (Parm. 8.29). Prose, the Zenoan paradoxes nevertheless activate a poetic dynamism like that operative throughout the Parmenidean poem, one that pierces the seemingly closed horizon for thought and opens possibilities.

Translationally, Zenoan prose stresses the differing that animates translation as a re-imagining and rethinking, a thoughtful return to the starting points for thinking. Nowhere in the extant fragments of Zenoan thinking does mere repetition-of-the-same emerge, while everywhere the dynamic of differing-in-relation—which is to say, *translation*—makes itself felt as the intimacy of thoughtful engagement. Like a poetry shorn of its music, Zenoan thinking opens possibilities through translational actions involved with the Parmenidean poem. A dance of gestures contouring, but never modelling or detailing Parmenidean thinking, the charged language of Zenoan thinking lets sound and appear the woven tensions of multiplicity:

> If multiplicities are [πολλά ἐστιν], necessity [ἀνάγκη] determines such things to be as many as they are [ὅσα ἐστί] and neither more nor less than themselves [αὐτῶν]. Yet, if such things are [τοσαῦτά ἐστιν] as many as they are [ὅσα ἐστι], they would be limited-as-enclosed [πεπερασμένα...εἴη].
>
> If multiplicities are [πολλά ἐστιν], the beings are [τὰ ὄντα ἐστίν] unlimited-as-open-expanse [ἄπειρον]; indeed, always are [ἐστί] others in-between the beings, and once-more others [πάλιν...ἕτερα] between those others, and in this way the beings are [ἐστί] unlimited-as-open-expanse [ἄπειρον] (Simpl. *in Phys.* 140.29-33= Zenon 4 Graham)

The weave of multiplicity and unity admits no outside, no resolution, just as the Parmenidean poem stages the irreducibly multiple throughout its own statements on unity and its conditions.[87] The poeticized language of Zenoan paradox concretizes this in its diction that emphasizes the bind of (neuter) plural (subjects) and (third-person) singular (verbs), the refrain of πολλά ἐστιν [many are/is] and the other phrases staging this bind. To be sure, this is an ordinary

---

87 Further articulation of this tension emerges as a central concern of the next chapter.

CHAPTER 1

feature of Greek, but the Zenoan context thematizes it, rendering legible and visible the tension active in this way of speaking. As they pull thinking horizontally, laterally, limit [πεπερασμένα...εἴη] and open-expanse [ἄπειρον] thread one another as the motion of opacity in Zenoan paradoxes.

A Parmenidean echo resonates in Zenoan (re-)translation of ἀνάγκη [typically translated: necessity]. In the Parmenidean poem, Ἀνάγκη exerts a hold on being, cinching its self-identity-as-self-repetition-othering [τὸ αὐτόν], the continual self-differing Parmenidean thinking on identity along Cassin's interpretive lines, where each articulation of self repeats, and so opens difference within-as, that self: τὸ αὐτόν, τὸ αὖ τό, *le re-le* [the once-again-the] or *ce re-ce* [this once-more-this]. Similarly, in the Zenoan prose excerpt quoted by Simplikios ἀνάγκη determines the bind of multiplicities and unity(-ies), where beings both remain self-enclosed in themselves (neither more nor less than themselves [αὐτῶν])—as if in the Parmenidean bonds of a limit (Parm. 8.30-1)—and, equally determined by ἀνάγκη, in a condition of ever-beyond themselves, ever-exceeding themselves as a site of continual self-differing. As with the Parmenidean force of Ἀνάγκη, Zenoan ἀνάγκη propels identity into the manifold relations of re-iteration. Such self-differing jolts thinking, shakes loose pre-established and received certainties and animates further thinking in a radically unsettled condition: not asserting unity as a lesson granted by the master Parmenides and the Thea of the poem, Zenoan thinking translates towards continual differing-in-resemblance, remaining unmoored, adrift and alert, tidal. "Thus it was said," reports Simplikios, "that Zenon used to say that if anyone could deliver to him what the one is, that person could handle [ἕξειν] the laying-out [λέγειν] of beings [τὰ ὄντα]" (Simpl. *in Phys.* 97.12-13= Zenon 9 Graham). Ontology [λέγειν τὰ ὄντα] restlessly churns in the surge and withdrawal of paradox disclosing unity as unclosed, a movement spoken in ἄπειρον as ever-exceeding the determination of number.

Releasing being from the constraint of limitation with which ἀνάγκη seems to enclose it in the Parmenidean poem, Melissoan thinking voices the open-expanse of possibilities [ἄπειρον] pulsing within being's totality. Where Zenoan thinking putatively encloses being [τὸ ὄν] by showing that, while members of a plurality fluctuate between greatness and smallness of size [μέγεθος (Simpl. *in Phys.* 139.8-9=Zenon 6 Graham)], size forms a condition and definite enclosure of being [εἰ μὴ ἔχοι μέγεθος τὸ ὄν οὐδ᾽ ἂν εἴη (Simpl. *in Phys.* 141.1-2=Zenon 7 Graham)], in Melissoan thinking being takes place as a continuously opening-expanse [ἄπειρον]. Being's greatness will not be a measurable size, not a self-enclosure, but an ever-self-opening expanse [τὸ μέγεθος ἄπειρον ἀεὶ χρὴ εἶναι (Simpl. *in Phys.* 109.31-2= Mel. 11 Graham)]. Withdrawing thought from a plurality, which amounts to a series of ones (unities), the un-closing of being from Parmenidean and Zenoan self-enclosure (and its paradox[es]) takes place as an

PHILOSOPHY AS TRANSLATION

open-expanse of multiplicities that defy singular and plural. Melissoan thinking re-activates through translation Anaximandrean ἄπειρον, keeps the open-expanse located on the site of any unity and opens it to ever more numerous possibilities, so that being's open-expanse of multiplicity constitutes its unity. In Melissoan thinking, the meaning of unity says: open-expanse, multiplicity, or, one-is-many. Once sung in hexameter thinking as the spiralized complex of Mousa(i)-Mnemosyne-singer, Melissoan thinking voices this experience as: open-expanse-multiplicity as being... unity as being [ἄπειρον δὲ τὸ ὄν...ἓν ἄρα τὸ ὄν (Simpl. *in Phys.* 103.29-30= Mel. 8 Graham)]. In the translational action Melissoan thinking activates, just as open-expansive-multiplicity *and* unity translate being, so does being translate each, and so too does each translate the other. The translational interface quickens more and multiple translational relations, each opening and disclosing differing facets of one another.

An ancient term already swelling the tides of the Homeric poems, ἄπειρον streams in multiple directions. Along with the valences of vastness, inexhaustibility, endless expanse "encircling the spherical body of our star-studded heaven" sounded by Kahn from the verbal base περ- and its manifestations as πείρω [pierce], περάω [drive through and across], περαίνω [complete, bring to an end],[88] ἄπειρον in its Anaximandrean translation also moves in the direction of experience (πεῖρα, experience, trial; πειράω, experience through making an attempt) and, as sounding a negation of experience [ἀ-πεῖρα, ἀ-πειράω], towards an irreconcilable dimension, an untranslatable element that animates the expansive abundance of being. In unpredictable ways, Anaximandrean ἄπειρον—as ἀ-πειράω, ἀ-πεῖρα, *without* experience—gives voice to unforeseeable possibilities somehow unified *and* differentiated, singular and plural. As that which remains outside of experience [ἀ-πειράω], ἄπειρον charges thinking with the circular or spherical energies involved in speech, turning within language the thought of a zone of abundance beyond or other than that within language, raising turbulence inside the zone of speech as a critical reminder of the abundance in excess of experience—the sprawl of heaven and earth past the dream of philosophy.

Involved with the language of Milesian and hexameter thinking, Melissoan translation re-turns in its own way to an experience of being as already in advance of thinking, surpassing experience even as it presses continually and always-already on experience. On this, Melissoan translation opens as differing from Parmenidean thinking, letting the self-differing play in the saying of the same. Retracing the open circle of Parmenidean thinking along which

---

88 Kahn, *Anaximander and the Origins of Greek Cosmology*, 232-3, 234 (quotation). The entire appendix, "The ΑΠΕΙΡΟΝ of Anaximander," is significant (231-9).

beginnings turn and return (Parm. 5), Melissoan thinking stresses the blur upon that circle, the way(s) its very circularity wears away the edges of beginning and ending, fraying into the open-expanse of ἄπειρον. For Parmenidean thinking, the anarchic-unbegunness of being remains entwined in the threefold of awareness-speaking-being [χρὴ τὸ λέγειν τε νοεῖν τ' ἐὸν ἔμμεναι (Parm. 6.1)]. In speaking being as ἄπειρον, Melissoan thinking stresses a differing and emphasizes the apartness on the span of the Parmenidean threefold, letting voice the ahead-ness of being, its outspanning and untranslatable dimension. Being surpasses an experience of being in a manner that leaves being radically open-ended [οὐδὲ τελευτήν], anarchic [ἀρχὴν οὐκ ἔχει (Simpl. *in Phys.* 109.20-1=Mel. 10 Graham)], a horizon whose drift recedes with each movement of approach: not invisible, nor hidden, but ever-in-motion, adrift, *e-merging* and the out of which all emerging might rise.[89] Distinct from the motion of emerging, the out-of-which horizon of being-emerging that Melissoan thinking hears as indistinguishable from γενόμενον [typically translated: coming to be, becoming], Melissoan thinking voices being-emerging instead as the ever-outspanning ἄπειρον.

Melissoan thinking uncloses being from the determinations of number and the limitation of completion, just as it unmoors being from something like a bind to or identification with a specific being or beings, as in the Pherekydean triad whose being(s)—like Melissoan being in its temporal span [ἀεὶ ἦν καὶ ἀεὶ ἔσται (Simpl. *in Phys.* 109.20=Mel. 10 Graham)]—remain(s) temporally expansive [ἦσαν ἀεί] as discrete entities Zas, Khronos [Χρόνος], and Khthonie (Diog. Laert. I.11)]. For Melissoan thinking, this Pherekydean plurality, an arrangement of discrete, atomistic unities remaining ever-themselves, fixed in their durable identities as none-other-than-themselves,[90] results in a limiting in the direction of and against an other [περανεῖ πρὸς ἄλλο (Simpl. *in Phys.* 110.5-6=Mel. 13 Graham)], which would reduce to isolated fixed identities being's unity-as-open-expansive-multiplicity [ἄπειρον]. Detaching being from *a being*, Melissoan thinking further releases being from determination as a *that*.

Not a thing to be altered, to be translated, to be enclosed in a strict, metaphysically determined identify of self-sameness, Melissoan being translates, or, is translating:

---

89 Maly offers "emerging" as a translation of τὸ ἐόν in the Parmenidean poem. Maly, "Parmenides: Circle of Disclosure, Circle of Possibility," 12-13.
90 With the compelling exception of the one female-feminine being Χθονίη, who undergoes translation—is translated by Ζάς—into Γῆ. For a discussion of this transformation (violence of translation), see Spitzer, "Divining," 441-4.

If it were to render-itself-other [ἑτεροιοῦται], by the press of necessity's double-bind [ἀνάγκη][91] being would not be differing-with-itself-in-similarity [ὅμοιον)] but rather the before-being [τὸ πρόσθεν ἐόν] would be utterly destroyed, while non-being would arise (Simpl. *in Phys.* 111.22-23=Mel. 15 Graham)[92]

The translational action that would sever being from its having-been—what Thea prohibits explicitly in the Parmenidean poem (Parm. 4.2)—thinks differing as something else, as if a wholly alien event enforced from the force of some other force, here called ἀνάγκη, required to enact a becoming-other. Such translational action has the character of a transfer from one self-enclosing identity of self-sameness to another. Melissoan thinking thinks a translational event of being otherwise, not in the manner of a fixed identity transformed from without to another fixed identity, but as the already-active differing that translates and (re-)names being: ὅμοιον: similar, a similaic dynamic, differing-with-itself-in-similarity. In so doing, Melissoan thinking translates the Parmenidean poem and its other-voicing of being as simile and similaic dynamic [πᾶν ἔστιν ὁμοῖον (Parm. 8.22)]. Melissoan being does not differ and change itself, nor harbor difference and change within itself as some other discretely differentiated thing isolable, detachable, something resembling the purported meaning to be delivered from one to another language by way of translation's "classical determination." Rather, being [τὸ ὄν] names and translates differing-as-being-itself [ὅμοιον] as the open-expanse undetermined, ἄπειρον, multiplicitous and expansive as its ownmost "tautological" figure, spoken otherwise in the Parmenidean poem as the folding-unfolding of τὸ ἐόν (Parm. 8.29).[93]

Embers still can return to flame, smoldering can be stirred into blazing fire. In Zenoan and Melissoan thinkings prose once more—as with the Milesians—translates singing while remaining enmeshed in the tradition of hexameter thinking through the re-beginning in experience of an encounter. The translating prose trembles with the tensions of paradoxes and of a relentless torque of repetition-as-differing. In all its transformations—from Homer and Hesiod through the Milesians and across the sun-touched waters of seas dark as wine to the Italian peninsula, Sicily, back eastward to the Aegean island of Samos—archaic thinking's translational action promotes differing and multiplicity. Early

---

91 ἀγκών: bend, as in the elbow for an embrace; ἄγχω: clutch, throttle, constrict. Cassin, *Parménide: Sur la nature ou sur l'étant*, 57.
92 Just a minor variation between this and Graham's text, which presents ὁμοῖον in place of ὅμοιον in this passage. Daniel W. Graham, *The Texts of Early Greek Philosophy: The Complete Fragments and Selected Testimonies of the Major Presocratics*, vol. 1. (Cambridge: Cambridge University Press, 2010), 472.
93 Maly, "Parmenides: Circle of Disclosure, Circle of Possibility," 14.

Greek thinking enacts elemental translation, the dynamics of thought-in-motion, the happening(s) or event(s) of *thinking* that (re-)sounds "not through logic or the metaphysics of rational assertion,"[94] but through a dynamic experience of open-awareness and alertness to the translational folding(s) of thinking, thinking that resists a reduction to unified and stabilized statements taken as fixed starting points. Elemental, this translational protocol does not settle earlier thinking into doctrines and mere assertions stripped of their fluid and fire-like mobile language(s), seeming instead to activate dimensions of what other thinking has thought in the differing-through-repetition of *tautology*, its re-turnings and re-beginnings that manifest as multiple versions, multiplicities.

Fire to Stone

Hephaistos, the mountain of flame, site of earth's translations—through this divinity and along the way of fire converge two translational pathways. From the western settlements of Hyele-Elea and those on Sicily into the emerging center and its putative stability in the form of autochthony (Hdt. VII.161.3, VIII.55.1),[95] at Athens Platon re-performs the elemental translation by fire undertaken by Empedokles, offering his poetry to the god of the mountain of fire and devoting himself to philosophy as distinct from singing, from poetry:

> He was planning to compete for a prize in tragedy when he heard Sokrates before the theater of Dionysos; he burnt down the poems, saying: "Hephaistos, come forth to this place, Platon now longs for you!" He was twenty. From then on, they say, he learned from Sokrates. (Diog. Laert. III.5-6)

Unlike Empedokles, whose elemental translation binds him to thinking as singing, Platon—at least in the tradition conveyed by Diogenes—destroys singing but preserves thinking in another mode: *philosophy*. According to Nightingale, by way of opposing other types of literatures and discourses Platon constructs philosophy's disciplinarity to be an exclusive area in the fourth century.[96]

Hephaistos, the mountain of flame, site of earth's translations—singing already has perished, burned to ash by the time the young Platon summons

---

94 Maly, "Parmenides: Circle of Disclosure, Circle of Possibility," 12.
95 Elsewhere, Athenian progenitor Erekhtheos is said to be earthborn [γηγενέος (Hom. *Il.* II.546-51)].
96 Andrea Wilson Nightingale, *Genres in Dialogue: Plato and the Construct of Philosophy* (Cambridge: Cambridge University Press, 1995), 18-19. Along these lines, Kraut suggests that because of Plato's sustained concern with establishing boundaries around the field and determining its proper performance, it can be understood as "his invention." Richard Kraut, "Plato," in *The Stanford Encyclopedia of Philosophy* (Spring 2022 Edition), ed. Edward N. Zalta, https://plato.stanford.edu/archives/spr2022/entries/plato/.

Hephaistos. Written in ash, the fragile remains and earthen residue of early Greek thinking as singing, Platonic dialogues compose figures of durability, figures of stone from the collections of sayings that reduce earlier Greek thinking to statements of doctrine. Reaching into earlier compendia of *epitomes* and selected quotations, Platonic writings sketch outlines or contour drawings of early Greek thinkers: the fifth-century sophists Protagoras, Hippias, and Gorgias all produced compendia from which Platon draws for the figures or shapes of the earlier Greek thinkers.[97] Hippias' collection underlies both the presentation in Platon's *Theaitetos* of "all the selective thinkers [σοφοί]" who agree that "all things are born from flux and movement" (Pl. *Tht.* 152d.2-e.9) and the opening survey of philosophy's history in Aristoteles' *Metaphysics*.[98] Quoted by Klemens of Alexandria in the second or early third century c.e., the introduction of Hippias' compendium declares its practice of cutting away selections of texts to illustrate the views of many early Greek thinkers:

> having collected [συνθείς] what is greatest and most alike from all these thinkers, I will produce this gathering [λόγον] new and with many views [πολυειδῆ] (Clem. Al. *Strom.* 6.2.228C)

Such epitomes simplify and reduce radiant early Greek thinking into statements of durable, easily transmissible—which is to say, *translatable*—positions, effectively limiting the range of early thinking, its "variegated and polysemic forms and expressive resources" that flow "in multiple directions beyond static doctrines."[99] Early Greek thinking becomes static thought shorn of thinking as a dynamic re-sounding and voicing of experiences, a singing in tension with itself, to borrow from Herakleitos, a singing converging diverging consonant dissonant (Hera. 10), differing with itself as its ownmost [διαφερόμενον ἑωυτῷ ὁμολογέει] in the manner of a lyre or a bow (Hera. 51).

In the dialogue called *Parmenides* Platon develops and integrates a second pathway by way of a translative gesture that renders Parmenides a figure of his own philosophy directly—and not unnamed as in Zenon and Melissos and other early Greek thinkers taken to respond (translate) to Parmenidean thinking, such as Anaxagoras. Valentine reads in the dialogue a certain violence, a

---

97 Jaap Mansfeld, "Aristotle, Plato, and the Preplatonic Doxography and Chronography," in *Studies in the Historiography of Greek Philosophy* (Assen/Maastricht, The Netherlands: Van Gorcum, 1990), 25-7.
98 Bruno Snell, "Die Nachrichten über die Lehren des Thales und die Anfänge der griechischen Philosophie- und Literaturgeschichte" *Philologus* 96 (1944): 170-82.
99 Spitzer, "Trans-philosophy," 566.

CHAPTER 1

forced migration imposed on Parmenides by Platon.[100] By locating Parmenides within the orbit of dialogic philosophy and the centrality of Athens and its more familiar idiom (Attic prose), Platon seems to enact an assimilative translation or, to use Casanova's term, an "annexation" of Parmenides that takes place "through a denial of difference."[101] Such a translative gesture unfolds as a version of Schleiermacher's "author-to-reader" translation, in which the foreign becomes other than itself, familiar and no longer foreign.[102]

On the other hand, the appropriative gesture might be complicated by the manner in which Platon lets the Parmenidean poem reverberate into multiple outcomes of dialectical investigation, leaving room for the poem to be more and other than the translative elaborations: in the *Parmenides*, Platon has the character Parmenides engage in dialectics that identify eight variations on themes of being, unity, and plurality. Furthermore, the detachment from place Valentine notes is in the first place *fictional*, expressive of action and play, two aspects that constitute the *drama* of Platonic writing. Place is semantically active in the dialogue, though differently than in the Parmenidean poem; Platon's *Parmenides* is in another place. Within the fiction, place and movement quicken some subtle tensions and implications. For example, those who seek out the drama are foreign to Athens, having arrived from Klazomenai in the Greek east (Pl. *Prm*. 126a.1-b.4), while within the narration given by Antiphon—son of Pyrilampes [Πυριλάμπης (Pl. *Prm*. 126b.4)], a very subtle gesture towards Parmenides' father Pyres [Πύρης (Diog. Laert. IX.3.21)]—those who seek Parmenides and Zenon must travel to the western part of Athens (Pl. *Prm*. 127c.1). These movements result in a curious reversal whereby the foreigners (Zenon and Parmenides) become the hosts, and an even more curious rendering of the foreign-hosts as foreign also to themselves by way of, and as a feature of, their own writings: Zenon's writings, a product of his youth, had been stolen and published involuntarily (Pl. *Prm*. 128d.7-e1); Parmenides is absent for much of the reading (Pl. *Prm*. 127. c6-d5); the readings themselves become the energy for discussion beyond their limits, i.e. into extra-terrestrial, foreign zones (Pl. *Prm*. 127d.6ff).

The house where the events recalled in the *Parmenides* occurred lay beyond the city walls, evoking the passage through the gates of the paths of Night and Day

---

100 Valentine, "The Archaeology of Parmenides," 29-30.
101 Pascale Casanova, "Consecration and Accumulation of Literary Capital: Translation as Unequal Exchange," trans. Siobhan Brownlie, in *Critical Readings in Translation Studies*, ed. Mona Baker (London: Routledge, 2010), 301.
102 Friedrich Schleiermacher, "On the Different Methods of Translating," trans. Douglas Robinson, in *Western Translation Theory: From Herodotus to Nietzsche*, 2nd ed., ed. Douglas Robinson (Manchester: St. Jerome, 2002), 229.

(Parm. 1.11). In the *kerameikos* (Pl. *Prm.* 127c.1), which was a neighborhood and a burial ground, the Platonic translative gesture echoes with the chariot's movement from east to west, its downgoing and associations with the underworld.[103] Situating the dialogue in proximity to that region, among the dead, adds nuance to Platon's interpretation and representation of the Parmenidean poem. The kerameikos was also the starting point of the great civic-religious procession in Athens.[104] Chief ritual among the Athenians, the Panathenaia reaffirmed their connection to and citizenship in the *polis* of Athens. That is, moving as it did from west to east, from extremity to center, from the burial site of the dead to a site of deathless divinities, the Panathenaiac procession led each citizen and the community as a whole symbolically from death, through the mundane and ordinary activities of life in the polis, to a sacred mountain at the heart of the city on which the principal and tutelary goddess was presented with the *peplos* and other offerings, renewing the sacred and ancient bond between humans and the goddess.[105] Arriving thus at the center and highpoint of the polis, Athenians gave themselves to a life beyond their own private lives, a life as citizens of Athens. The journey of the Parmenidean poem makes similar movements, seeking the goddess and a relationship with the divine beyond the ordinary, far from the human path (Parm. 1.27), perhaps with the goddess Athene.[106]

In Platon's *Parmenides* the destination is the home of Antiphon, a man concerned, like his grandfather, with horsemanship (Pl. *Prm.* 126c.7-8, 127a.1-2), a

---

103 See Peter Kingsley, *In the Dark Places of Wisdom* (Inverness, California: The Golden Sufi Center, 1999), 93-100, with notes on 233-4.
104 Whitaker notes these references in his translation of the dialogue. Whitaker, *Plato's Parmenides*, 23-4.
105 This point has been inferred from the lecture, "The End of Athens," given by Professor Will Freiert (University of Arkansas, February, 2004), particularly from his metaphorical use of the journey *from* the city *towards* the academy by way of, or through, the cemetery. Other information on the Panathenaiac procession comes from Jenifer Neils, "The Panathenaia: An Introduction," in *Goddess and Polis: The Panathenaiac Festival in Ancient Athens*, ed. Jenifer Neils (Hanover, New Hampshire: Hood Museum, Dartmouth College, 1992), 13-27; Jon D. Mikalson, "Erechtheus and the Panathenaia," *American Journal of Philology* 97, no. 2 (Summer, 1976): 149-51; and *OCD*³. s.v. "Panathenaia."
106 Miranda interprets several fragmentary inscriptions as dedicated to Athene and Zeus, for the former pointing back to Phokaia's Temple to Athene, and suggests that "the Phokaians, having fled from their homeland, transplanted or founded at Velia [Hyele, Elea] a cult of the Greek Athene and Zeus," Elena Miranda, "Nuove inscrizioni sacre di Velia," *Mélanges de l'Ecole française de Rome, Antiquité* 94, no. 1 (1982): 164 (Phokaian Temple to Athene), 168 (quotation). My interpolation. Athene figures also into Valentine's range of identities radiantly surrounding the poem's goddess, Thea. Valentine, "The Archaeology of Parmenides," 109.

subtle literary detail attaching the scene to the horses of the Parmenidean poem (Parm. 1). Horses are further emphasized by the fictional Parmenides himself:

> And yet I seem to be troubled by the Ibykeian horse [τὸ τοῦ Ἰβυκείου ἵππου πεπονθέναι]. The poet likened himself to an older champion horse who is preparing to compete in the chariot race [ἅρματι] and who, from experience [ἐμπειρίαν], shudders [τρέμοντι] at what is to come. Likewise, the poet, elderly and unwilling, approaches sex under compulsion [εἰς τὸν ἔρωτα ἀναγκάζεσθαι]. (Pl. *Prm.* 136e9-137a.4)

Having the character Parmenides quote the line from Ibykos, Platon enacts a translative gesture that might work through an association with place towards an implication about poetry: Ibykos began at Rhegion in Sicily, one moment on the fragmentations of the Phokaian-Hyelean diaspora (Hdt. 1.166.3), though seems to have traveled throughout Greece and the Greek east.[107] Formed from that emplacement, an especially subtle implication might underlie this quotation. Ibykos was associated with the tyrant Polykrates of Samos and, on those grounds, seemed to avoid "overtly political poetry."[108] Might Parmenides be implicated as tyrannical in his status as poet, from which he is ousted by, and into, the more democratic conditions of dialectics?

In the language of the dialogue Platon's translative gesture moves beyond horses to several elements of the Parmenidean poem echoing in the translation of Ibykos:

- the passive construction in which the horse is the agent (compare Parm. 1.1)
- the chariot [ἅρματι; compare ἅρμα (Parm. 1.5)]
- the horse's trembling [τρέμοντι; compare the τιταίνουσαι [straining] (Parm. 1.5])
- the presence of compulsion [ἀναγκάζεσθαι; compare ἀνάγκη (Parm. 8.16, 30)]
- a subtle resonance in experience [ἐμπειρίαν] with the limit [πείρατος (Parm. 8.31)]
- the presence of ἔρος [eros] as the destination towards which he is compelled (compare the erotic element at the center of the *kosmos* and first among divine beings [Parm. 13])

---

107 Ewen Bowie, "Early Expatriates: Displacement and Exile in Archaic Poetry," in *Writing Exile: The Discourse of Displacement in Greco-Roman Antiquity and Beyond*, ed. Jan Felix Gaertner (Leiden: Brill, 2007), 31-2.
108 Eva Stehle, *Performance and Gender in ancient Greece: Nondramatic Poetry in its Setting* (Princeton: Princeton University Press, 1997), 250.

By way of a shared vocabulary, Platon seems to be drawing attention to the similarities between the Parmenidean and Ibykean poems, linking the former to the cultural matrix of Western Greece by (translative) means of the latter. Might Platon's suggestion throughout these translative gestures imply a separation of poetry and philosophy? Parmenides has been asked to guide the way through various hypotheses on being and unity to show how investigations prepare a person for the philosophic task of defining stable entities in their formal being.[109] In response to this request, Parmenides quotes Ibykos as a way to remind himself of the arduous task he is being asked to demonstrate and to articulate his (Parmenides') own reticence to undertake it on account of his advanced age. That is, Parmenides invokes the Ibykean horse (poetry) prior to the work towards philosophy as a way to recall the effort such work requires. With all the verbal echoes between the Parmenidean and Ibykean poems in play, Platon's gestures may link the two in terms of poetry's mnemonic role prior to, but not directly involved in, the task of philosophy. Might this moment open a glimpse onto Platon's evaluation of the poetry of Parmenidean thinking as something like an *aide-mémoire* or preparation for philosophy, yet separate and ultimately separable from it?

Athenian Platon has Parmenides perform the translational action from poetry to prose that is applied in the philosophy of the fifth century to the Parmenidean song, reducing the singing to prose.[110] Parmenides is depicted not only translating the poem of Ibykos into prose, but also producing a self-translation into the dialectical idiom of Platon and into the dialect of Athens. The problem is not paraphrase or translation or so-called misquotation, but rather the homogenization of philosophic discourse, even in a fictional dialogue and all its complexities, into prose and the establishment of doctrine attributed to the subject of translation. Put another way, the *Parmenides* stages a translational action in which the translation is signed (by another) in the name of the original author, concealing the translator's presence and, further, the translation itself: the problem of invisibility.[111] This becomes especially clear when Platon's character

---

109 Parmenides tells Sokrates that anyone who lacks a view onto the forms would lack understanding, since the form of each being remains ever-itself [ἰδέαν τῶν ὄντων ἑκάστου τὴν αὐτὴν ἀεὶ εἶναι (Pl. *Prm.* 135b5-c2)].

110 Robb regards this as central to Platon's translational protocol of *Republic*, particularly in the tenth book: the "counter-charm" protecting audiences depends on the translation of "those wondrous ancient verses into plain everyday prose" so that their deceptive powers are exposed. Kevin Robb, *Literacy and Paideia in Ancient Greece* (Oxford: Oxford University Press, 1994), 226.

111 Berman, "Trials of the Foreign," 241 (repression, concealment, negation of a mode of translation that would expose translation and translator[s]); Venuti, "Invisibility," chap.

Parmenides begins his engagement with Aristoteles from his own hypothesis (Pl. *Prm.* 137b.2-3).

In the *Parmenides*, the layered images and literariness of Platon's writing perform a complex translation as the dialogue presents an image of Parmenides. Overall, the gestures and actions in Platon's *Parmenides* work in two ways. First, the dialogue lets a variety of interpretations of the Parmenidean poem remain in play, so that Parmenides appears less a source of doctrine than of a way of thinking. Second, in the implication that the thinking carried out in and as the Parmenidean poem can be translated *simpliciter*, that is, according to the "classical determination," into prose, Platon assumes a doctrine *available to be translated*. The second assumption resurfaces in the translation of Parmenides undertaken by Platon in the well-known passage from *Theaitetos*. With characteristic and subtle writerly flourishes, Platon layers the figuration of a Parmenidean doctrine of the one and static being by staging Parmenides as single and alone in the dramatic speech of the dialogue—alone against many *sophoi* (Pl. *Tht.* 152e.2-5)—and by formulating that doctrine in the negative:

ὡς ἄρα ἓν μὲν αὐτὸ καθ' αὑτὸ οὐδέν ἐστιν

(Pl. *Tht.* 152d.2-3)

to be sure nothing is a unity, itself by itself.[112]

In the phrase ὡς ἄρα ἓν μὲν αὐτὸ καθ' αὑτὸ οὐδέν ἐστιν [nothing is a unity, itself by itself] Platon issues a shadow of the Parmenidean saying ταὐτόν τ' ἐν ταὐτῷ τε μένον καθ' ἑαυτό τε κεῖται [the same staying in its sameness remains with sameness (Parm. 8.29)] and leaves the doctrine in shadowed silence, unspoken and absent, but present as the shadow of what all others say.[113] Again, Platon's

---

1 in *The Translator's Invisibility* (New York: Routledge, 1995); Theo Hermans, "The Translator's Voice in Translated Narrative," *Target* 8, no. 1 (1996): 23-48. See also the new collection engaged specifically with this problem, Larisa Cercel and Alice Leal, eds. *The Translator's Visibility*: New Debates and Epistemologies (New York: Routledge, 2025).

112 Another Platonic subtlety resonates in the συμφερέσθων [drawn together (Pl. *Tht.* 152e.3)], which gestures in the direction of the Herakleitean phrase ὅλα καὶ οὐκ ὅλα, συμφερόμενον διαφερόμενον [whole and not whole converging diverging (Hera. 10)] and follows immediately Parmenides' name.

113 On an eccentric reading a shadow of dactylic hexameter emerges in Platon's line: if read with stress on the accented syllables there sounds a shadowed dactylic rhythm over five, and not six, feet: — ˘ ˘ / — ˘ ˘ / — ˘ ˘ / — — / — ˘.

translation is complex:[114] shadowing the Parmenidean poem gives it in the negative, available as *what is not*, quietly and playfully disturbing the Parmenidean poem's repeated apparent denial *and* affirmation of negation (Parm. 2.3). While Platon's presentation of the positive statement of being in relief may subject it to slight ridicule, insofar as the very statement itself as it sounds in the Parmenidean poem seems to advance the negation it denies, it may also be a show of respect to the Hyelean thinker of being. For, Platon's translation makes Parmenides the standard against which all other thought is measured.

The alleged doctrine of Parmenides comes to light in a line of *Theaitetos* that has been construed as a variation on a line from the Parmenidean poem, though it is presented as an amalgam, attributed to "many Melissoses and Parmenideses" (Pl. *Tht.* 180e.2), intimating the enduring resistances of singing and its translations to a simple reduction:

οἷον ἀκίνητον τελέθει τῷ παντὶ ὄνομ' εἶναι (Pl. *Tht.* 180e.1)
Since it is wholly motionless, being is the name for the all.[115]

This translates the Parmenidean line:

οὖλον ἀκίνητόν τε ἔμεναι· τῷ παντ' ὀνόμασται[116]
(Parm. 8.38)

To be whole and changeless; wherefore it has been named all things.[117]

Sokrates speaks the composite translation then translates it to prose as follows:

ὡς ἕν τε πάντα ἐστὶ καὶ ἕστηκεν αὐτὸ ἐν αὑτῷ οὐκ ἔχον χώραν ἐν ᾗ κινεῖται (Pl. *Tht.* 180e.3-4)
that unity both is all things and has set itself in itself, not having a place in which it can move.

Exercising the translational action of philosophy, Sokrates' translation voices a twofold doctrine of unity of being and its accompanying stasis. Putting in

---

114 Repetitions: Parm. 6.1-2; 7.1; 8.9, 46.
115 Translation is from Joe Sachs, *Plato's Theaetetus* (Newburyport, MA: Focus, R. Pullins, 2004), 76. Sachs comments on this line that "Socrates seems not so much to be misquoting as engaging in free variation on a theme."
116 Another reading of the final foot: ὄνομ(α) ἔσται. Hermann Diels and Walther Kranz, eds. *Die Fragmente der Vorsokratiker*, vol. 1. 6th ed. (Berlin: Weidmannsche, 1951), 238 (28 B8.38).
117 Translation is from Gallop, *Parmenides of Elea*, 71.

view a haphazard quotation attributed across multiple thinkers and following that with a further prose translation that encapsulates in a single statement what many thinkers and thinkings thoroughly assert [διοχυρίζονται (Pl. *Tht.* 180e.3)], the reduction of manifold into singular restates the translational protocol motivated by an attempt to extract and "to reveal the unity of being under the differences of languages."[118]

As a translational action, assertion and establishment of doctrine reduces complexity and asserts identity of thinking and thought, of thought with itself: it takes place as a philosophy of the same. This has been termed "essentialism" and has been aligned with Platon.[119] Van Wyke links a notion of "ideal form" with "original works" whose "'essence' is treated with a reverence similar to that which Sokrates shows towards forms."[120] However, reading along these lines hypostasizes and homogenizes Platonic texts that themselves elude easy doctrinal readings by way of a treasury of formal and literary resources that keep thought and thinking in motion, enacting dialogue in which "every claim is presented for examination, every claim is provisional, and nothing gets settled once and for all."[121] That is to say, critique of essentialism folds into its own essentialist movement in extracting and presenting philosophic doctrine, as it must do under the compulsion of metaphysics and "the medium of the concept."[122] Yet, following Adorno, that "magic circle" will not be undone by referring essentialism to itself, but instead will take another turn into "micrology" whose action produces fissures in the identity yielded by the translational action of subsumption.[123] To assert that Platon's "is a philosophy of sameness" is to excise much important complexity and to reperform that impulse towards stabilized identity that animates the criticism.[124] In Platon and in the translational and translative movements of archaic thinking, as the readings of early Greek thinkers and the Platonic *Parmenides* and *Theaitetos* have attempted to contour

---

118 Cassin, "Philosophising in Languages," trans. Yves Gilonne, *Nottingham French Studies* 49, no. 2 (Summer, 2010): 19.
119 Arrojo, "Philosophy and translation," *Handbook of Translation Studies*, vol. 1, ed. Yves Gambier and Luc van Doorslaer (Amsterdam: John Benjamins, 2010), 247-8.
120 Ben Van Wyke, "Imitating Bodies and Clothes: Refashioning the Western Conception of Translation," in *Thinking Through Translation with Metaphors*, ed. James St. André (Manchester: St. Jerome, 2010), 32.
121 Anne Ashbaugh, "Consuming Knowledge," in Spitzer, *Studies in Ancient Greek Philosophy*, 135-6.
122 Theodor Adorno, *Negative Dialectics*, trans. E. B. Ashton (New York: Bloomsbury, 1973), 406.
123 Adorno, *Negative Dialectics*, 407-8.
124 Van Wyke, "Imitating Bodies and Clothes," 20.

on the level of small (the *micrologic*), thinking appears to continue its resistance to essentialism itself even as it produces the conditions for its formulation and its afterlife. In this sense, Platonic philosophic translational actions might be understood as transitional, participating in and extending the resistance to reductions animating archaic Greek thinking while also subjecting that sinuous thinking—singing—to the "classical determination" of translation.

Aristoteles both receives and transmits particular readings—translations—of the Parmenidean poem, making use of existing doxographic sources that classified archaic thinking in various ways while adjusting them through his own philosophic engagements with them. Of the three fifth-century sophists mentioned above, Gorgias' presentation was oriented by what Mansfeld has termed a "systematical point of view," while Hippias arranged thinkers in relation to questions, and Protagoras' collection aimed specifically at a critical assessment of Eleatic monism.[125] At once accepting and establishing a doctrinal reading of the poem, the thinking of *Physics* attributes to Parmenides a static unity [μίαν...ἀκίνητον (Arist. *Ph.* 184b.15-16)]. On the basis of this translation, Aristoteles eliminates Parmenides (and Melissos) from the discourse on φύσις [upsurge and withdrawal; typically translated: nature] because an investigation of one static being is *not* an investigation around φύσις: a static unity cannot be an ἀρχή [source, principle], since the ἀρχή is of something or of somethings (Arist. *Ph.* 185a.3-5). In *Physics*, if the static unity of the Parmenidean poem gave rise to some other thing it would be self-destructive on two counts: it would erase its own unity; it would be involved in the change of generation. While opening an insightful engagement with implications of the unity of being Aristoteles discerns in Parmenidean thinking, the translational action works exclusively from doctrines assigned to *Parmenides* with little direct involvements with the Parmenidean poem itself: few quotations, no sustained response to the multiple figures and densities of the Parmenidean Song of Being.

In the history of philosophy opening *Metaphysics*, Aristoteles' translational action(s) towards Parmenides for the most part severs the poem from the richness and fluid, supple multiplicities of its language. Initially, Aristoteles quotes part of a line from the Parmenidean poem in tandem with a fragmented passage from Hesiod's *Theogony* as the first steps towards articulating a cause of motion and change (Arist. *Metaph.* 984b.20-32). The translational action both reduces the two sayings and their poetic resonances to a repetition of the same—where both are candidates for being the first to establish [ἔθηκεν] eros or desire

---

125 Mansfeld, "Aristotle, Plato, and the Preplatonic Doxography and Chronography," 27.

[ἐπιθυμίαν][126] as a source and principle [ἀρχή]—and eliminates important and meaningful aspects of the poetic narratives: that Thea voices the phrase from the Parmenidean poem within a section of the narrative she herself terms deceitful [ἀπατηλόν (Parm. 8.52)] and that, in the Hesiodic *Theogony*, Mousa(i), whose concealments remain indistinguishably entwined with their disclosures (Hes. *Theog.* 27-8), along with Mnemosyne work as the wellspring of the genesis narrative from which Aristoteles quotes and then translates. Later in the inquiry, Aristoteles presents a translation along similar lines, minus the partial quotation. Best of the unifiers [ἑνίσας (spoken of Xenophanes, first of a group)], Parmenides is assigned the view that

> since deeming that besides being non-being could not be, compelled-from-necessity [ἐξ ἀνάγκης] he thought that being is one and no other thing is...while being compelled by necessity [ἀναγκαζόμενος] to follow what-shows-itself-in-its-own-light [τοῖς φαινομένοις], and accepting that being was one on account of *logos* and more than one on account of perception, he re-established two causes and two sources. (Arist. *Metaph.* 986b.27-33)

Perhaps gesturing subtly to the Parmenidean poem, Aristoteles summons the divine Ἀνάγκη [typically translated: Necessity] by way of the repetition of ἀνάγκ— terms, but the translation recasts this as logical necessity rather than the potent divinity [κρατερὴ Ἀνάγκη] whose grasp on τὸ ἐόν [typically translated: being] secures its reflexive self-touch-contact, its foldedness and enmeshment that encompasses, haptically keeps totality in-touch (Parm. 8.29-31).[127]

Presumably based on the verses that now form the eighth fragment, the translational action at work in Aristoteles' presentation effaces all the figures of the Parmenidean song—the singing Thea, the divinities *Ananke* [Ἀνάγκη] and *Moira* and their bonds [or, shackles: πέδῃσιν] and the tensions built from the image of restraining τὸ ἐόν—and the song's narratological alienation and distancing are extinguished,[128] transformed from the smoldering ash of a once blazing fire into the silent and heavy stone of established doctrine through a translational action

---

126 Here, too, the translational action shows its commitment to reduction of difference into repetition of the same: Eros, last of the originary beings in Hesiodic *Theogony* (Hes. *Theog.* 120-22), Eros, first of divinities to be unfolded into the divinely-generated totality (Parm. 13), with their differing evacuated turn out to be equivalent to a non-divine ἐπιθυμία [desire], which also encompasses the translation of Empedoklean φιλότης [sex] to φιλία [closeness, intimacy (Arist. *Metaph.* 985a.2-7)].

127 Spitzer, "Being-in-touch," 3-4.

128 On the alienation of narration, see Cassin's discussion of the "bifurcation du sujet" [bifurcation of the subject] based on an insightful comparative reading of the Sirens scene from the *Odyssey*. Cassin, "Le chant des Sirènes dans le Poème de Parménide: quelques

that, "far from being the trials of the Foreign" instead unfurls as "its negation, its acclimation, its naturalization."[129] Yet, the Parmenidean song stages such a trial within its own limits, translating within itself "the relationship of the self-same (*Propre*) and the Foreign,"[130] layering *oratio recta* "as a mimesis of live speech within the context of live speech,"[131] but also voicing its own shiftings, intralingual translations on the very name of being, between πέλ- and εἶναι. While both are typically translated with forms of "to be," Smith discloses the latter as voicing "what comes to pass...a kind of being that 'is' at rest within its 'stirring,' 'arising,' 'coming to the fore'."[132] In the introduction and presence of Thea's voice as "speech within speech" and in the ways in which that "secondary voice" inextricably entwines foreignness of the self-same with itself,[133] the song already activates the translational energies of *l'épreuve de l'étranger* [trial of the foreign]:

IT is indivisible [οὐδὲ διαιρετόν ἐστιν], an homogeneous whole,
not more in one place
        which would prevent its coherence
and less in another
        a plenum of existence
continuous gravitation [πελάζει] of being towards being (Parm. 8.22-5)[134]

In the πελάζει formulation and the active condition spoken in -ιζω- verbs, πελ- actively turns, resonant of the broad sea's ceaseless active motion [πέλαγος, πελάζει, πέλειν]; Lombardo activates a force of motion in his "continuous

---

    remarques sur le fr. VIII, 26-33," in *Études sur Parménide*, vol. 2, *Problèmes d'interprétation*, ed. Pierre Aubenque (Paris: Libraire philosophique J. Vrin, 1987), 165-6.
129 Antoine Berman, "Translation and the Trials of the Foreign," trans. Lawrence Venuti, in Venuti, *The Translation Studies Reader*, 241.
130 Berman, "The Trials of the Foreign," 240.
131 The "context of live speech" is performance. Victor Bers, *Speech in Speech: Studies in Incorporated Oration Recta in Attic Drama and Oratory* (Lanham: Rowman and Littlefield, 1997), 3.
132 P. Christopher Smith, "Parmenides and Poetry: Taking Gadamer's Reading One Step Further," *Journal of the British Society for Phenomenology* 34, no. 3 (October, 2003): 273-4. In unfolding an understanding of πόλις, Heidegger articulates the mobility voiced in πέλειν as "aufgehend ins Unverborgene ragen" [rising, to rise towerlike into unconcealing]. Heidgger, *Parmenides*, 133.
133 "Secondary voice" borrows from Bers, *Speech in Speech*, 7. Thea's addresses to the interlocutor suggest a dialogics, an atmosphere of orality.
134 Lombardo's translation puts on view the self-estrangement of the Thea's song with the breaks creating uneven lines against the statements on homogeneity. Lombardo, *Parmenides and Empedocles*, 16; my interpolations.

gravitation." Even as being does not differ from itself [οὐδὲ διαιρετόν ἐστιν] its tidal pulls and swells turn it towards itself, performing the self-differentiation of reflexivity and a self-translation from and into itself-as-differing.

Such translative differentiation surfaces most notably in the lines stressing sameness while fanning into diversity:

ταὐτόν τ' ἐν ταὐτῷ τε μένον καθ' ἑαυτό τε κεῖται

(Parm. 8.29)

remaining the same and in the same [it] lies by itself [same][135]

Heavy, spondaic opening feet in the hexameter, with five consecutive long syllables, draw attention to the *sameness* in repetition and its modulations attached to the dental -τ-, adding emphasis to the in-built differentiation of reflexivity and of translation. Maly's translation highlights such differentiation: "the selfsame, together with itself, just as it is in this very place, is situated within the core movement/tension of itself."[136] The second sense of Berman's trial comes forward in the song's self-translations, as its language flashes the song's own "most distant from itself."[137] The Aristotelian translation of the Parmenidean poem extinguishes the flames of thinking-as-singing, enacting the "classical determination" of translation, its work (and conceptual possibilization) of reducing to doctrine minimizes the foreignness permeating the Parmenidean song. This translational mode attempts to make an analysis of the other's thinking "down to its innermost core, to disregard the constitutive role played by a language and then, as it were through a new chemical process compound this 'prelinguistic' core with the essence and the power of another language."[138] Aristoteles' translational action attempts to move such a "prelinguistic core," not only prior to language but also "an unchangeable core or essence,"[139] from singing into a rigid, unmoving prose, a petrification of elemental translation, of thinking.

The "classical determination" of translation and its rootedness in the attempt at repetition of the same also resounds in Zenoan thinking as it undergoes

---

135 Gallop's translation with interpolation in brackets added. *Parmenides of Elea*, 69.
136 Maly, "Parmenides: Circle of Disclosure, Circle of Possibility," 14.
137 Berman, "The Trials of the Foreign," 240. See Jacobs's reading of αὐτός (same) as the center of the poem, which he takes—after Heidegger's insights—to say "belonging together." David C. Jacobs, "The Ontological Education of Parmenides," in *The Presocratics after Heidegger*, ed. David C. Jacobs (Albany: SUNY Press, 1999), 186-7.
138 Schleiermacher, "On the Different Methods of Translating," 234.
139 Arrojo, *Fictional Translators: Rethinking Translation through Literature* (London: Routledge, 2018), 50.

transformations in Aristoteles' translation. Platon's Sokrates regards the Zenoan paradoxes and the Parmenidean poem as asserting the same thing [ταὐτόν] veiled by deceitful changes (Pl. *Prm.* 128a.6-8), already revealing his inclination to locate the one, as he requests of Meno in a different dialogue, "in which many do not differ but are all the same [ταὐτόν]" (Pl. *Meno* 72c.3-4). In Aristotelean translation the Zenoan Akhilleus seems to register as a fully translatable figure. For instance, rehearsing "the so-called Akhilleus," Aristoteles finds that it differs from the first of the four paradoxes only in the omission of the half measure, the dichotomics [τῷ διχοτομεῖν, τῇ διχοτομίᾳ] by which what is ahead cannot be overtaken by what follows (Arist. *Ph.* 239b.14-20). Aristoteles finds them interchangeable, even ὁ αὐτὸς λόγος [the same discourse], with the one exception noted. This alteration suggests the presence of the same meaning repeated with inconsequential differences regardless of how it is expressed. The vibrant dance of repeated words and parallel constructions, as well as the vivid images and figures of Zenoan thinking, becomes a mere play of costumes pulled away from a putative core of stable meaning to be exposed, evaluated, and (re-)solved. Focalizing the paradoxes through the topic of motion, for example, Aristoteles reduces the subtleties of Zenoan thinking to a logical refutation of motion's possibility. The spread of Zenoan thinking undergoes radical translation into elements, mere letters that stabilize the tensions motivating the paradoxes (e.g. Arist. *Ph.* 239b.33-240a.18). In so doing, the Aristotelean translational scheme dissolves or sets aside a practice of the early Greek thinkers that, as Simplikios articulated, "brings to light [ἀποφαίνεσθαι] in a darkly-gestural way [αἰνιγματωδῶς][140] their projections-towards-understanding [γνώμας]" (Simpl. *in Phys.* 36.30-1).[141]

Water to fire, fire to stone—bearing the complexion of the perduring and static result of a translative process—classical philosophy translates early Greek thinking according to a different translational mode formed in the sophist compendia and adopted by philosophers as they consolidate their discipline by way of shaping a history and protocol. Statements of doctrine supplant the fluidities of the first mode, the elemental pathway voiced from the experience of Mnemosyne—Mousa(i). Early Greek thinking *is translated* to philosophy as a practice of advancing doctrines to be defended through reasoned argumentation,

---

140 See Marciano on the Aristoteleian reconfiguration (translation) of αἴνιγμα according to the primary criterion of clarity. M. L. G. Marciano, "Images and Experience: At the Roots of Parmenides' *Aletheia*," *Ancient Philosophy* 28, no. 1 (2008): 23-4.

141 The translation of γνώμας as "projections-towards-understanding" attempts to evoke the way such understanding sets-up and locates its beginning or starting-point, in the manner of a gnomon, that will enable and generate fruitful relations projected by means of what is located.

with special emphasis on unity and clarity,[142] putatively isolating an abstract or conceptual content as "a meaning which transcends its form, circumstances and history, and which could be forever protected from difference and change."[143] As philosophy takes shape as a distinct field around Platon and Aristoteles and their schools through the course of the fourth century, its translational protocol seeks to consolidate views of earlier thinkers gathered into the emerging disciplinary range, such that "the origin of philosophy," as Derrida observed, "is translation or the thesis of translatability."[144] Accordingly, the predominate translational action pursues "immediate intelligibility and the absence of any linguistic or stylistic peculiarities that might preempt the illusion of transparency."[145] Water, fire, air—swift, coursing elements—are arrested through the translational action of classical philosophy into earthen sculptures of themselves, immobile and static in a putative core or essence, fully translatable, as if their mobilities become superficial coverings—fully translatable conceptual content that can be installed in different garb. Indeed, enacting this translational intent constitutes a characteristically philosophic task in identifying and articulating the unmoving and singular essence. Water, fire, air—swift, coursing elements—undergo a different elemental translation, a transformation to durable, translatable, transparent statements, a transformation from movement to stillness, from fire to stone.

Stone to Ice

Philosophy's mode of translation, oriented towards reproduction of the same, insists on the separability of ideas from language, a schism or detachability Derrida thinks as "the unique thesis of philosophy."[146] The transmission of doctrine, as the principal movement of this mode, flows from the compendiasts through Platon and Aristoteles into doxography and thence to the modern and contemporary periods. Restatement of established doctrines—the putative core and essence of early Greek thinking—tends to supplant intimate engagement with the myriad facets of thinking-as-singing, the suppleness and swift agility

---

142 For a discussion of clarity as a criterion for philosophy, see Spitzer, "Divining," 427-8 with notes.
143 Arrojo, "The Revision of the Traditional Gap Between Theory & Practice & the Empowerment of Translation in Postmodern Times," *The Translator* 4, no. 1 (1998): 28.
144 Jacques Derrida, *The Ear of the Other: Otobiography, Transference, Translation: Texts and Discussions with Jacques Derrida*, trans. Christie McDonald (New York: Shocken, 1985), 119-20.
145 Lawrence Venuti, *The Scandals of Translation: Towards an Ethics of Difference* (New York: Routledge, 1998), 114.
146 Derrida, "White Mythology: Metaphor in the Text of Philosophy," *Margins of Philosophy*, trans. Alan Bass (Chicago: University of Chicago Press, 1982), 229.

of its language, its own movements and tensions within itself. In the case of the Parmenidean poem, singing and its vivid tensions are petrified, stilled and quieted into a rigid doctrine of stasis and unity of being alongside a multifarious and more liquid physical doctrine understood as δόξα [typically translated: opinion] separable from the "true" understanding, the doctrine on being.[147] In the late fourth and early third centuries, Aristoteles' associate and successor Theophrastos included in his work *About the Philosophers of Nature* [Περὶ τῶν φυσικῶν] the statement of doctrine: after commenting that Parmenides explored two pathways for inquiry of φύσις according to truth [κατ᾽ ἀλήθειαν] and popular opinion [κατὰ δόξαν τῶν πολλῶν], Theophrastos attributes a position to the section of the Parmenidean poem according to truth [κατ᾽ ἀλήθειαν] that the singular totality [τὸ πᾶν] is one [ἕν], ungenerated [ἀγένητον], and spherical (Alex. Aphr. *in Metaph.* A.3.984b.4-11=DK 28 A7).

The doctrinal interpretations spread throughout the diverse philosophical schools of the Classical and Hellenistic periods as well as through the Christian traditions in overlapping ways:

- in the late fourth century Eudemos, another associate of Aristoteles, seems to take a reduction of the doctrine of being—that whatever is besides being [τὸ παρὰ τὸ ὄν] is non-being, but also being is said univocally [μοναχῶς],[148] so being is one—as a starting point for logical reasoning (Simpl. *in Phys.* 115.13-15=DK 28 A28)
- Philodemos the Epikourean (ca. 110-35) gives a brief statement of the doctrine of being as ἕν τὸ πᾶν [one the totality] common to Parmenidean and Melissoan thinking (DK 28 A49)
- in the first-second centuries c.e., Plutarkhos the Platonist relays the doctrine of being as eternal and unchanging, a unity [ἕν] similar to itself and not accepting any difference (Plut. *Mor.* 1114d=DK 28 A34)
- the Christian Hippolytos (second-third centuries c.e.) summarizes the twofold ontological and natural position that makes the totality [τὸ πᾶν] a unity [ἕν] that is eternal, ungenerated, [ἀγέννητον], spherical, and motionless [ἀκίνητον], while also elaborating a physical theory Hippolytos articulates as involving two source-principles [ἀρχάς] fire and earth (Hippol. *Haer.* I.11=DK 28 A23)
- citing Theophrastos, in the third-century c.e., Diogenes Laertios mentions a two-part natural and ontological doctrine, but prioritizes the former in his summary (Diog. Laert. IX.3=DK 28 A1)

---

147 On ways the so-called δόξα permeates the whole poem, see Rose Cherubin, "'Mortals Lay Down Trusting to be True'," *Epoché* 21, no. 2 (2017): 251-71.
148 The translation of μοναχῶς as "univocally" is Gallop's translation, *Parmenides of Elea*, 113.

- Christian scholar Eusebios (third-fourth centuries c.e.) summarizes the Parmenidean doctrine of being as an unmoving [ἀκίνητον] aspect of the eternal and ungenerated τὸ ἐόν (Euseb. *Praep. evang.* I.8.5=DK 28 A22)

By the time of Simplikios in the sixth century c.e., the position on the unity of being comes to be elaborated through textual citations that indicate clearly [δηλοῖ τὸ σημεῖον αὐτοῦ] the doctrine that being is one, ungenerated [ἀγένητον], imperishable [ἄφθαρτον], incorporeal [οὐδὲ σωματικόν], and indivisible [ἀδιαίρετον], where Simplikios adduces different passages for each part of the doctrine (Simpl. *in Phys.* 142-3).

Content detached from form assumes primary significance under the rubric of rational argumentation: beneath the gaze of a philosophy of self-sameness poetic elements become allegorical vehicles for the reinforcement of philosophic argumentation, or as Plutarkhos phrased it in the early second century c.e., the phrases [ἔπη] are reasonings [λόγοι] that make use of poetic features in the manner of a vehicle [ὄχημα] adopted so as to flee from pedestrian, ordinary language [πεζόν] (Plut. *Quomodo adul.* 16c-d=DK 28 A15)]. In a few rapid strokes of allegoresis aptly termed a "radical translation,"[149] Sextos Empirikos renders transparent the opening sequence of the Parmenidean poem, reducing the poem's diverse and polysemous figures and images into stable rational components and declaring that the so-called proem narrates a passage towards "intelligence [τὴν διάνοιαν] which holds safe the apprehension of things" and the "cognitive reason" [ἐπιστημονικὸν λόγον] distinct from sense (Sext. Emp. *Math.* VII.113-115).[150] The doctrinal reductions of the Parmenidean poem isolate a purportedly rational or logical content and consolidate its position within the field of philosophy.

Already by Platon and Aristoteles the Parmenidean poem has been translated from its own hexameter language to prosaic statements of doctrine within the domain of philosophy. Through philosophy's traditions the poem comes to rest within the discipline, so that even when interest in the poem's own language resurfaces in the Renaissance it remains within that field, albeit somewhat expanded by the project of Stephanus' sixteenth-century c.e. collection *Poesis Philosophica* [*Philosophic Poetry*]. As philosophy's history takes shape in European modernity, the emphasis on content severed from form resurfaces. Within the strain of dialectics in Hegel's nineteenth-century c.e. *Vorlesungen der Geschichte der Philosophie* [*Lectures on the History of Philosophy*] this translational protocol operates on early Greek thinking. From the outset, the sweep of dialectics

---

149 Cassin, *Parménide: Sur la nature ou sur l'étant*, 15.
150 Translation is from Bury, *Sextus Empiricus*. Vol. 2, *Against the Logicians*, 61, 63, respectively.

PHILOSOPHY AS TRANSLATION

generates "the Eleatics" within which Xenophanes, Parmenides, Zenon, and Melissos are gathered. On Aristoteles' recommendation the latter, Melissos, is eliminated from further consideration.[151] After translating biographies into a composite narrative of each of the remaining three Eleatics, Hegel enters the "purer field" [*reineres Feld*] on which the principal teaching [*Hauptlehre*] can be seen: "It is only One, Being; all else has no truth, is only opinion [*Meinung*], appearance [*Schein*]." The dialectical movement surfaces in the rapid move away from particularities of place and biographic minutiae and into the *Hauptlehre*, the chief lesson. As translational mode, elimination constitutes the task. Elimination entails identification and selection and the production of schisms on the fabric of thinking's history. In action, the second dialectical moment of Hegel's translation carves philosophy out of and away from history: after completing the translation of Zenon's biography, Hegel introduces philosophy in the purified field, i.e. the region of philosophy demarcated from that of bodies, "colonization," particular cities: after this, Hegel can begin: "What now concerns the philosophy of the Eleatics, thus we enter here a purer field [*ein reineres Feld*]."[152] This open country [*Feld*] is more pure [*reineres*] than the political fray Hegel has just translated concerning Zenon and the tyrannicide at Elea.

Through dialectics Being and One translate one another with no remainder and no friction as full presence obtains across the terms *das Sein, das Eine,* τὸ ὄν, τὸ ἕν.[153] The initial translation, rendered a moment in dialectical inquiry, accumulates through the translational work and reaches another stage in the phrase "The true is only the One, Being. Everything else is not." All the poetry of Xenophanes and Parmenides, all the richness, the subtleties and interplay of images in Zenon's paradoxes, these form the mere excess and matter that has been shorn from the innermost, "the universal statement of the Eleatics."[154] Dialectics has churned these as concepts as it also has churned the thinkers out of the initial synchronic presentation (where this translation of equivalence occurs) into a diachronic relation, so that Xenophanes is eliminated, then Parmenides, until the final paragraphs of the chapter feature Zenon alone. The two temporal relations then dialectically converge such that Zenon and Kant form a dialectical

---

151 G. W. F. Hegel, "Die Eleaten," in *Vorlesungen über die Geschichte der Philosophie*, Teil 2: *Griechische Philosophie I. Thales bis Kyniker*, ed. Pierre Garniron and Walter Jaeschke (Hamburg: Felix Meiner Verlag, 1989), 49.
152 Hegel, "Die Eleaten," 51.
153 Hegel, "Die Eleaten," 52. Venuti articulates the importance of the remainder from the standpoint of translation theory as deviations from standardized or the "major form" of a language that disrupt the dominant form. Venuti, *The Scandals of Translation*, 10.
154 Hegel, "Die Eleaten," 67.

pair, with the greater achievement bestowed on the former for his reformulation, his translation through Hegel's translation, into a subjective, but not yet objective, configuration of the dialectic: "The world is in itself shining appearance [*Erscheinen*], and only the One [*Eine*] Being [*Sein*] is the true."[155] In the chapter's synthetic movement *Eine* and *Sein* have been translated into a synthesized substantive that bears, even through all the magic of dialectics, the markings of the translation of singing into doctrine, the core available to any language.

While focusing on singular personalities and the unique experiences they voice, Nietzsche nevertheless gives a translation of the twofold doctrine of stasis and unity. After styling Parmenides essentially un-Greek and nearly inhuman— insofar as he experiences an "entirely bloodless abstraction" [*völlig blutlosen Abstraktion*],[156] a personality governed by "logical rigidity" and suffused by a contempt for embodiment and phenomena,[157] Nietzsche develops a biography of Parmenides to reconcile the apparent gap between cosmology and ontology in the Parmenidean poem. Unlike Hegel, for whom the residue of history constitutes impurity and must be purified through dialectics, Nietzsche, in pursuit of the singular personality that voiced an only ever partially translatable experience,[158] translates Parmenides with reference to biography. On the other hand, the biography Nietzsche embeds in his critical translation is the product of his own interpretation, a fiction that serves a purpose in translating the text to itself, spanning the distance between *Aletheia* and *Doxa*. Moving over and across the seemingly incongruous parts of the poem, Nietzsche attends, unfolds, and translates the conventional doctrinal reading:

> It can be neither infinitely large nor infinitely small, for it is perfect, and a perfectly given infinity is a contradiction. Thus it hovers: bounded, finished, immobile, everywhere in balance, equally perfect at each point, like a sphere, though not in space, for this space would be a second existent. There cannot be several existents. For in order to separate them, there would have to be something which is not existent, a supposition which cancels itself. Thus there is only eternal unity.[159]

---

155 Hegel, "Die Eleaten," 69.
156 Nietzsche, *Die Philosophie im tragischen Zeitalter der Griechen*, 187.
157 Nietzsche, *Philosophy in the Tragic Age of the Greeks*, trans. Marianne Cowan (Washington, D. C.: Regnery, 1962), 69-70, 80, respectively.
158 See above, p. 23. Drawing from Kirkland's insights on Nietzsche's involvements with the early Greeks. Kirkland, "Nietzsche and Drawing Near to the Personalities of the Pre-Platonic Greeks," 417–37.
159 Nietzsche, *Philosophy in the Tragic Age*, 78.

The twofold doctrine of an eternally unchanging unity [*Eine und ewig Ruhende*],[160] in Nietzsche's translation, emerges from the translational action that silences and represses language's "own foreignness to itself" in order to render a text into a veneer of glassine ice, "to make it," as Johnson has put it, "the transparent expression of a great philosophical thought."[161] Without reference to the language of the poem and the richness and semantic spread of its figures, Nietzsche's translation makes Parmenides into a "thinking machine" through whom a logical process operates upon the insight most characteristic and determinative of philosophy: *Einheit des Seienden* [unity of Being], a translation from the basic and definitive statement of philosophy issued by Thales, *Alles ist Eins* [all is one].[162]

Translated from fire to stone and from stone to ice, the Parmenidean poem has solidified into "the earliest philosophic text which is preserved with sufficient completeness and continuity to permit us to follow a sustained line of argument."[163] The criterion of argumentation as a way to differentiate philosophy from other ways of thinking in the Greek Archaic period guides much interpretation, a criterion developed from the idea that philosophy primarily involves argumentation in support of claims to which a thinker commits. While the narrative of the Parmenidean poem itself challenges this criterion and its basis through the summoning of another voice—the voice of Thea—to let thinking sound in the manner of the Mousai-Mnemosyne tradition, doctrinal-philosophic interpretation expands the translational protocol of detachability towards minimizing or excising Thea or, as Marciano observes, applying a "reverse procedure" that works from extracted "supposedly logical arguments" towards analysis and then, perhaps, to some commentary on the "problematic nature of the proem."[164] Sedley, for instance, identifies "laws" established in the poem, the first of which prohibiting "ambivalence about a thing's being," that he attributes to Parmenides, disposing with Thea—although she voices them.[165] Detaching Thea's centrality, and in spite of the thematic emphasis on

---

160 Nietzsche, *Die Philosophie im tragischen Zeitalter der Griechen*, 191.
161 Barbara Johnson, "Taking Fidelity Philosophically," in *Difference in Translation*, ed. Joseph Graham (Ithaca, NY: Cornell University Press, 1985), 146-7. Johnson sees this as constitutive of Western philosophy.
162 Nietzsche, *Die Philosophie im tragischen Zeitalter der Griechen*, 187, 191 (Parmenides), 164 (Thales) respectively.
163 Kahn, "The Thesis of Parmenides," *The Review of Metaphysics* 22, no. 4 (June, 1969): 700.
164 Marciano, "Images and Experience," 21.
165 David Sedley, "Parmenides and Melissus," in *The Cambridge Companion to Early Greek Philosophy*, ed. A. A. Long (Cambridge: Cambridge University Press, 1999), 115. *Ambivalence*, however, whether understood broadly as an expansive horizon of possibilities for meaning and interpretation, a certain openness in the poem that refuses

mutual aid and being-in-the-world, Sedley writes that Thea, the poem's central figure, the chief (or only) speaking character, "may be taken to represent the god's eye view of being that *Parmenides' arguments have enabled him to attain for himself.*"[166] The procedure not only divides the poem from itself, excavating a purported content from the poetic form containing it, but also flattens the poem, homogenizing its multiple voices (i.e. the narrating voice and the voice of Thea), its own foreignness to itself.

The doctrinal translation and reception of the Parmenidean poem also guides contemporary editions for and by philosophers seeking to study the Parmenidean poem. With their frequently used English-language edition Kirk, Raven, and Schofield have introduced many readers to the Greek text, which integrates "fragments" with commentaries providing glosses and outlines of arguments. The summary of the poem's "radical and powerful" argument follows the conventional lines: Parmenides "proves in an astonishing deductive *tour de force* that if something exists, it cannot come to be or perish, change, or move, nor be subject to any imperfection."[167] Graham's recent edition similarly reinforces and reiterates the doctrinal reading of the Parmenidean poem. Where the hexameter "sometimes obscures the argument" that the poem presents in a "strange mixture" of what are now distinct disciplinary strands (e.g. philosophy, literature, myth, science), the attribution of "the first extended argument in Western philosophy" and the operation of extracting "the most philosophical part" from the rest of the fragmentary poem take place in an unproblematic manner that never seems to acknowledge the translational force of those categories.[168] *Philosophy* and *philosophical* Graham seems to take as primarily advancing arguments in support of positions and being involved with investigations that are translated-translatable into contemporary categories. Accordingly, Graham arrays the presentation of the poem's text of the eighth fragment in numbered sections keyed to Thea's four descriptions of being (Parm. 8.3-4), which he terms "four properties, or sets of

---

decisive interpretation, or more narrowly as an expression that appears to make two opposing assertions, may appropriately describe the opening journey-narrative. See Jenny Bryan, "The Pursuit of Parmenidean Clarity," *Rhizomata* 8, no. 2 (2021): 225-6. See also Mansfeld, "Insight by Hindsight: Intentional Unclarity in Presocratic Proems," *Bulletin of the Institute of Classical Studies* 40 (January 1, 1995): 230-1.

166 Sedley, "Parmenides and Melissus," 114 (italics added). But this perspective, too, is a specific one; see Mackenzie, *Poetry and Poetics in the Presocratic Philosophers*, 82-3; and Spitzer, "Being-in-touch," 15.
167 G. S. Kirk, J. E. Raven, M. Schofield, eds., *The Presocratic Philosophers: A Critical History with a Selection of Texts*, 2nd ed. (Cambridge: Cambridge University Press, 1983), 241.
168 Graham, *The Texts of Early Greek Philosophy*, 203-4.

properties" and attributes to an argument made by Parmenides.[169] Indeed, the edition organizes the text of the Parmenidean poem under current disciplinary sub-headings such as "cosmology," "astronomy," "psychology."

Yet, the poem's refusal to release thinking from images and figures—what seem to be understood as *mythological* features—exposes attempts to make it a paradigm of logical procedure as performing the translational action according to the "classical determination." Though often interpreted as advancing arguments, the poem can also be read as developing not a program of "logical deduction" but rather one of persuasion,[170] which is to say that reading the Parmenidean poem as "the first extended argument in Western philosophy" constitutes not a "proper, standard, neutral mode or approach," but instead just one way of accessing the poem among numerous other ways of understanding and practicing philosophy.[171] Rather than applying some kind of "god's eye view" or objective description and analysis of the poem's putative stable core of argumentative content, the logico-analytic approach brings to bear its own perspective, tradition, and history, and falls into place along a spectrum of perspectives on and accesses to the Parmenidean poem.

*

* *

Fluid as waters coursing and shimmering, early Greek thinking rises in multiple voices as a hearkening to and singing from the experience of an already-there and its openness in the source(s) Mnemosyne-Mousa(i). Through multiple translations as sounding of such experiences, the tidal flow of early Greek thinking blazes, catches fire in diverse elemental translations.

From the fire's blaze of thinking as singing, its movements and flourishes, its spiralized drifts into and out from (re-)beginnings, Parmenidean thinking assumes in Nietzsche—procedurally drawn from the classical translational protocols—a character "formed of ice rather than fire, pouring cold light all around."[172] The earlier translational moments, particularly the compendia and Platonic and Aristotelian integrations of them, have oriented philosophy towards stabilized doctrines that replace and petrify the multiplicities of thinking-as-singing, its poetry of openings and summons for more and further translations.

---

169 Graham, *The Texts of Early Greek Philosophy*, 215, 217 (text), 237 n. F8.3-4(comments).
170 Smith, "Parmenides and Poetry," 266, 271.
171 Spitzer, "Trans-philosophy," 580.
172 Nietzsche, *Philosophy in the Tragic Age*, 69.

This translational reduction of other thinking to a fixed set of doctrines, enables another, further translational action that insists on the portability of these stabilized doctrines through languages, cultures, places, etc. The presentations in Platonic and Aristotelian texts take place in such a manner and are illustrative of that basic gesture, what Cassin has thought as the action "to communicate as quickly as possible the thing underlying the words, to reveal the unity of being under the differences of languages, to reduce multiplicity to the singular."[173] Nevertheless, even here, faint echoes of the poem *as* poem, in its manifold and paradoxic harmonies and counterpoints, still tremble, however slightly, as the poetic thinking of the Parmenidean poem resists the doctrinal reductions to motionless unity, pulsing from within its statements of this one with its own tensions of multiplicities.

---

173 Cassin, "Philosophising in Languages," 19.

CHAPTER 2

Philosophy through Translation
A Weave of Voice & Text

> τῷ ξυνεχὲς πᾶν ἐστιν· ἐὸν γὰρ ἐόντι πελάζει (Parm. 8.25)
> holding itself together
> totality is since being draws
> near to being

Two assumptions shape interpretation of the Parmenidean poem: (1) that it is primarily a text to be read (2) that a singular, definitive text of the poem existed. Circling the poem, the doctrine of unity and stasis associated with Parmenides guides the presentation of the Parmenidean poem, while the presentation of the poem reinforces that doctrine. Yet, the Parmenidean poem unfurls within a tradition of hexameter poetry, its dynamic practice of performance and-as re-composition, its winged phrases shaped and flown on the breath of a living voice and its pulses and rhythms. Approached principally as a text to be read, the poem's multiple voices sound no more, the possibility of its shifting and multiple phrasings through different performances remains closed, silent. How might attention to the ways the largely oral archaic Greek culture and its tradition of orally performed poetry resonate in the poem and open more numerous pathways for inquiry? What tensions do the reverberations and energies of oralcy generate with the poem's own statements on the unity and stability of being?

Singing

Multiple pathways and currents bear across the Mediterranean Sea elemental translation and its songs of beginning on the scudding tide of dactylic hexameters, ceaselessly translating. Along the pathway from the Milesians, through Xenophanes, Parmenides, and Empedokles to Zenon and Melissos, singing hexameters rise and fall as the tides of the sea, as the turnings of fire, now rising, now falling, now bursting into flame, now settling into smoldering embers of dense prose. As a member of the diasporic community set in motion from the Ionian city Phokaia by the rising Persian encroachments of the mid-sixth century, Parmenides flourished among the Hyelean-Elean inhabitants who had embarked with more than their moveable belongings (Hdt. I.164.3); they boarded their long black ships with an Ionian Mnemosyne and her treasury of songs.

CHAPTER 2

Migrating westward to Hyele-Elea from the Greek east, hexameter singing flows not only from Xenophanean thinking, but also from a more remote history in the figures of Phokylides the Milesian (early sixth century), Mimnermos of Kolophon (*fl.* 632-29), and an early Phokaian epic poet named Thestorides to whom was attributed the *Ilias parva*.[174] Phokylidean hexameter thinking praises Night, letting her hover like the simile joining radiant Apollo and deep Night in the *Iliad* (Hom. *Il.* I.43-9) as both the darkness of the daily temporal span and the ancient figure emerged from Khaos (Hes. *Theog.* 123):

> to share in thinking [βουλεύειν] by Night, by Night
>   bodied-sense [φρήν][175] narrows, quickens [ὀξυτέρη][176]
> for human beings stillness [ἡσυχία]
>   a good for a seeker [διζημένῳ][177]
>
> (Phokyl. 8 Gerber)[178]

Night in Phokylidean thinking harbors differentiated modes of thinking: a sharing in togetherness [βουλεύειν] and an embodied sense [φρήν] that can be heard in both Xenophanean thinking, which situates it both in the divinity [νόου φρενί (Xenoph. 25)] and in himself [ἐμὴν φροντίδ᾽ (Xenoph. 8.2)], and in the Parmenidean poem, which locates this mode of awareness [φρονέει] in the living-composition [φύσις] of Night and Light suffusing totality (Parm. 16).[179] Echoes of Mimnermos may resonate (among others) in the Parmenidean figure

---

174 Gregory Nagy, "Oral traditions, texts, and authorship," in *The Greek Epic Cycle and Its Ancient Reception*, ed. Marco Fantuzzi and Christos Tsagalis (Cambridge: Cambridge University Press, 2015), 61-3.
175 A willing or yearning, felt and active in the midriff, φρήν pulses almost viscerally: with a yearning like seeking, Telemakhos feels with his φρήν the absence (to his gazing [ὀσσόμενος]) of his father (Hom. *Od.* I.115); later, Telemakhos' awareness opens to Athene's transformation from Mentes to a bird by-with-in his φρήν (Hom. *Od.* I.319-23); from her upper chambers Penelopeia is drawn to a divine song by the yearning [φρεσὶ σύνθετο θέσπιν ἀοιδήν] stirred by the tale of other Akhaians' return voyages (Hom. *Od.* I.325-9).
176 The double-translation of ὀξυτέρη as "narrows, quickens" looks to the sense of narrowing from sharpening [ὀξυ-] and, for *quickens*, to the connection of ὀξύ- and ὠκύ- [swift].
177 Throughout the Parmenidean poem might run some connection to the seeking [διζημένῳ] that benefits in Phokylidean thinking from the stillness of Night (Parm. 2.2 [διζήσιος]; 6.3 [διζήσιος]; 7.2 [διζήσιος]; 8.6 [διζήσεαι]).
178 Gerber's text prints νυκτός, the miniscule concealing the hovering of Night.
179 Both link φρήν to the mode of open-awareness [νόος, νοεῖν]: Xenoph. 25; Parm. 16, where φρονέει seems to name a mode of open-awareness [νόος], a concentrated willing of always-already enmeshed situated within the very ownmost movements [φύσις] of human embodiment.

of the chariot:[180] Mimnermian singing presents Helios making a circuit from west to east, where his chariot and horses stand ready (Mimn. 12), while horses in the Parmenidean song bear the first-person narrator to the domain of Thea with assistance from the Daughters of Helios ['Ηλιάδες κοῦραι (Parm. 1.1, 9 respectively)]. Homer also teems in the depths of hexameter thinking and its surfacing on the shores of the eastern Aegean and its resurfacing on the western shores of the Italian coast, opening from the beginning as a source of learning for all (Xenoph. 10). Source and origin, Homeric thinking is like the great Okeanos, source of all things (Hom. *Il.* XIV.201).

Hexameter singing, along with all archaic poetries, implies a context of oral performance. Aristocratic culture remaining "dominantly oral, and musical, well into the fifth century,"[181] the symposion offers one such context for hexameter thinking to be performed as song. *Theognidea* contours the symposion as the location of memory where, amidst the tones of the *aulis* and the erotic encomia of young men, the magic of poetic speech bestows immortality to human beings as it comes to being ἐν στόμασιν [in the mouths] of those whose singing gives it voice (Thgn. 240-3 West). In Xenophanean thinking too, the context comes into view as the archaic Greek cultural institution of the symposion (Xenoph. 1; 22), a setting that grew increasingly private under the emerging social and political changes energized by the polis. Even so, symposia continued to harbor luxuriant aristocratic cultural practices, including an important paideutic function in ancient Greek culture through the Archaic and Classical periods, and cultivated an atmosphere that "fostered both composition and performance of sung poetry."[182] One of the Xenophanean songs describes a relaxed and relaxing atmosphere of soft couches, wine, and conversation (Xenoph. 22). As Lesher puts it, it is likely "that these hexameters were created for the purpose of leading off the after-dinner entertainment."[183] Such entertainment has more solemn facets,

---

180 Diels gives a concise review of the chariot image in the ancient Greek tradition(s) from Homer through lyric poetries and into Platon's *Phaidros*. Hermann Diels, *Parmenides Lehrgedicht* (Berlin: Georg Reimer, 1897), 20-2. For an investigation focused on this specific image in transcultural context(s), Alexander S. W. Forte and Caley C. Smith, "New Riders, Old Chariots: Poetics and Comparative Philosophy," in *Universe and Inner Self in Early Indian and Early Greek Thought*, ed. Richard Seaford (Edinburgh: Edinburgh University Press, 2016), 186-203.
181 Robb, *Literacy and Paideia*, 13.
182 On symposion and luxuriant lifestyle, Oswyn Murray, "The *symposion* as social organization," in *The Greek Renaissance of the eighth century B. C.: tradition and innovation*, ed. Robin Hägg (Stockholm: Swedish Institute in Athens, 1983), 198. On paideutic and musical importance, Robb, *Literacy and Paideia*, 35.
183 Lesher, *Xenophanes of Colophon*, 72.

too, that come to speech in the opening Xenophanean song as an attention to making orderly arrangements throughout the setting—including preparation of table, hands, and cups and the orderly arrangement of special attire (Xenoph. 1.1-2) to the careful setting of the altar (Xenoph. 1.11)—that spread order across and through the entire meaning-rich setting. These ordering—*poetic*—tasks prepare the way for not just amusing or diverting tunes, but a singing that avoids the shaping-influences [πλάσματα (Xenoph. 1.22)] of ancient tales narrating disarray [μάχας, στάσιας (Xenoph. 1.21, 23 respectively)], a singing that instead gives voice to those things which Memory [Μνημοσύνη][184] and well-crafted poetic speech [τόνος (Xenoph. 1.20)] grant to the singer. At least for Xenophanean thinking, the symposion not only opens a zone for singing, but also becomes a resonant atmosphere of attunement, reverberating with the meaningfulness that, as Xenophanean thinking discloses, is wrought [τέτυκται] as the very fabric of totality (Xenoph. 34.4).

Other channels, too, even earlier than the Phokaian diaspora carry hexameter thinking on the sea's undulating back dark as wine, as archaic Greek communities reach distant Italic shores, hexameter in the fabric of their language and culture embodied by merchants and colonists of the eighth century as well as in their wares: hexameters arise etched into the fabric of ceramics such as the "Cup of Nestor" from the western Greek colony or emporion Pithekoussai, an island off the western coast of Italy, as they also bear along with the hexameter the aura of the Greek Homeric-epic-mythic imaginary.[185] The cup illustrates a fusion of writing and singing in the Archaic period—where *singing* encompasses a range of performed vocalization from chants and song (in its ordinary sense) to the sort of reading aloud depicted in Platonic writings. On one interpretation, the writing on the Cup of Nestor presents a "bona fide magical incantation inscribed with the serious intent of inducing erotic seizure in another individual."[186] Archaic Greek writing summons the voice's singing, in this case chanting the inscription-as-incantation so as to enchant another through performative speech, rendering untenable a rigid dichotomy of orality and literacy.[187]

---

184 Capitalizing Μνημοσύνη is a minor adjustment to Lesher's text.
185 Malkin gives a date ca. 720 for the cup and takes it, along with a seal impression from Pithekoussai, as indicative of wide familiarity with the Homeric poems in the archaic period. Irad Malkin, *The Returns of Odysseus: Colonization and Ethnicity* (Berkeley: University of California Press, 1998), 156.
186 Christopher A. Faraone, "Taking the 'Nestor's Cup Inscription' Seriously: Erotic Magic and Conditional Curses in the Earliest Inscribed Hexameters," *Classical Antiquity* 15, no. 1 (1996): 79.
187 On the synchrony of literacy and orality, see Rosalind Thomas, *Literacy and Orality in Ancient Greece* (Cambridge: Cambridge University Press, 1992), 13-14.

Unsinging—Song as Text

From fire to stone and ice, translation transforms the Parmenidean poem from the deeply folded tradition of hexameter singing, in which thinking en- and un-folds as the hearkening to and intentional openness towards an-other, into a set of rigid statements: a doctrine. In a doubled movement, the poem's textualization both accompanies and quickens this translational pathway. Already translated from song to text or summaries and excerpts in the compendia of the fifth century that present a stabilized doctrine, through four centuries following the collections and commentary of Theophrastos the Parmenidean poem goes under; the song's shadow fades upon a background of darkness.[188] In the period from the second to the end of the sixth centuries c.e., as Cordero has articulated, the poem resurfaces as fully instrumentalized: authors mobilize lines or sections of the poem to bolster the concerns of whoever happens to be making use of the text. A cessation of new passages appearing in the texts transmitting the Parmenidean poem signals a transition to a new phase in Cordero's history of the text: by Simplikios' time at the end of the sixth century c.e. the Parmenidean poem has been reduced to those sections most useful for the articulation of the doctrine—or most useful for the enrichment of others' doctrines.[189] Sometimes taken as an announcement that a complete text of the rare poem lies before him, the statement in Simplikios on the scarcity of the poem gestures towards a line of textual transmission not necessarily any more complete than the passages he himself transcribes and not necessarily stemming from the already ancient figure of Parmenides (Simpl. *in Phys.* 144.25-9=DK 28 A21).

In the prolific activity of Henri Estienne (a.k.a. Henricus Stephanus, 1531-1598 c.e.) and his associates the practice of collecting the writings of archaic Greek thinkers resurges in early Renaissance Europe. Under the new conditions of the sixteenth century c.e. the task is translated: by producing at Geneva in 1573 c.e. *Poesis Philosophica*, the first effort to extract the poem from the "'vehicles of a lost text,'"[190] Stephanus and Joseph Scalinger follow a philological drive towards a singular authoritative text. On the principle that any diversity across

---

188 Cordero indicates a "closure" of what he terms the "première étape de l'histoire du texte de Parménide" [the first step of the history of the text of Parmenides] just past Aristoteles, in his successor Theophrastos. Néstor-Luis Cordero, "L'histoire du texte de Parménide," in Aubenque, *Études sur Parménide*, vol. 2, 5. What follows summarizes Cordero's thorough and useful tracking of the poem from Platon to Diels (8, 10-18).
189 Cordero, "L'histoire du texte de Parménide," 6.
190 Cordero, "L'histoire du texte de Parménide," 8. The translational layers begin to accumulate, as texts become conveyors (translations) of other texts that translate the *vox universalis* into the *ipsissima verba*.

texts shows corruption,[191] Stephanus' notes on variations among manuscripts illuminate not only the extent of the bind joining translation, interpretation, and textualization, but also a drive towards unity. Lloyd-Jones sees in the emergence of a veneration for originals a characteristic of Renaissance philological and translational practice rooted, on his reading of Stephanus, in the figure of the *vox universalis* that transcends rational and linguistic categories yet forms an intimate connection with the words in which it is spoken or written according to an analogous spirit-body relationship.[192] Original words, *ipsissima verba*, enable access to the *vox*, which leads Stephanus towards a commitment to "lexical precision" pivoting between a "linguistic obligation toward the authority of the source language, and a conceptual service rendered to, and shaped by, the target language's inherent insufficiencies."[193]

A framework for subsequent arrangements of the text emerges in Fülleborn's eighteenth century c.e. edition, positing the familiar bipartite form of *Aletheia* and *Doxa*;[194] the division itself can be heard in early, ancient commentary.[195] The poem as a separate textual entity was further articulated in editions through the eighteenth century c.e. to Stein's "acutely hyper-critical" version.[196] The path down to Diels and other presentations of the Parmenidean poem now opens as an attempt at "restoring the pristine qualities of material that the passage of time, like all other kinds of transformation, has altered."[197] The will to restore involves both construction and preservation, with the result that the poem's language remains in view, endowed with special value and significance. Though

---

191 *Alicubi aute[m] duae lectiones occureru[n]t, quarum una, & diversa & simul perversa manifeste erat* [Moreover, anywhere two readings occur, one of which will be manifestly at once both different and corrupt]. Henricus Stephanus, *ΠΟΙΗΣΙΣ ΦΙΛΟΣΟΦΟΣ: Poesis Philosophica* (n.p. 1573), 221.
192 Stephanus' analogy. Stephanus, *ΠΟΙΗΣΙΣ ΦΙΛΟΣΟΦΟΣ: Poesis Philosophica*, 3-4.
193 Kenneth Lloyd-Jones, "The Tension of Philology and Philosophy in the Translations of Henri Estienne," *International Journal of the Classical Tradition* 1, no. 1 (Summer, 1994): 2. The page numbers refer to the digital version of this article and do not correspond to those of the original publication.
194 Cordero, "L'histoire du texte de Parménide," 12-13.
195 This division can be heard in Aristoteles' treatment in *Metaphysics*, where Aristoteles reads Parmenidean thinking on being and the one as κατὰ τὸν λόγον [unity in definition (Arist. *Metaph.* 986b.19)] to belong together with a thinking of φύσις—which, Aristoteles writes, Parmenides has been compelled [ἀναγκαζόμενος] to follow by the way things show themselves [τοῖς φαινομένοις (Arist. *Metaph.* 986b.31)]. A pair of causes [αἰτίας] or principles [ἀρχάς] Aristoteles then aligns with Parmenidean thinking as hot and cold or fire and earth (Arist. *Metaph.* 986b.33-4).
196 Cordero, "L'histoire du texte de Parménide," 17.
197 Lloyd-Jones, "The Tension of Philology and Philosophy," 6.

Diels recognizes that elements of the Parmenidean poem are lost irretrievably, particularly its dialect and its "artistic and conventional poetic-language [*Dichtersprache*]," he nevertheless sees the task of this philological effort as a restoration of "Aristoteles' book [*Codex*]."[198] Through creative editorial enterprise Diels crafts a text of Parmenides, ordered and reconstructed in the direction of archaic Greek, that achieves a status Cassin describes as "more or less standard or stabilized."[199] Indexing their own numbering systems for arranging the fragments to the Diels-Kranz system, twentieth- and twenty-first-century editions take their bearings from Diels's construction of the text *as text* with little attention to the conditions of archaic Greek oralcy. In the first edition of their mid-twentieth-century collection of presokratika, for example, Kirk and Raven announce that "Parmenides wrote exclusively in hexameter verse," with the additional comment that, in spite of the verse form, "his subject-matter is of the most prosaic order."[200] The note links their commentary and interpretation to the ancient translational protocol that severs form and content; in this case, Kirk and Raven's remark echoes the fifth-century Proklos, who asserts that the Parmenidean text resembles a prose [πεζόν] more than a poetic discourse [ποιητικὸν λόγον (Procl. *In Ti.* 665.30-1=DK 28 A18)]. Along similar lines, in their recent edition of presokratika Laks and Most introduce Parmenides as "the author of a single poem in dactylic hexameter" whose text survived intact and complete at least until Simplikios,[201] though it may equally be the case that the surviving text by Simplikios' time amounted to more or less what survives now, having been culled long before the sixth century c.e. With a less explicit position on the subject of Parmenides and writing, in the introductory remarks on Parmenides and notes Graham's twenty-first-century edition implies that Parmenides wrote the poem.[202]

Song unsung—the Parmenidean poem has been transformed—*translated*—to be primarily a text, a work of writing to be read, a song unsung. Modern editors and scholars tend to minimize the position of the song in a tradition of oralcy and, as a result, to pass over in silence the poem's native setting in performance. The linkages between orality and writing surfacing in the context of orally-performed poetry might alert today's readers as to a great deficiency

---

198   Diels, *Parmenides Lehrgedicht*, 26-27.
199   Cassin, *Parménide: Sur la nature ou sur l'étant*, 12.
200   Kirk and Raven, *The Presocratic Philosophers*, 265.
201   André Laks and Glenn Most, eds. and trans., *Early Greek Philosophy*, vol. V, part 2, *Western Greek Thinkers* (Cambridge, MA: Harvard University Press, 2016), 3.
202   Graham, *The Texts of Early Greek Philosophy*, 203, 234 n. 7-9.

of an interpretive practice that does not attend to both facets.[203] As Havelock observed, among twentieth-century philologists a tacit interpretive principle was that "Greek literature by definition had to be a written literature composed for readers," even as the poem itself "never once assumes a situation of books and readers, but always of reciters and listeners."[204] The conventional editorial silencing—the *unsinging*—of the poem mutes a whole dimension of its meaning-bearing facets and enables a translational protocol characterized by an implicit "ease of accessibility to the meaning(s) of the original text that ignores the inevitable interpretations and alterations that are a result of its translation into another language."[205] Through this translational "ease of accessibility" a twofold doctrine is established and reinforced: "the eternity of identity and the impossibility of difference."[206]

Archaic Greek writing summons the voice, its singing. Bringing into view the tangled helix of writing and singing in the Archaic Greek period can open fresh perspectives onto the Parmenidean Song of Being. Specifically, two root assumptions rise into awareness, assumptions that guide and orient interpretation of the Parmenidean poem: (1) that the poem was primarily a text to be read and (2) that there was a single, authoritative version of the poem. These two critical presuppositions engender and reinforce the conventional interpretation of the poem, generated through a reductive translational mode, as presenting a fixed doctrine of stasis and unity. Challenging and suspending the primacy of textuality and the impulse towards a unified textual source and emphasizing the poem's oral and multiple character can release tensions at work in the Parmenidean poem that, in turn, quicken different pathways for understanding.

Text & Stasis

Approaching the Parmenidean song as a singular text aligns its form with the statements made about being in the poem. Particularly for modern readers, who are likely to read the work silently, the presentation of song-as-text produces a univocity whereby the *content*, having been separated from the language, is restated in and by the textuality itself. The textualization of the Parmenidean

---

203 Wilkinson, *Parmenides and* To Eon, 3-4.
204 Eric Havelock, "Pre-Literacy and the Pre-Socratics," in *The Literate Revolution in Greece and Its Cultural Consequences* (Princeton: Princeton University Press, 1982), 225, 248, respectively.
205 Kathryn Batchelor, "Invisible Untranslatability and Philosophy," *Nottingham French Studies* 49, no. 2 (Summer, 2010): 49-50.
206 Leonardo Tarán, *Parmenides: A Text with Translation, Commentary, and Critical Essays* (Princeton: Princeton University Press, 1965), 181.

poem endorses the reading of being-as-stasis through a (re-)inscription of the stability and stasis attributed to being:

> ...that what-is is ungenerated and imperishable (Parm. 8.3)

> ...for, what coming-to-be of it will you seek?
> In what way, whence, did [it] grow? (Parm. 8.6-7)

> And what could have impelled it to grow
> Later or sooner, if it began from nothing? (Parm. 8.9-10)

> For, if [it] came-to-be, [it] is not, nor [is it] if at some time [it] is going to be.
> Thus, coming-to-be is extinguished and perishing not to be heard of (Parm. 8.20-1)

> Moreover, changeless in the limits of great chains
> [It] is un-beginning and unceasing, since coming-to-be and perishing
> Have been driven far off, and true trust has thrust them out.
> Remaining the same and in the same, [it] lies by itself
> And remains thus firmly in place (Parm. 8.26-30)

> ...Since it was just this that Fate did shackle
> To be whole and changeless (Parm. 8.37-8) [207]

These selections voice the stasis and stability of being. When textualized, the lines gain a stability of textual presence that reinforces the statements themselves, such that the materiality and the phrases together form a unison and single path towards a single interpretation: being is stable, static just as the text itself remains unchanging, same with and in itself, etc. As the stable textual form confirms its statements on the stasis of being the Parmenidean poem comes to be what Hejinian names a "closed text," that is, a poem "in which all the elements of the work are directed toward a single reading of it."[208] The reader, at least apparently, encounters a text whose identity remains unchanged and intact through multiple readings, a text that remains as it is and in place in a way separate from the reading.

Against the apparent stability of textuality and its support of a doctrinal position on being as motionless twists a range of movements from the meter itself, as well as the contexts of oral performance and composition towards

---

207 The translations here are from Gallop, *Parmenides of Elea*, 66, 68.
208 Lyn Hejinian, "The Rejection of Closure," in *The Language of Inquiry* (Berkeley: University of California Press, 2000), 42.

performance, possible facets of the poem's performance and its reception, and the poem's own figures and images that develop an "aesthetics of clashing" through the nuanced tensions between motion and stasis.[209] Dactylic hexameter implies motion in its association with the "traveling bard,"[210] situating the Parmenidean poem within a tradition of orally performed poetry and the movement(s) joined to that tradition. Publication of ancient poems and-or texts involves movement in the form of public oral performance and circulation of written texts, borne by performers across multiple contexts: cities; sanctuaries; competitions; courts; city-sponsored occasional events, for which poems are specifically composed; patronage; diplomatic missions.[211] Archaic Greek poetry implies motion; movements constitute the way in which archaic Greek poetries were published and flourished as they reached audiences through performance contexts. An image of such motion(s) reverberates in the Parmenidean poem as it voices the movement of the traveling narrator whom the way of the *daimon* bears along every city [κατὰ πάντ' ἄστη (Parm. 1.3),[212] reminiscent of the expansive travel Xenophanean thinking narrates (Xenoph. 6; 8). In order to be heard in various oral-performance contexts, ancient poetry moves, so that poetry as poetry shimmers with the aura of motion.

Oral performance and written texts converge, enhancing the aura of motion in which the Parmenidean poem blazes. In late archaic Greece, performance settings could range from small and exclusive audiences—from symposia to something like an "Eleatic school" where students might have "had to learn the poem by heart" to be initiated to its esoteric teaching,[213] or again to a relatively local ritual context associated with Orphic traditions,[214] or to the broader audiences of public festivals for performance of longer hexameter compositions through which the poem might swiftly and widely travel through the expanse

---

209 G. O. Hutchinson, "Parmenides, On Nature," chap. 6 in *Motion in Classical Literature: Homer, Parmenides, Sophocles, Ovid, Seneca, Tacitus, Art* (Oxford: Oxford University Press, 2020), 192. Hutchinson also explores ways the poem develops "clashes" through different kinds of movement.
210 Stehle, *Performance and Gender*, 171-2.
211 Richard Hunter and Ian Rutherford, introduction to *Wandering Poets in Archaic Greek Culture: Travel, Locality and Pan-Hellenism*, ed. Richard Hunter and Ian Rutherford (Cambridge: Cambridge University Press, 2009), 17-19.
212 Text here is from Diels and Kranz, *Die Fragmente der Vorsokratiker*, 228 (DK 28 B1.3). This text also appears in Mutschmann's Teubner edition of Sextos Empirikos (Sext. Emp. *Math.* VII.213.11). Hermannus Mutschmann, ed. *Sexti Empirici opera*, vol. II (Leipzig: Teubner, 1914), 26. On the so-called variants for this line, see below, pp. 82-84.
213 W. J. Verdenius, *Parmenides: Some Comments on his Poem* (Amsterdam: Adolf M. Hakkert, 1964), 2.
214 Valentine, "The Archaeology of Parmenides," 141-2.

of the archaic Greek world, which compasses a vast swath of the Mediterranean Basin; Diogenes Laertios' comment that Empedoklean poetry was performed at Olympia recommends the festival context for philosophic poetry (Diog. Laert. VIII.2.63).[215] Whatever the specific performance sphere(s) may have been, the Parmenidean poem itself pulses with the energies of a primarily oral setting.[216] This is not to suggest that Parmenides did not write, but that the production of a text in archaic Greek settings is not distinct from, and by no means exclusive of, performance: the two belong together. Even as the order and scope of the Homeric epics reach a state of relative fixity *within* and *for* the purpose of their major public performance in the *agones* of the Panathenaic festival under the Hipparkhic rules of the late sixth century,[217] it may be that the "recomposition-in-performance" quality of oral poetry courses in tandem with the crystallization of the poems.[218] By the archaic period singers-poets likely performed a combination of memorized texts and recomposition,[219] and the performance may have outspanned such a text to present "a complex combination of words, music and dance."[220] Writing and performance entwine and coil in the archaic period.

Composition towards and within performance settings gives rise to images of movement that place emphasis on the *making* and *doing* of poetry, which is to say, its generation and enactment. Rushing along the daimon way, the chariot of the Parmenidean poem's opening scene voices an "image for the process of composing of enacting a poem."[221] Some of the details of the song's overall movement take place in the form of what Calame calls "self-referential allusions" that are "internal references to musical activity," rendering the poem a "song-act" that generates a temporal and spatial "transference" into the "*hinc et nunc* of ritual song performance."[222] For example, in the opening scene the axle sounds like a σύριγξ [musical pipe (Parm. 1.6)], and later in the fragment the hinges of the doors turn ἐν σύριγξιν [in the pipe-like sockets (Parm. 1.19)]. Letting the

---

215 Mackenzie, *Poetry and Poetics in the Presocratic Philosophers*, 66-7.
216 Havelock, "Pre-Literacy and the Pre-Socratics," 248.
217 H. A. Shapiro, "Hipparchos and the Rhapsodes," in *Cultural poetics in archaic Greece: cult, performance, politics*, ed. Carol Dougherty and Leslie Kurke (New York: Oxford University Press, 1998), 104.
218 Nagy, "Homer and the Evolution of a Homeric Text," in *Homeric Questions* (Austin: University of Texas Press, 1996), 69-70.
219 Stehle, *Performance and Gender*, 170; Thomas, *Literacy and Orality*, 4, 13, 62; Robb, *Literacy and Paideia*, 223.
220 Thomas, *Literacy and Orality*, 124.
221 Hunter and Rutherford, introduction to *Wandering Poets in Archaic Greek Culture*, 7.
222 Claude Calame, "Metaphorical travel and ritual performance in epinician poetry," in *Reading the Victory Ode*, ed. Peter Agócs, Chris Carey, Richard Rawles (Cambridge: Cambridge University Press, 2012), 306.

making of poetry reverberate from the poem's own images sustains a theme of generation that, in its turn, produces torque with the poem's later statements on being as ἀγένητον [ungenerated] and ἀνώλεθρον [not-destroyed (Parm. 8.3)]. Having heard the opening and closing of the poem, listeners' own experiences of the performance will have generated their own tensions with such statements.

The helix of performance-composition-text excites a dynamic torque of speech-as-fluid and text-as-stable in the production of a song that also functions as a text. If the Parmenidean song of being is approached solely or primarily as a text to be read, the mode of access itself delivers into the poem the stable presence presented by a text.[223] For readers in the ancient Greek world, who performed texts through the sociality and orality that characterized the practice of reading,[224] continual access to what has already passed in the voicing of the reader(s) can return: the poem's presence answers to the summons of readers. This immanent presence of the text could give rise to a view of language as both static, or stabilizable, and separable from speakers, so that, as Wilkinson puts it, "the emerging objective character of language" arises along with the possibility of "concepts like Being, One, and Form."[225] Writing instigates a metaphysics of the word. The hexameter word, however, flies, takes flight as the Homeric soaring words [ἔπεα πτερόεντα (e.g. Hom. *Il*. I.201)], complicating the metaphysics of stability by the oralcy and performative qualities of reading.

The oralcy of archaic poetry haunts the imagined fixity of writing. As a performance, the poem's motions turn within the dynamics of the poet's voicings. In the Parmenidean song, the performer will inhabit and undergo a dramatic translation, a kind of ek-static transformation from their own identity/-ies to the minimized first-person who is carried—transported, translated—in the song's opening scene: "The horses that take me [ἵπποι ταί με φερούσιν] to the ends of my mind / were taking me now" (Parm. 1.1-2).[226] The ek-stasis continues through another transformation, as the performer shifts suddenly—within the space of a single line—from the narrator to Thea and her first-person speech and its own shifts from plural [ἡμέτερον δῶ (Parm. 1.25)] to an emphatic first-person singular

---

223 Ford recounts an ancient example of editing between singer and hearer in the setting of a performance, then writes that "to focus on the stable text behind such contexts is to impose our textualist values on more complex social practices." Andrew Ford, "From Letters to Literature: Reading the 'Song Culture' of Classical Greece," in *Written Texts and the Rise of Literate Culture in Ancient Greece*, ed. Harvey Yunis (Cambridge: Cambridge University Press, 2003), 23.
224 Mathilde Cambron-Goulet, "The Criticism—and the Practice—of Literacy in the Ancient Philosophical Tradition," in *Orality, Literacy and Performance in the Ancient World*, ed. Elizabeth Minchin (Leiden: Brill, 2012), 213.
225 Wilkinson, *Parmenides and* To Eon, 12.
226 Translation from Lombardo, *Parmenides and Empedocles*, 11. My interpolation.

[ἐγὼν ἐρέω (Parm. 2.1)]. Along the poem's circular movement the narrator announces Thea [Θεά], a feminine divine being who begins speaking to him (Parm. 1.23-4). This point marks a narratologically significant moment: the narrator's account encircles Thea's speech, while the voice of the poem's performance encircles both of these, mortal and immortal narratives. On a parallel with the narratologics of Homeric poetry, the performer acts as a primary *Fokalisator*, while the secondary focalization shifts here from the first-person narrator to Thea. Three voices, or three narratological layers, can be heard, since the narrator himself narrates action retrospectively yet urges the point of view of the first-person narrator, which creates a distance between the narrator-performer ["wahrnehmendes Subjekt (Fokalisator)"] and the narrator-character ["Subjekt wahrgenommen wird ('le focalisé')"].[227] The narratological shift from narrator to Thea may also have resulted in an alteration in the performer's voice, "a shift in register a vocal quality," to mark different speakers as in epic poetry.[228] That is, the performance itself may have stressed the change through vocal shifts. Such shiftings make a counterturn to the poem's declarations of homogeneity (e.g. Parm. 8.22), and decisively against the conventional interpretation according to which the poem forecloses the possibility of differentiation.[229]

Even when written, hexameter thinking sings within a predominantly oral cultural atmosphere, opening the possibility of the Parmenidean poem (among other early Greek thinking) to unfurl as a multimodal event. Gesture or use of props may have been enacted in poetry performances to emphasize narratological shifts.[230] The Parmenidean poem's references to a musical instrument might suggest some musical accompaniment during performance (Parm. 1.6, 19). Additionally, if dance or movement accompanied the poem's performance, the effect would be a scene full of motion, perhaps activating vivid memory of festive ritual procession and its richly multifarious range of "sensuous, phenomenal experience,"[231] dance and song among them, as the painted metopes at the Temple of Athene in Poseidonia suggest.[232] Special attire, such as that

---

227 I. F. J. de Jong, "Fokalisation und die Homerischen Gleichnisse," *Mnemosyne*, 4th series, 38, no. 3/4 (1985): 259 (quotation), 261.
228 C. B. Davis, "Distant Ventriloquism: Vocal Mimesis, Agency and Identity in Ancient Greek Performance," *Theatre Journal* 55, no. 1 (March, 2003): 65. More recently, and specifically concerning the Parmenidean poem in performance, Mackenzie, *Poetry and Poetics in the Presocratic Philosophers*, 83.
229 E.g. A. A. Long, "Parmenides on Thinking Being," in *Proceedings of the Boston Area Colloquium in Ancient Philosophy*, vol. 3, ed. John J. Cleary and William Wians (Lanham: University Press of America, 1998), 147.
230 Bers, *Speech in Speech*, 14, 20.
231 Valentine, "The Archaeology of Parmenides," 90-1.
232 The scene is of young women processing in pairs, "almost dancing," and led by a solo feminine figure. John Griffiths Pedley, *Paestum: Greeks and Romans in Southern Italy*

attributed in ancient sources to performers of epic—as in Sokrates' description of intricately-decorated clothing and golden crowns (Pl. *Ion* 535d.2-3)— as well as early philosophers and *sophoi*, would gain attention through the unusual design, combinations, ornamentation, and colors.[233] When set in motion by the performer's movements, the poem's performance would produce a vivid and visual contrast with the Parmenidean poem's statement seeming to deny changes of place and color (Parm. 8.41).

Transformations arise from performing the text, giving it voice as one's own voice(s), the voice(s) of the reader performing the text. While the text remains silent it is still—a *quietus* hovers over and in the text, whereas in order to speak it must be spoken, to be set in motion by the reader's performed voicings, so that performing the text also activates the dynamics of motion and rest. The written text is a site of re-enactment just as the performance of a poem takes place as a re-enactment. Writing and reading aloud belong together, as Bakker noted, in the web of performance, "related to each other as performance and reperformance."[234] Viewed through this complex lens of writing and performance, the surviving text of the possibilities for interpretation are minimized when the Parmenidean poem is taken to be a static, fixed text. For the poem's auditors, within the emphatic being and the torque generated by its vocalization the near-polyptotonics energize statements that, when read and so taken within an overall setting of stability and stasis, declare the immobility or static nature of being. Listen to the rapid transitions across forms of εἶναι [to be]:

...one *muthothumos*[235] of a way
still left, how *is* [ὡς ἔστιν]; on this way signs *are* [ἔασι],
many, many, how ungenerated *being* [ἐόν] and
indestructible *is* [ἔστιν],

(London: Thames and Hudson, 1990), 71 with illus. 44, 75. In discussing the procession of the metopes Pedley notes the eastern Greek attire they wear and links this to the "fugitives from Phocaia." Valentine brings out the close associations between this iconography and the Parmenidean poem. Valentine, "The Archaeology of Parmenides," 67-9. Funerary ritual processions, with which the Parmenidean poem may have associations, may also open fruitful comparisons involving movement, music, differentiated attire, and feasting. On funerary ritual, see Christiane Sourvinou-Inwood, "A trauma in flux: Death in the 8th century and after," in Hägg, *The Greek Renaissance*, 39, and description passim.

233 Håkan Tell, "Sages at the Games: Intellectual Displays and Dissemination of Wisdom in Ancient Greece," *Classical antiquity* 26, no. 2 (2007): 252-5.

234 Egbert Bakker, "Activation and Preservation: The Interdependence of Text and Performance in an Oral Tradition," *Oral Tradition* 8, no. 1 (March, 1993): 16.

235 This term merges the two words reported in this position [μῦθος (Sext. Emp. *Math.* VII.111); θύμος (Simpl. *in Phys.* 145.1)].

whole both single-limbed and unmoving and complete;
never *was* [ἦν] nor *will be* [ἔσται], when now *is* [ἔστιν] on the
   whole everything

—one—held together (Parm. 8.1-6)

Even as the poem declares a stability of being the language nevertheless figures the motions of being in its entanglements with speaking-as-differing. When voiced and heard, particularly under conditions of archaic oral performance, the very core of stasis tremors with the recoil quickened earlier in the poem by the constellation of speaking, attentive openness, and being:

χρὴ τὸ λέγειν τε νοεῖν τ' ἐὸν ἔμμεναι· ἔστι γὰρ εἶναι (Parm. 6.1)]

according to involvements [χρή][236] being-arising [ἐόν]:[237]
to assemble [λέγειν], to open [νοεῖν], to be-otherwise [ἔμμεναι]; for, to be-differently [εἶναι][238] is [ἔστι]

Here too the quick transitions—in a single hexameter—from participle (ἐόν) to infinitive (ἔμμεναι) to third-person singular (ἔστι) to a different infinitive form (εἶναι) infuse the staged vocalization of being in its mobility and mutability, its figures of motion. This line stages and reconstitutes the presence of everything, the tension of *now*, in its continuous passage out of itself through the performance of the text; that is to say, the line translates and is translated by Thea's later statement: ἐπεὶ νῦν ἔστιν ὁμοῦ πᾶν [since now *is* at once everything (Parm. 8.5)].

Unlike readers of a text who can "pause, reflect, go back or forward" in their engagement with the text that seems to remain steadily in place and in a sense unbegun or ungenerated, auditors of the song cannot make such returns.[239] Yet, this inaccessibility of a return might not necessarily mean the poem prohibits an auditor from the mode of reflection that roams across and through the stable

---

236 Translating χρή as *involvements* summons the engagedness in which *use*—*Brauch*, Anaximandrean τὸ χρεών—comes to pass. "Usage" is Krell's translation of Heidegger's *Brauch*, which in turn translates Anaximandrean τὸ χρεών. Heidegger, "Der Spruch des Anaximander," in *Holzwege* (Frankfurt am Main: Klostermann 1950), 367-8); "The Anxaimander Fragment," in *Early Greek Thinking: The Dawn of Western Philosophy*, trans. David Farrell Krell (San Francisco: Harper & Row, 1984), 52-3.
237 Translating ἐόν as being-arising draws on Maly, "Parmenides: Circle of Disclosure, Circle of Possibility," 14.
238 Different translations intend to activate the difference voiced in the two infinitives ἔμμεναι and εἶναι.
239 Wilkinson, *Parmenides and To Eon*, 94.

text, but instead that the poem's movements in an oral-performance setting force a listener to choose to engage in such reflection—something like a repetition and consideration of what one has just heard—*or* to remain attentive to the motion of the performance, the tide of its now. The poem raises a decision at several moments within Thea's teaching:[240]

> may the common-pathway of habit [ἔθος]
>   never force you along
> this way of vast experience [πολύπειρον]
> to guide unseeing eye and hearing
> and tongue echoing, but to decide [κρῖναι]
>   with laying-out-in-speech [λόγῳ] a vastly-
>   experienced-[πολύπειρον]-contested [πολύδηριν][241] challenge
> from those things voiced from me (Parm. 7.5-6)

Listener's might hear the poem staging a decision they themselves face when hearkening to the poem's foreignness. Thea directs an auditor to resist the ordinary way [ἔθος] and the experience accrued to it [πολύπειρον] and, through the twofold of speaking-and-hearkening [λόγῳ], to reach a decision concerning the challenge arising from her speech, which also has accrued both great experience [πολύπειρον] and great conflict [πολύδηριν]. Attempts to confine Thea's unusual way of speaking within habitual understandings would constitute a choice that would distort the senses (unseeing eyes and echoing hearing and speech) and prevent awareness of her challenging way of speaking. Might the decision Thea poses to auditors require the difficult double-task of both suspending the translational inclination to refer and resolve the foreign to the familiar-habitual [ἔθος, πολύπειρον]—which would disrupt a listener's involvement in the movement of Thea's difficult speech by rummaging around in the debris of accumulated habit from experience in an attempt to determine a correspondence, a way of resolving the foreign into the familiar—and remaining alert to the motions of her difficult way of speaking?

A second call to decide Thea issues to hearers in the wake of an image of Dike [Δίκη, typically translated: Justice] holding in bonds generation [γενέσθαι] and destruction [ὄλλυσθαι (Parm. 8.13-14)]:

---

240 Implicitly, the poem calls for decisions at various other moments in the inquiry (e.g. Parm. 2; 6).

241 To retain the multiplicity of the fifth line, where Sextos presents πολύπειρον (Sext. Emp. *Math.* VII.114) and Diogenes gives πολύδηριν (Diog. Laert. IX.3.22), the texts from these sources have been combined.

> On that account neither to be born
> nor to perish did Dike release, slackening the shackles,
> but holds. Around such matters, the decision [κρίσις]
>   is in this:
> is or is not? Already it has been decided [κέκριται] as if
>   Necessity,
> the one to leave without-awareness [ἀνόητον] and
>   nameless [ἀνώνυμον] since it is not a disclosive
>   pathway, but the other one so as
>   to turn-up [πέλειν] and
>   to be [εἶναι] genuine [ἐτήτυμον].
> How then would being [τὸ ἐόν] turn-up-ruined [πέλοι, πέλοιτο, ἀπόλοιτο]?[242] (Parm. 8.13-19)

This decision point forms a confluence of multiple *ruptures*,[243] challenges confronting listeners:

- The image of Dike as separate enough from being so as to enable her to restrain its generation and destruction (Parm. 8.13-15), ruptures—or generates tensions with—the description of being's completeness and unity (Parm. 8.4-6). The image likewise spreads a tremor of uncertainty on the absence of generation and destruction, which the poem presents not as an inherent aspect of being, but rather as a prohibition upon being, implying that being tends towards generation and destruction (hence the need for Dike's restraint).
- The subjectless *is* and *is not*, as Wilkinson discusses, produces ruptures in the Parmenidean poem—or, rather, between the Parmenidean poem and the sound-sense bond of earlier archaic traditions—where being, the poem's ἐστιν [is], "resists all names," opening a new avenue for thinking "against the impulse to name" that Thea attributes to mortals (Parm. 6; 8.38-9, 53-9; 9.1 [implicitly]).[244] An additional tremor raised by these ruptures brings being into close contact with non-being through this resistance to names and naming: Thea discloses that *is not* has the character of nameless, unspoken (Parm. 2.7-8; 8.8), so that the referents of Thea's μέν-δέ construction hover indeterminately, leaving open the possibility that Thea calls ἀνώνυμον [unnamed, nameless]

---

242 This translation works on a composite text, keeping three suggestions in play: πέλοι in Gallop, *Parmenides of Elea*, 66 (8.19); πέλοιτο in Graham, *The Texts of Early Greek Philosophy*, 216 (17.F8.19); ἀπόλοιτο in Diels and Kranz, *Die Fragmente der Vorsokratiker*, 236 (28 B8.19). The phrase *turn-up* translates πέλοι and πέλοιτο; see above, pp. 50-2 and n. 132.
243 Borrowing *ruptures* from Wilkinson as a way to address the poem's foreignness, which Wilkinson hears in the phrasings of the subjectless ἐστι throughout the poem rupturing sound and sense. Wilkinson, *Parmenides and* To Eon, 96.
244 Wilkinson, *Parmenides and* To Eon, 97.

the pathway ἔστιν [is (Parm. 8.16). A further possible rupture then opens on the site of Thea's earlier articulation of the belonging together of νοεῖν and λέγειν (Parm. 6.1; 8.35-6), since the namelessness or resistance to names and naming joins *is* and *is-not* with a νοεῖν [open-awareness] unmoored from λέγειν [gathering-in-speech], or at least apart from any λέγειν or *logos* that attempts to affix names to being's *is* and-or *is-not*.

- By turning being through intralingual translations in the phrases "the other one so as to turn-up [πέλειν] and to be [εἶναι] genuine" and "how then would being [τὸ ἐόν] turn-out-ruined [πέλοι, πέλοιτο, ἀπόλοιτο (Parm. 8.18)], the poem activates ruptures-yet-to-be, pointing towards and disrupting Thea's thinking of undifferentiated being a few lines later in the poem (Parm. 8.22).

Might the poem enact another reflexive moment here, this time on its own mobility, its moving character, calling attention to auditors' involvements in the formation of meaning and the movements of such meaning-making? Might Thea confront listeners with the decisions to isolate and petrify the motions of being and speaking in an attempt to shake loose the linked pair of being and speaking from its traditional tendency towards "fixity" through assignment of static names and narratives?[245] Shimmering [αἰθόμενος] like the chariot's axle in its hubs (Parm. 1.5-8), or again like φύσιν [upsurge and withdrawal; typically translated nature][246] in its unfixed shimmering [αἰθερίαν τε φύσιν τά τ' ἐν αἰθέρι πάντα / σήματα (Parm. 10.1-2)], might Thea offer a performance of a lesson in the "movement of emergence as it emerges," the moving, rising, *e-merging* spoken by τὸ ἐόν that moves continuously without decisively established points?[247] Would the ruptures activated by Thea's voicings here redirect—*translate*—an auditor's awareness towards a choice during the performance of a very challenging and *disruptive* poem, whether to remain with the ever-turning horizon of the now of performance in its ek-static motions or to attempt to arrest the event of the poem's movements by encircling with names "that which resists names," a nameless resistance that at last contours the moving border of *is* and *is-not*?

Stirred from the helix of writing-reading-composition-performance, all the various figures of being's motions teeming within the Parmenidean poem generate significant torsion with its descriptions of a stable and enduring being. In its theme of travel and journey, which Mourelatos takes to be both pervasive

---

245 Wilkinson, *Parmenides and To Eon*, 100.
246 On this translation of φύσις, see above, p. 16 n. 36.
247 Maly, "Parmenides: Circle of Disclosure, Circle of Possibility," 13-14.

and the key to philosophic interpretation of the poem,[248] the Parmenidean song draws attention to such motions, evoking movement that permeates and bears all Thea's teachings. From the outset the Parmenidean Song of Being unfolds as an astonishingly persistent motion: the chariot speeding to the point of collapse and its axle's noise sounding the "strenuous tumult of the motion" (Parm. 1.6-8),[249] the Sun-daughters who rush out in an apocalypse of movement (Parm. 1.8-10), the strangely mobile keys of Dike (Parm. 1.14), the opening of the gates (Parm. 1.16-17), the whirling gates and their chasm (Parm. 1.17-18), all the way through the poem's more subtle movements, such as the association of being with wheels or circles-in-motion in the εὐκύκλου σφαίρης [well-turned sphere (Parm. 8.43)],[250] and the action of simile-formation itself—a kind of motion in its joining or drawing together differences.

While the assumption of the Parmenidean song as principally text will recommend and empower an interpretation involving a static quality of being, approaching the song both as performance *and* as text will let the poem's radiant and vivifying tensions charge the poem with differentiating energies. Torque generated by the fluidity of oral performance and the relative fixity of a written text animates the Parmenidean Song of Being. This interaction opens the text: the motion of singing pierces each seemingly stable assertion, setting it adrift into a field of possibility where each statement exceeds itself. As if turning the poem on itself, early in Thea's discourse the poem bestows an image of such piercing and exceeding:

> But nevertheless you shall learn these things as well, how things which seem
> Had to have genuine existence, permeating all things completely [διὰ παντὸς πάντα περῶντα-περ ὄντα] (Parm. 1.31-2)[251]

The language transposes or blends the aurally indistinct περῶντα and περ ὄντα,[252] so that the terms "hover indeterminately in near-homophony, converging

---

248 Alexander P. D. Mourelatos, *The Route of Parmenides: A Study of Word, Image, and Argument in the Fragments* (New Haven and London: Yale University Press, 1970), e.g. 14-25, 46.
249 Hutchinson, "Parmenides, On Nature," 198.
250 Nagy brings out the resonance of *kuklos* as wheel in the Homeric "cycle" and its connection with fitting-together of artistic making and, finally with the name of *Homeros* itself as "a global metaphor that pictures the crafting of the ultimate chariot-wheel by the ultimate carpenter or, better, 'joiner'." Nagy, *Poetry as Performance: Homer and Beyond* (Cambridge: Cambridge University Press, 1996), 74.
251 Translation is from Gallop, *Parmenides of Elea*, 53. Gallop's edition gives περῶντα in the main text and περ ὄντα in his notes. Gallop, *Parmenides of Elea*, 52 n. 2.
252 Graham notes that "in a non-Ionic alphabet and without word-breaks" the two variants would be "ambiguous," both appearing as ΠΕΡΟΝΤΑ (he ultimately decides in favor

as they pass through one another in the very manner the lines describe,"[253] the image sending a multiplicity [πάντα] shooting through a singular totality [παντός], exceeding the limits of its unity.[254]

Text & Unity

Scholarly disputes continue to develop according to a basic program of establishing a superior text, that is, one that conforms to a putative standard for the poem's language and philosophy, ostensibly grounded on both the *ipsissima verba*, the "best" reading of manuscripts and overall philological soundness. In this manner, for example, Gallop proceeds under the cautions that fragments may have been misquoted and-or misinterpreted.[255] The very notion of *mis*-readings or *mis*-interpretations implies the presence of a singular and genuine text in comparison with which quotations and interpretations might be co-ordinated and scrutinized in order to establish the textual points and extent of their deviations. This, however, is not the only or even the best way to think about the poem's text(s); as Cassin has illustrated, from each fragment radiates a multiplicity of sources, manuscripts, citations, readings (interpretations), as well as translations. The practice of attempting to locate the (single) best source for a term or phrase amounts to a drive for unity.[256] Editors' selected variants often indicate a desire to unify the text according to an overall interpretation of the poem. For example, two disputed phrases can be heard in the opening lines of the Parmenidean poem:

- a singular or plural form of δαίμων [*daimon* (Parm. 1.3)]
- one of several phrases in the middle of the third line, including most notably κατὰ πάντ' ἀσινῆ [everywhere unharmed], κατὰ πάντ' ἄστη [along/over all cities], κατὰ πάντ' ἄτη [along /according to every madness (Parm. 1.3)].

For both phrases, an interest in an overall unity guides interpretation, translation, and presentation of the text in editions of the Greek.

Following Stein's mid-nineteenth century c.e. conjecture, Wilamowitz-Möllendorff advanced the nominative plural δαίμονες [*daimons*][257] in place of

---

of, and promotes to the main text of his edition, περ ὄντα). Graham, *The Texts of Early Greek Philosophy*, 235.
253 Spitzer, "Trans-philosophy," 578-9.
254 Spitzer, "Archaic Images of Totality," in Spitzer, *Studies in Ancient Greek Philosophy*, 50-1.
255 Gallop, *Parmenides of Elea*, 5.
256 Cassin, "The Relativity of Translation and Relativism," trans. Roland Vésgő, CR 12, no. 2 (2012): 24-6, and fig. 1.
257 Ulrich Wilamowitz-Möllendorff, "Lesefrüchte," *Hermes* 34, H 2 (1899): 203-4.

the genitive singular δαίμονος [of a *daimon*] attested in the source manuscript and presented both in Bekker's 1842 c.e. edition of Sextos Empirikos and in a 1621 c.e. edition produced by Petrus and Jacob Chouët that included Stephanus' sixteenth-century c.e. Latin translation.[258] Incorporating the plural noun, the Diels and Kranz translation—translated—gives:

> The mares, which take me further than they were pulling me—only so far as desire [*die Lust*] overcame me—the Daimones [*die Dämonen*; δαίμονες] (the Goddesses [*die Göttinnen*]) driving brought me to the very famous path that carries the knowing man over all inhabited places [κατὰ πάντ' ἄστη] (Parm. 1.1-3)[259]

Accepting the emendation of the manuscript, Diels and Kranz transliterate δαίμονες as *die Dämonen* and then translate *die Göttinnen*. In their apparatus and notes, they further emphasize the translation, making explicit their identification of δαίμονες with the Ἡλιάδες [daughters of Helios] who appear in the poem (Parm. 1.9).[260] In forging this link between the two terms, the translation introduces a decisive unity to the text in preference to its own textured diversity and uncertainty.

In more recent editions, editors have tended towards a reversion to the manuscript reading and present the singular δαίμονος in their texts.[261] The translation in the collection by Kirk, Raven, and Schofield reads:

> The mares that carry me, as far as my heart ever aspires sped me on, when they had brought and set me on the far-famed road of the god [δαίμονος], which bears the man who knows over all cities [κατὰ πάντ' ἄστη] (Parm. 1.1-3)[262]

Of the editors of recent editions, Tarán's argumentation in defense of this reading foregrounds the impulse towards unity on several levels. Tarán makes intertextual appeals to sequences in Pindar in order to conclude that the manuscript

---

258 Henricus Stephanus and Gentianus Hervetus Aurelius, eds. *Sexti Empirici: Opera quae extant* (Geneva: Petrus and Jacob Chouët, 1621), 157c.7; Immanuel Bekker, ed. *Sextus Empiricus* (Berlin: Reimeri, 1842), 213.
259 Translation and text from Diels and Kranz, *Die Fragmente der Vorsokratiker*, 228. The parenthetical phrase the Goddesses [*die Göttinnen*] is part of the Diels-Kranz translation. Other interpolations are mine.
260 Diels and Kranz, *Die Fragmente der Vorsokratiker*, 228 n. 19.
261 Kirk and Raven, *The Presocratic Philosophers*, 266 (342.fr. 1.3); Tarán, *Parmenides: A text*, 7 (1.3); Kirk, Raven, and Schofield, *The Presocratic Philosophers*, 242 (288 fr. 1.3); Gallop, *Parmenides of Elea*, 48 (1.3); M. R. Wright, *The Presocratics: The Main Fragments* (London: Bristol Classical Press, 1985), 13 (1.3); Cassin, *Parménide: Sur la nature ou sur l'étant*, 70 (I.3); Graham, *The Texts of Early Greek Philosophy*, 210 (10.F1.3); Laks and Most, *Early Greek Philosophy*, V.2:32 (D4.3).
262 Translation and text from Kirk, Raven, Schofield, *The Presocratic Philosophers*, 242-3 (288 Fr. 1.1-3). My interpolations.

should be accepted and that "the δαίμων is the same as the goddess of line 22."²⁶³ Reinforcing a unity through the text, Tarán develops an interpretation of Thea as exclusively "a literary device"—effectively bringing to rest the indeterminacy and instability of her identity(-ies)²⁶⁴—in order to maintain the logical consistency of the poem because, on his reading, to Parmenides "there exists only one thing, the unique and homogenous reality." ²⁶⁵

Concerning the other disputed phrase in the opening three lines, there is wider variation among editors, perhaps because the linguistic possibilities themselves are more numerous.²⁶⁶ In the poem's third line occurs a phrase that has posed difficulties to editors to the extent that, in her edition and translation of the line, Cassin presents an ellipsis within chevrons indexed to an entry in the apparatus providing various readings and to a note on the translation explaining some possibilities.²⁶⁷ Three of the numerous phrasings are:

1   κατὰ πάντ' ἀσινῆ: Gallop follows Jaeger in accepting the phrase. Jaeger posited the adjective ἀσινῆ [unscathed] and appealed for support to a similar phrase in Aiskhylos' *Eumenides* that he interpreted as religious in orientation and so compatible with his wider project declared by the title of his lectures collected in *Theology of the Early Greek Philosophers*. Particularly, Jaeger takes this reading on the grounds that salvation alone can result in the traveler's condition of ἀσινῆ.²⁶⁸ For Gallop, who reads the narrator as an "initiate into mysteries" that both take place in and have to do with a transcendence of "all difference or contrast," the safe passage of the traveling

---

263 Tarán, *Parmenides: A text*, 10-11.
264 Valentine opens the text into widening semantic possibilities as she approaches Thea in terms of "flexibility and fluidity rather than fixity in her identity." Valentine, "The Archaeology of Parmenides," 109.
265 Tarán, *Parmenides: A text*, 30-1.
266 Additional possibilities include: κατὰ πάντ' ἄντην ["straight on through all things"]. Graham, *The Texts of Early Greek Philosophy*, 210 (10.F1.3 and n.4). Bekker prints κατὰ πάντα τῆ in the main text of Sextos (Sext. Emp. *Math.* VII.111.11) with a reference in the apparatus to various readings. Bekker, *Sextus Empiricus*, 213 and n. 11. In a nineteenth-century c.e. printing of Stephanus' text and translation emended by Fabricius, the reading is κατὰ πάντ' ἀτηφέρει (Sext. Emp. *Math.* VII.111.9) with additional possibilities in the apparatus. Albertus Fabricius, ed., *Sexti Empirici Opera Graece et Latine* (Leipzig: Kuehn Library, 1841), 300 and n. d. The seventeenth century c.e. Chouët version of Stephanus offers a very difficult text to discern [approx. ἣ κατὰ πολύτα], rendered in Stephanus' translation as *via quae fert per singula* [whose singular way carries through] (Sext. Emp. *Math.* 157c7). Stephanus and Aurelius, *Sexti Empirici*, 157.
267 Cassin, *Parménide: Sur la nature ou sur l'étant*, 70-1.
268 Werner Jaeger, *The Theology of the Early Greek Philosophers*, trans. Edward S. Robinson (Oxford: Clarendon Press, 1947), 98 and 225, n. 20-3.

narrator "through descent into a magic region" gathers significance.²⁶⁹ That is, the destination must be assured because it is in that "magic region" of Thea that the *kouros* can receive what Gallop sees as the legacy of Parmenides, namely, an "explicit and self-conscious argumentation." Such argumentation renders Parmenides, in Gallop's view, "the first extant author deserving to be called a philosopher in a present-day sense of the word."²⁷⁰

2   κατὰ πάντ' ἄστη: Mutschmann presented this text in his 1914 edition of Sextos (Sext. Emp. *Math.* VII.213.11).²⁷¹ Looking to intertextual parallels, a construction they take as an intratextual recommendation for this reading, and the trustworthiness of the manuscript, Diels and Kranz opt to include this phrase in their edition.²⁷² However, Coxon dismissed κατὰ πάντ' ἄστη as having "no manuscript authority at all" and as "a simple misreading of the manuscript,"²⁷³ and more recently Pelliccia has interrogated an intertextual support alleged by Diels, determining the source for comparison to be "almost entirely Diels' invention."²⁷⁴ The phrase's inclusion in Kirk, Raven, and Schofield's edition builds toward their reading that "Parmenides' chief purpose in these lines [sc. all of fragment 1] is to lay claim to knowledge of a truth not attained by the ordinary run of mortals;" thus their suggestive translation *"over all cities."*²⁷⁵ Wright, too, elects this reading in order to bolster her reading of the journey as following the path of the sun.²⁷⁶ Finally, Mourelatos, after dismissing κατὰ πάντ' ἄτη (3) on the assumption that the text must be corrupt, takes κατὰ πάντ' ἄστη (2) as "closer to the text."²⁷⁷ The image of travel generated by this variant supports his interpretative concentration of the journey.

3   κατὰ πάντ' ἄτη: Coxon described this phrase, which he determines to be the authoritative reading of the manuscript, as "meaningless" yet "completely clear."²⁷⁸ Though not an editor, Lombardo may be unique among translators into English in electing to translate the phrase as it is reported and read in the manuscript (κατὰ πάντ' ἄτη): "through every delusion,"

---

269 Gallop, *Parmenides of Elea*, 6-7.
270 Gallop, *Parmenides of Elea*, 3.
271 Mutschmann, ed. *Sexti Empirici opera*, II:26.
272 Diels and Kranz, *Die Fragmente der Vorsokratiker*, 228 n. 19.
273 A. H. Coxon, "The Text of Parmenides fr. 1.3," *The Classical Quarterly* 18, no. 1 (May, 1968): 69.
274 Hayden Pelliccia, "The Text of Parmenides B1.3 (D-K)," *The American Journal of Philology* 109, no. 4 (Winter, 1988): 509, 508, respectively.
275 Kirk, Raven, Schofield, *The Presocratic Philosophers*, 243; italics added, my interpolation.
276 Wright, *The Presocratics*, 77.
277 Mourelatos, *The Route of Parmenides*, 22.
278 Coxon, "The Text of Parmenides fr. 1.3," 69.

which conforms to his reading of the poem as shamanic with links to other spiritual practices aiming for enlightenment or, at least, seeking "to exercise compassion and advance in wisdom." About translating ἄτη, Lombardo acknowledges the textual problems and articulates his decision to avoid the emendation ἄστη (2) because it both lacks witness in the manuscripts and "it trivializes Parmenides' experience as that of a philosopher on tour."[279]

A desire for and from a unified interpretation impels editors and translators to construct a text of the Parmenidean poem most appropriate to that interpretation. The assumption of a singular, authoritative text finds itself reiterated in the statements on the unity and homogeneity of being within the Parmenidean poem:

> It never was nor will be, since it is now, all together, one,
> continuous. For what birth will you seek for it? (Parm. 8.5-6)
>
> Nor is it divided, since it all exists alike; nor is it more here
> and less there, which would prevent it from holding together, but it is all full of being. So it is all continuous: for what is draws near to what is. (Parm. 8.22-25)[280]

Being and the poem-as-text again repeat one another, here in their unity. Just as the approach to the poem as an exclusively or primarily written composition enables and supports a homogeneity of text and textualization, the approach that assumes a singular, authoritative text produces a kind of monotony, where interpretation that seeks a unity of content or message runs strictly parallel to the singularity of a presumed textuality of the poem; the interpretation and the textuality repeat one another, enact a repetition of the same, a refusal of difference. This repetition stands as both cause and result of an alleged connection of writing and the unitarity of truth.[281]

Returning to the poem's situation within the oral tradition can dissolve such monotony and awaken the poem's vibrancy and dynamism. Situating the poem in the lineage of oral poetry involves opening its textual history to the possibility of multiplicity. Since the poem formed in the late sixth and early fifth centuries in a performance mode and setting, the poem's textualization may incorporate features of that tradition beyond what can be gathered through textual comparison with other poems. That is, following Lentz, the position of the Parmenidean poem within the tradition of oral poetry raises

---

279 Lombardo, *Parmenides and Empedocles*, 11 (translation), vii (on shamanic traditions), 3 (discussion of the choice).
280 Translation comes from Kirk, Raven, Schofield, *The Presocratic Philosophers*, 249, 250-1, respectively.
281 Charles Segal, "Spectator and Listener," in *The Greeks*, ed. Jean-Pierre Vernant (Chicago: University of Chicago Press, 1995), 194.

PHILOSOPHY THROUGH TRANSLATION

the possibility that the early Greek philosophic poems may have been published orally and only written much later according to a sensibility in which the "exact wording" was of little importance.[282] The diversity of epic poetry forms the current in which the Parmenidean poem flows. If the Parmenidean poem belongs within the tradition of epic poetry, and if that poetry "easily tolerates multiple versions of tales,"[283] then the Parmenidean poem also may have existed as multiple versions, some of which echo in what are now considered textual variants. Again, it may be the case that memory of "the sequence of arguments" would take priority to a "word-for-word reproduction of the entire treatise."[284] And if composition takes place on multiple occasions and after different performances, perhaps even by different performers, each composition or transcription would differ accordingly. That is, the cultural conditions of epic poetry at least open the possibility of a variety of written texts—perhaps, transcriptions of performances—of the Parmenidean song that have left traces of their differences in the apparatus of modern compilations under the heading of *variants*. In short, there could be no single, authoritative version because of the "primacy of the oral version."[285]

Of equal importance to the diversity of epic poetry is the creativity of each instance of a poem, the *re-creation* of each performance.[286] This founding creativity, shaped through what Lord called a "poetic grammar" that is "based on the formula,"[287] forms the basis of the re-creation-in-performance of epic speech. In Bakker's terms, the song of Parmenides "activates" being through its repetition,[288] and the character of being as plural and changing in this activation sustains a tension of the *said* and the *(re-)enacted*. Voicing the situation of the Parmenidean poem within a tradition of epic speech, Kurfess urges that editors, as well as readers and critics, should "be prepared to accept that, like Hesiod and Homer before him, and Empedocles and Lucretius after (and imitating) him, Parmenides repeated phrases, whole lines, and even runs of multiple verses at various points

---

282 Tony Lentz, *Orality and Literacy in Hellenic Greece* (Carbondale: Southern Illinois University Press, 1989), 93-4. Thomas agrees with this assessment and goes on to say that a written text of poetry, in an era that predates the invention of an orthography for poetry, would have been "comparatively unhelpful." Thomas, *Literacy and Orality*, 92-3.
283 Segal, "Spectator and Listener," 194.
284 Lentz, *Orality and Literacy*, 92.
285 Thomas, *Literacy and Orality*, 161.
286 Bakker, "Activation and Preservation," 11.
287 Albert B. Lord, *The Singer of Tales* (Cambridge, MA: Harvard University Press, 1960; reprint, New York: Atheneum, 1973), 65.
288 Bakker, "Activation and Preservation," 13. Bakker does not discuss Parmenides; here the term "activate" is re-enacted towards the song of Parmenides.

in his poem."[289] Reconstituting the extent of repetition in the song of Parmenides will raise within the poem what Nagy calls the "paradox of repetition" that involves a heightened sense of differentiation with each instance of apparent sameness.[290] Specifically, the torque of *said* and *(re-)enacted* makes itself felt in Thea's disclosure of the two ways for inquiry:

> Come now and I shall tell, and do you receive through
>   hearing the tale,
> which are [εἰσι] the only ways of inquiry for thinking:
> the one: that it is [ἔστιν] and that it is not possible not to be
>   [οὐκ ἔστι μὴ εἶναι],
> is [ἔστι] the path of Persuasion (for she attends on Truth);
> the other: that it is not [οὐκ ἔστιν] and that it is [ἔστι] right it
>   should not be [μὴ εἶναι],
> this I declare to you is [ἔμμεν] an utterly inscrutable
>   [παναπευθέα] track,
> for neither could you know [οὔτε γὰρ ἂν γνοίης] what is
>   not [μὴ ἐόν] (for it cannot be accomplished),
> nor could you declare it [or: point it out] [οὔτε φράσαις]. (Parm. 2.1-8)[291]

Ten times εἶναι [typically translated: to be] sounds in this fragment, voiced in four different forms. Of these, three are spoken as strong negations (μὴ εἶναι; μὴ ἐόν) and two as less intense negations (οὐκ ἔστι), so that the negation of being composes half of the passage's articulation of being. Nevertheless, the poem declares with those very words that non-being is not and that, further, it cannot be learned at all [παναπευθέα] and it cannot be known or spoken by the second-person subject-object present in Thea's speech [οὔτε γὰρ ἂν γνοίης, οὔτε φράσαις (Parm. 2.6; 2.7-8)].

On another level, the multiplicity of being that the poem "preserves," again, according to Bakker's terms, as it "activates" being, keeping being (partially) in view and maintaining its presence through repetition,[292] speaks against the unity implicit in the textual presentation of the poem even as it creates an atmosphere of being's unity:[293] the unity voiced by Thea takes place not as a simple and

---

289 Christopher Kurfess, "Restoring Parmenides' Poem: Essays Toward a New Arrangement of the Fragments Based on a Reassessment of the Original Sources," (PhD. diss., University of Pittsburgh, 2012), 25.
290 Nagy, *Poetry as Performance*, 100.
291 The translation is from Graham, *The Texts of Early Greek Philosophy*, 213. Interpolations of Greek are mine, but the bracketed alternative in the final line ("or: point it out") and the parenthetical phrase in line 7 are Graham's.
292 Bakker, "Activation and Preservation," 13-14.
293 Wilkinson, *Parmenides and* To Eon, 99.

undifferentiated unity, but as a differentiated manifold. Indeed, the language of the poem itself makes a reflexive statement on the dynamic of preservation-activation and its underlying multiplicity:

> Come, I will speak [ἐρέω], and you, hearkening to a traditionally arranged speech [μῦθον ἀκούσας], gather it into your care [κόμισαι (Parm. 2.1-2)]

Only through a basic manifold constitutive of speaking and hearing can Thea's μῦθος [*muthos*; translated as *traditionally arranged speech*] be preserved in and by another. This initial differentiation of speaker and hearer widens into a field of differentiation as the performance of a μῦθος [*muthos*] for and towards others, such widening spoken in the polysemy of the verb κόμισαι [translated as: gather it into your care], another valence of which is registered in Gallop's translation, "convey."[294] Once heard within its culture of multiplicity, the text-as-singular also begins to fragment internally by means of the language. Not only does each statement concerning singularity within the poem take place *as* plurality, the plurality constitutive of speaking, but the emphatic manifold of the poem's whole atmosphere also problematizes any unity that is declared. The wholeness and unity spoken in the phrase οὖλον μουνογενές-μουνομελές-οὐλομελές [whole formed-as-one—single-limbed—whole-limbed (Parm. 8.4)][295] depends on the continual torque both of the emphatically numerous signs or gestures [σήματ' ἔασι / πολλὰ μάλ' (Parm. 8.2-3)] along the one way and the abundance of language figuring the unity, that is, the compound adjectives of such unity as μουνογενές-μουνομελές-οὐλομελές. On an aural-oral layer, if a performance of the hexameter entails rests after the final foot of each line, the friction of the third line's plosive and more rapid dactyl (πολλὰ μάλ') with the smooth closed vowel and slower spondaic opening of the fourth line (e.g. οὖλον μουνογενές) encourage a continual play of the plural and the singular. Such friction also closes the second and third lines: the third person plural ἔασι [are (Parm. 8.2)] of the second line inaugurates a staged movement from many to one through the following line ending in the third person singular ἐστιν [is (Parm. 8.3)].

*

* *

Wilkinson's statement that the presupposition or expectation of "something like an oral definitive version of the epics is to impose the rigidity of text upon the

---

294 Gallop, *Parmenides of Elea*, 55.
295 The multiple possibilities are given in Cassin, *Parménide: Sur la nature ou sur l'étant*, 84 n. VIII 4.

artistry of oral poetry" resonates with the poem of Parmenides.[296] Both as text and as epic speech, diversity and multiplicity animate the Parmenidean poem. The philological impulse towards a single, authoritative text shapes a reading of the poem as offering a vision of being as a singular unity, and the impulse itself is, cyclically, reinforced by such a reading. Resituating the Parmenidean poem in oralcy and awakening the tensions arising from that position amplifies the dynamics operative in the poem. Instead of a unison of images, form, and ideas in which each agrees with and reinforces the other according to what Valentine has called a "self-replicating circularity" that adduces from the poem itself reasons for disassociating it from historical specificities and then uses the "paradigm" of such disassociation to interpret the text,[297] the Parmenidean poem begins to open itself to more numerous interpretive accesses and possibilities.

"Within the possibility in Parmenides," Maly writes, "is difference; within that difference is possibility, for us."[298] Promoting a reception of multiple, diverse versions of the song opens further pathways for thinking the poem as driven by the energies of a moment of synchrony between orality and literacy, but with a primacy of the former; a moment of complex performance stimulating and drawing attention to, rather than disavowing, various bodied senses—and as a locus of numerous possibilities. How might translation set in motion the dynamics of poetry-in-performance, the tensions developed through the movements of oralcy and a written text? Might translation activate some of the features of the poem's oralcy and its constitutive variation and self-differentiation? Can expansive translational engagement create openings for the Parmenidean poem to be thought with fresh perspective from outside or beyond the limits of philosophy and philology?

At times, an engagement that enacts a wide divergence from accepted translational norms may take place as a gathering and putting on display of the divergence of the text from itself—its self-translational torque—as it has been channeled through philological and philosophical attempts at integration of a single, unified, unchanging whole. Whereas the impulses of consistency and singularity jointly guide much effort to establish a text and, on its grounds, a doctrine of the Parmenidean poem, translation might make an antistrophe—a counter-turn—in order to reanimate interpretive possibilities that refuse the decisions of textual variation. This antistrophe involves allowing differences across the apparatus criticus to sound forth in translation, re-sounding the possibilities of diversity in the early history of the poem's performance.

---

296 Wilkinson, *Parmenides and* To Eon, 26.
297 Valentine, "The Archaeology of Parmenides," 9-10.
298 Maly, "Parmenides: Circle of Possibility," 10

CHAPTER 3

Translating Philosophy

Figures of Motion, Figures of Being

...τῇ φερόμην (Parm. 1.4)
—there was I translated

orientation

[1]   forces draw   the object of primary
                          self to the outer limit of self

swept onto a pathway of speech & madness among the din the crush

                                        pulls | for all time
                                along the sacred way to ecstasy
                                         where human light
                                                &
                                            vision end

  i am torn   a shadow | from | a shadow of a self forces strain
                         every harmony of the living world every syllable of
                                           thought ignites shimmering
            from within a music sings the mind's whole grammar of becoming

   beings of fire roar out of darkness   an apokalypse
                                        from the halls | of night
                                              where all paths lead

en-trance

[1.11]   gates | secure | being   at the world's
                                              edge trimmed by stone full
                          of the mysteries of air & light | opposition
                                        locks the twilight land

CHAPTER 3

    where dis-
           -semblance opens a path closed | in flame
                               beings of fire unclose an emptiness
                                                  be-
                           yond the gates of day & night
                        chasm | tremulous wings of bronze
                          echoes spirals of light & sound
                      &
                      passage of first | self over
                                      the boundary
temple of   thought & speech
                        i

entranced   ecstatic   translated

abyss

[1.22]   —a self of   primacy drawn under
                                        by a force of unhuman
                                                light
                                      seized handinhand of

            a shimmering a divine a glance
     the song of being | suddened | over the abyss:
strove past the edge   *of awareness*
                                        & ceaseless togetherness
        drawn by forces an object of second self reaches for belonging an
                    otherness of first selfmanyselves
        an open hand of greeting joins neither malice nor doom
                sent pathway unjoined
                    one—distance & estrangement
                the object of second self a return into
              a foreignness both settled & gestural

          seek everything—
                what opens   *&*   *closes itself*
                      in its cycle of oblivion
                             &

what surfaces on the bright quick slope of going
                under most of all learn the surfacing the woven
                      shimmering its violence its translation

[2] *now –*
    the song will sing you
                under figures of being   *pathways of images luminous*
                beneath the   opening   *light of awareness opening*
                shelter & passage   *in the mouth of a second self*
                                            over the lapsing
                                                    expanse two
                                                     paths curve
                                                     awareness
     one splits   *isisnotnotturningits way to the center of oblivion*   *along the*
              other   *flowtogetherthe streams of isisnottogether*
  speaking   *a phrase that can never be spoken*

[3] *since awareness & being open the same on the circle of the same in its turnings its repetitions*

cycle

[4] *where distances vanish into presence not*   *isolation not*
                                                                                     belonging

[5]
                                  together - ness
                        is a fold of   *being granted*
             a primary self   *for*   *bestowals begin*
                turned any   *where*   *again*
                    turned   *&*   *re-*
                              turned

[6]   *desire uncloses being—gatheringawarenessopening*
                                beingis
                     while   *nothingisnot*
          urgethesephrasestowards   *a second*
              selfalong a path   *of inquiry as*
                      thought alone clogs
                            the way

its two-heads risen from a single neck gnash each other in folly desire for what has been silences the living world drives phantom minds into the blindness of habit where being & nothingness mergesplinterapathcurving againagainintoitself

[7]
$$\text{not}$$

never   not

beingovercoming itselfitsnon
awareness an arrow opening sky opening aether breaks
breaks the circleof thoughtdrawn
taut by habithabit'sforce
&

experience
its creases its
seams
its many folds—

a circle   of eyes
without sight   of ears and
tongues ringing with their own noise
within the gathering experiencehardship a
gauntlet from primary selffrom
joiningspeech has been
spoken

the way of makings & doings

[8] *only creation creating again a way into being everything points to this all signs signs numberless signs an uprising unmoveable enduringly fragile eternally perishing*

listen
song's unity trembles
inside a moment of bringing
forth what beginning a folding of one
togetherwith itself a second
self chases
source

what is source ofallthatisfallnotintochasmintonothing

           nihil silences
          cover the opening
            awareness
             through
         a moment | without
              then
               or
              then

lack the emptiness of doubt yokes
        thought to generation
a mouth forever speaking an oracle turning turningbeingintobeingturning
              a voice
          of no beginning
           opensitself
     from everywhere the innerness
     of beingwithdrawsfromawareness

       voice
      a bell a
    toll of silent   thunder
   an omen never spoken
   light of opening lighthuman
    light as if ever as if
     always as if a span
       opening

          in the instant | before
         thought an emptiness filled
         by desire summoned undone

triptych: time being change
[8.9]   *oracle lunges*

    region with-
       -out then or then without involvements
what carves a hollow into being
      where desire as   prophecy
          upsurge of the un-
            -begun
     being-turning emptiness counter-turn
            & returns

CHAPTER 3

                      being cloaks

                                              emptiness always

everywhere

                    or   *there*   *is*   *only*

negation

[8.12]   *force*   *of*   *persuasion's turnings*
               will never launch   *anything*
                     beyond   *itself beside another*
                                   from   *adamant*
       silence   *always*   *an edge*
                 of speech   *growth*   *&*
                                                                      decline

                    emergence   *&*
                                         down-
                                                    -going-   *col-*
-lapse beneath the grasp the bonds of a fixed direction

                        a crisis of is&isnot
                                 one
                isnamelessisawarenesscovered
                                 &
a   *hidden center secretly pressingasanxietyasa lost wayapathlosing itself*
          before the opening & closing of oblivion (which is called truth)

other path unwinds   *as being translated turningsvoiced from within*

        speaks the question of being folded-un-folded through all the tenses
genesis   *on fire*
         & the serpentine   *catastrophe*   *of human tongues*
burning burning
no other self to trans-
-late & part the self everything simile

            full of beingbeingintouchalwayssummonsbeingnolessthanbeing
                intouchbeingasturningbuildswavescrashesintobeing

[8.26]   *poised in limits like*
                shackles no sourceever-beginning's cusp genesis & catastrophe ab-
                                                                -and-
                                                                -oned
by the turnings of oblivion   *a   self*
        awaits within   *self   in-*
                                                        stant be-
                                                        -fore
                                                        beginning

                forced a great head lowered shackled body compressed
        all around time future bent the angle of time future already closing

identity

[8.32]   *never reaching itself   never*
                                                        absentfromitself
never hollowed all never
                                        once-more-it-self is open
since also is
                                                        openings
                                                        &
                                                        source of
openness awareness apart
                                                from beingalive
in what has been
                                        spoken unfolds all dissimilarity
second person second self discovery's
                                                        horizon
never or is or horizon of is other from being-
                                        -within as in the partition granted
each together binds the whole a wheel unturned to
                                being infinitive its open expanse its non
belonging other than
                                        there all guided into names set
down in the longings the demise turns without pause

CHAPTER 3

the opening
&
closing of oblivion

[8.40]   *from the outset of down-going to perishing*
infinitivebeingitsunclosed&not&placetochange&
translationsshiningsplendoritspageantryofcolors waving
within each risenappearing

                                             from the manifold of place
                                                  to the glare of hues

yet extension reaches its own edge limited & complete

               from   *everythingsimilarity*   *as*
        soliditysolidity   *as*   *massasphere's un-*
                                                                  -*broken*

      curve   *ex-*

                                                                                                                                   -*tending*

itself   *from*

                              the   *center in every*
                          direction   *into the hollow*
                               of each   *thing*

of necessity   *being flows*
     neither more   *nor less*
        in each place   *negation & being*
           do not   *touch—negation*
                          cuts off   *the re-*
                          -*turn*
                 of being
          into sameness would
    surge

       & retreat settle more
     in one place   *less*
elsewhere—being is asylum, refuge

         being a harbor
  within all things

a similarity from

   everywhere moving

    towards sameness

     at the moment

      of perception its

            borders

re-orientation
[8.50] *in this place the first self for the second*

    self an edge an opening of sound
     in its turnings its figures
       of being
speech around opening & closing its center of forgetting stops

  learn the future tipped from silences of collapsing awareness not yet
  said the given-ness of things their decrescendo hear the universe
   as flame everything in its hungry light on & on

     attend kosmos
    of dissemblance delusion
   shaped breath of the first self a source
   of shaped breath song as speech
    second self opens in
     hearkening

[8.53]

shapes gnomic dyad	*plural self moves*	*shapes to name*
morph and settled in		*unquiet naming*
one un-	*un-*	*involved*
hollowed		*use a storm*
in plural	*self again*	*a sea*
being		*a diaspora*
crisis made	*plural self*	*many bodies*
a scape of opposites		*against & signs*
& wonders	*grounded*	*plural self*
signs & wonders		*apart*
away a	*source*	*manifold*
region		*of bright things*
here	*burns the ether*	*the fire eclipses*
the same bright		*a unity with-*
-in self	*same*	*a circle of itself*
unclosed		*everywhere*
an other	*more*	*distant*
not itself		*yet*
this	*down*	*alongside*
itself		*as opposition*
un-flamed	*night*	*its*
opacities		*dense bodies*
enfolded	*weighed*	*upon*
earth		*its horizon*

first person with second self
the translated order of all resemblances
    speaks   *so a knowledge of hunger shadows inextricable togetherness*
                                                                             never astray

symbols
[9]
now then	*radiance*	*& night*
totality		*names*
those	*other*	*powers*
woven		*many others*
everything	*full*	*singular being*
is		*together*
of radiance	*of invisible*	*darkness*
together		*in each*
of many	*plural*	*others*
then		*not alongside*
not	*one*	*not one*

upsurge | withdrawal
[10]
second self	*sees*	*ether*
sees		*upsurge*
totality	*within*	*ether*
of signs & wonders		*pure*
doings & marvels	*unseen as if*	*a nether-*
		-ruined opacities
sun	*gleams*	*see*
origin		*raising*
& letting	*fall*	*all works & days &*
sky-signs		*behold*
moon	*a circle*	*of deeds*
of turnings		*& risings*

CHAPTER 3

	sees around	heaven	a second self embracing
	waxing -future	angle	of time- drives
	grips edges	to hold	borders stars
[11]	see moon	earth	& sun bright
	upper air together	see	galaxy see
	heaven fire of stars	eschatologies	of heaven plural surge
	heat second self	of force	to rise look
[12]	of fire stirred	un-	contained or pure
	filled numerous	numerous	& others of night
	something like bestowals	fate	or of fire
	take flight a cusp	halts	momentany then once
	again as if	shimmering	daimon effervescence
	in showing to occupy	a singular	one—she center a midpoint
	totality infinitive act	of numerous	others to steer

TRANSLATING PHILOSOPHY

as if	*a kosmos*	*a storm-*
raised		*body*
of waters	*churned*	*a buoyant*
drift		*of totality*
of many	*other*	*totalities*
feminine		*centered*
Eros shimmering	*to guide*	*sources-relations*
pairs		*of intimacies distances*
giving	*showing*	*a way*
as		*in beginning*
sources	*again*	*birth*
its		*pains*
delights	*of togetherness*	*sexed*
longing		*others*
seeking	*others*	*others*
longing		*a circle*
of desire	*at once*	*joins*
again		*in togetherness*
[13] *before*	*numerous other*	*shimmerings*
she		*arranges*
projected relations	*distance*	*intimacies*
broken		
[14] *signs*	*around earth*	*crests*
a halo of shadow		*of differing*
[15] *open-span*	*casting*	*sight*
directed		*looks*

CHAPTER 3

to shimmering beams	*visions*	*of sun-dust suspended*
[15a] *snapped solitary*	*frayed*	*line word*
	speaks	
roots water	*plunged*	*into water convergedwithearth*
[16] *mix limbs*	*each*	*other flailed*
many others &	*strain*	*of bestowals clutch*
mix for all	*awareness—*	*openness alongside*
self- self	*once more*	*repeats a third*
instance for human	*singular*	*each beings*
for turns	*human beings*	*whatsoever as upsurge*
& granted	*withdrawal*	*of bestowals for multiple*
for totality the heart	*for again*	*multiplicities opens*
itself singular	*overflows*	*a third thing*
a unity edges	*full*	*past its openings*

TRANSLATING PHILOSOPHY

awareness	*its noetic plenary*	*a readiness*
for everything fullness		*is awareness abundance*
[17] *down*	*through a*	*hollow*
center		*splits*
right	*masculine*	*left*
feminine		*a broken*
line	*drawn*	*an*
echo		
[18] *translated*	*the tongue*	*again*
feminine to		*begin*
joined	*togetherness*	*& masculine*
churned		*along*
another name	*a shimmering*	*of difference*
said		*otherwise*
she	*enshaping*	*the hand*
smoothing curves		*kernels*
in arteries	*of grace*	*translated*
of shine		*of numerous appearings*
potencies	*belonging*	*to love*
& from		*the blood*
multiplicities	*tempered*	*shapes*
offering		*bodies*
still	*a possibility*	*with joining*
with		*confluences*
clash	*numerous*	*others*
forces		*neither*

CHAPTER 3

    the many   *fashion*   *a unity*
    in bodies   *vex a horizon*

    the underworld   *its riches*   *its plenum*
    prophecies   *cataclysms*

    its bright   *motion*   *away*
    its divisions   *separations*

    numerous   *furies*   *a double*
    by power   *rising*

[19]   *and again*   *as if for a second*   *self*
    among shinings   *effusive*

    also now   *plural*   *others*
    beings   *also risen*

    past horizons   *the afterglow*   *from one*
    multiple others   *end*

    &   *for numerous*   *others*
    names   *human*

    beings   *settled*   *for one*
    another   *ensign*

[Cornford's]

                                as if one

                movement   *annulled*

         for one   *ends*

  for totality   *names*   *translated*

                         to be

       culled   *from an-*

                     other

CHAPTER 4

Translation through Philosophy

Translating the Parmenidean Poem

...κρῖναι δὲ λόγῳ (Parm. 7.5)
—to open a crisis
in the gathering

Access to the Parmenidean poem opens through translation alone. Translation, in its turn, *alters* and *reshapes* a text according to the language(s), experiences, orientations, and interpretations of a translator. Accordingly, the task cannot be simply to erase or eradicate the ways interpretation (re-)shapes and (re-)configures the text to be translated, what Hix has called "distortions,"[299] since these describe the very activity of translation. Rather, to shape, distort, draw the poem's figures of being from the experience of a thoughtful engagement, to draw such figures with alert awareness of their sources in and from experience, and then to chart some of that engagement, constitutes a task for translation. As a counter-turn to the prevailing doctrinal translation-interpretations of the Parmenidean poem, *Figures of Motion, Figures of Being* pursues as a goal "to reawaken dimensions of early Greek thinking that too often remain dormant in interpretation and translation."[300] Chief among these dimensions is the poetry of the poem, the foreignness and challenging—even baffling—language that gestures in many directions. Three aspects of the translational approach towards the Parmenidean poem at work in *Figures of Motion, Figures of Being* come to speech as *archaeologics, daimonologics, erotics*. What does not settle into these three dimensions of the translational activity of *Figures of Motion, Figures of Being* remains quickening in the unsheltered regions outside of any conceptual or categorical reach: the shadows, the recesses, the non-. Being aware of such presences forms one aspect of the translational daimonology, but the paradoxical—and Parmenidean—status of those presences as also absences lets them retain their distance from articulation.

---

299 H. L. Hix, "Fire at Night: A Version of Herakleitos," *The Yale Review* 103.2 (2015): 6-7.
300 Spitzer, "Trans-philosophy," 570.

Archaeologics

Down among roots and the magic of origins moves a translational archaeologics. Thought as a practice of archaeology, translation exhumes "words in such a way as to generate new works" that "become sources of generative translations."[301] The archaeologics of *Figures of Motion, Figures of Being* re-performs a founding gesture of philology, its quest for *radices*, monadic *Ur*-elements into which linguistic diversity can be reduced and out of which its development can be traced. Yet, instead of arriving at a ground or base level from which changes in linguistic elements shape themselves and to which such changes might be indexed, the roots become rhizomes, tangled relations multiply dispersed and in motion. A paradox of archaeologics energizes a poetics of translation: the impossibility of ever gaining something other than surfaces: beneath each stratum, another stratum.[302] Even as the downward motion of archaeologics takes place in the manner of excavation, which is to say, reduction and removal, it also accumulates. The negativity of excavation, that is, results in what Haroldo de Campos develops out of his critical encounters with Ezra Pound, the poetry of transcreation: "a continuous accumulation of heuristic strata."[303]

Within *Figures of Motion, Figures of Being* such accumulation stands out perhaps most visibly in the translation of fragment eighteen, which translates a Latin translation of a section of the Parmenidean poem. In this fragment can be seen both the extent to which translation forms and mediates any access to the poem and the absence of *originals* in an ontologically motivated sense. As a primary access to the Parmenidean poem, translation refracts, switches the conventional relation so that translation "*is* the original."[304] An absence of originals lets play the play of supplementarity, where an absence opens in the movement of supplement—of *translation* as alteration, of saying otherwise—that makes visible an absence of what previously occluded "the lack or absence of a center or origin."[305] The translation of this fragment in *Figures of Motion, Figures of Being* excavates

---

301 Lisa Rose Bradford, "Haunted Compositions: *Ventrakl* and the Growth of Georg Trakl," *Translation Review* 95 (2016): 41.
302 Echoing Van Wyke's formulation that "[t]he truth is in the veils." Van Wyke, "Imitating Bodies and Clothes," 39.
303 Here de Campos is specifically discussing Pound's translation practice. Haraldo de Campos, "Translation as Creation and Criticism," in *Novas: Selected Writings*, ed. Antonio Sergio Bessa and Odile Cisneros, trans. Diana Gibson and Haroldo de Campos, ed. A. S. Bessa (Evanston, IL: Northwestern University Press, 2007), 317.
304 André Lefevere, "Mother Courage's Cucumbers: Text, System and Refraction in a Theory of Literature," *Modern Language Studies* 12, no. 4 (Autumn, 1982): 16.
305 Derrida, "Structure, Sign, and Play in the Discourse of the Human Sciences," in *Writing and Difference*, trans. Alan Bass (Chicago: University of Chicago Press, 1978), 289.

poetic language from the only available ancient stratum of these particular lines of the Parmenidean poem. For example, archaeologic soundings of the word *dirae* exposed strata specific to philological directions of a Latin term:

the underworld	*its riches*	*its plenum*
prophecies	*cataclysms*	
its bright	*motion*	*away*
its divisions		*separations*

Locating *dir-* initially opens translational pathways towards a certain type of speech (the lexicon entry "curses" moves into the translation "prophecies, cataclysms"), while the stem's relation to *dis-, di-* reverberates with *Dis* (Lord of the Underworld) and the resonances of wealth and radiance that surround that term. In this way, with each *radix* discovered in the archaeologic movement of translation emerges a spreading multiplicity, not the linearity and upward directionality of the root into trunk, branches, and leaves, but rather, as Deleuze and Guattari have thought, a subterranean entanglement of filaments: a rhizomatics.[306]

Reconstruction also forms an inextricable action in the archaeologic movements of translation. In Privitello's evocative phrasing: "The poetic wisdom of Parmenides is built upon a cult of ruins that has dictated our philosophical-historical continuity."[307] Ruins, fragments, the detritus of a sundered whole, in this respect the poem resembles the objects of archaeological investigations, though an important difference arises in that whole artifacts often do reach a conclusive form that is ready for use, veneration, or display, while the wholeness of the poem varies: even if different in each performance, even if on some occasions only certain parts are performed, and even if there could be no definitive version, each version has a kind of wholeness in the trajectory of its performance. William Biers offers an example of the ways that interpretation and inclinations of the archaeologist shape reconstruction in the realm of material remains. Using a single sherd from a ceramic vessel from the Geometric period, Biers presents two very different reconstructions: one invokes a scene from Homeric poetry, the other, "a common activity having nothing to do with

---

306 Gilles Deleuze and Félix Guattari, "Introduction: Rhizome," 5-9.
307 Privitello, "Approaching the Parmenidean Sublime: A New Translation and Resequencing of the Fragments of Parmenides," *Epoché* 23, no. 1 (2018): 3.

myth or epic."[308] While Biers regards this as a cautionary tale about the need to restrain the interpretive impulse, it illuminates the already-there of interpretation, the in-built, inalienable interpretative movement of being-in-the-world and the fullness of involvements.[309] Interpretation and criticism adhere to, or form another dimension or side of, objects of study, what Berman thinks as an ontological belonging-together of texts and criticism, whereby "works of language" call for "criticism to communicate *themselves*, to manifest *themselves*, to accomplish *themselves* and perpetuate *themselves*."[310]

Section titles in *Figures of Motion, Figures of Being*, such as "orientation" and "en-trance," foreground the interpretation operative throughout the translation, while the presentation of the poem as a poetic sequence with marked internal divisions keeps in view the poem's fragmentarity. Absences form at least as much of the poem as do presences, and so fragmentation in the form of a poetic sequence works as a reminder of those absences and the poem's irretrievable elements.

Even within words, down to the syllabic elements themselves, graphic arrangement of language dispersed across the page similarly emphasizes the missing features of the poem:

in-
-stant be-
-fore beginning

As breaks remain visible on the text's surface they signal and remind a reader of the song's irrecoverable fragmentariness and the imprint of reconstruction on every presentation of the Parmenidean poem. Poeticizing the fragmentary status of the Parmenidean poem in this way highlights "not so much some deeply significant cultural find but the problem of engaging with histories that are at best only partially recoverable."[311] The breakages and tears rent in the fabric of

---

308 William Biers, *The Archaeology of Greece*, 2nd ed. (Ithaca and London: Cornell University Press, 1996), 111 with fig. 5.1 on 112.
309 What Heidegger unfolds in the "as-structure" and the "fore-having" within a totality of living involvements. Heidegger, *Being and Time*, trans. John Macquarrie and Edward Robinson (New York: Harper and Row, 1962), 189-95.
310 Antoine Berman, "The Project of a 'Productive' Criticism," ch. 1 in *Toward a Translation Criticism*, trans. Françoise Massardier-Kenney (Kent, OH: Kent State University Press, 2009), 26.
311 Mandy Bloomfield, "Archaeopoetics," chap. 1 in *Archaeopoetics: Word, Image, History* (Tuscaloosa: The University of Alabama Press, 2016), 2. Bloomfield is discussing Charles Olson's poem "The Kingfisher" in terms of its archaeologic modelling and the derived

translations Hermans views as "a kind of communicative short-circuit, a fissure within the discourse which draws attention to the linguistic and pragmatic dislocation that comes with translation," though he notes attention is not always granted to this rupture.[312]

Archaeologics produces breakages in its translational work, yet it also reassembles towards a semblance of wholeness marked by its very semblance. Just as much of the reconstructed ceramic vessel consists of noticeably distinct material from that of the sherds, such new and different materials are necessary for the display of a vessel as a vessel. In translation, an important distinction must be registered: *all* translating language assumes the complexion of the different materials, such that the reconstruction forms the whole work.

Daimonologics

A haunted text, the Parmenidean poem arrives at its current form by a series of translations that silence and finally eliminate the oralcy as and in which the poem takes shape. Yet, a singing or chanting voice haunts the Parmenidean song.[313] To let that invisible and silent voice somehow make itself felt in its absence through translating the song forms part of the task for translation. Yet, the task complexifies: this silence, this not-presence, this *absence* will not be brought into the circle of what is here and anchored there (here). Like the movements on a boundary that characterize the δαίμων (*daimon*), translation from a *daimonologics* will seek to let the silence remain as it is, an absence shimmering on the between—as-with-on-in the between—of translation, translating; a *shimmering* as "a flickering shining," the motions from the opened boundary as Maly has unfolded it.[314] The Song sings the absence alongside, as in the fourth fragment's saying: "unfold vision [λεῦσσε] towards absence in open-awareness [νόῳ] presence doubled in motion" [βεβαίως[315] (Parm. 4.1)].

"alternative epistemology" dealing in "concrete specificities" rather than, as in Pound and Eliot, "generalizing and totalizing aspirations" (2-3).

312 Hermans, "The Translator's Voice," 28.
313 For an inspiring account of responsive openness to this haunting voice and its translative-transformational power, see Privitello, "Approaching the Parmenidean Sublime—Part II," 105-9.
314 Maly, "Echoes at the Edge," 123-4.
315 βεβαίως can be unfolded and strained away from its conventional rendering as "firm, secure," by way of its reduplicated form from βαίνω, go, walk. The "firmness" and "certainty" associated with βεβαίως may come from this very doubling in the manner of, but also otherwise than, the perfect tense: have gone, have walked and then, with a stress on the doubling, walked repeatedly so that the walk has become familiar, one knows where the obstacles are and can avoid them *steadily*. The movement remains, but has become transformed into a movement with the sense of security. Compare this certainty

CHAPTER 4

The song gives its own figures of silent presences in the Ἡλιάδες κοῦραι [*Heliades*, daughters of the divine Sun (Parm. 1.9)]. While the chariot and axle-pipes have been already noted as reflexive moments in the poem, the Heliades can also be heard as commenting on the practice and performance of singing-thinking. As earlier epic opened with invocation, the Parmenidean song might voice the experience of being guided and aided by music towards the presence of language and song. The Heliades approach the traveler just as language comes of its own powers, arrives; the openness of thinking as-towards *arrival*, as the open-awareness called νοεῖν, surfaces as the thematic of *opening-disclosing* in the Song of Being. As the Heliades rush [σπερχοίατο (Parm. 1.8)] to the self in transformational motion of thought—a kind of translation—not only does their own movement flash into song as from umber Night [προλιποῦσαι δώματα Νυκτός] into light (Parm. 1.9-10)—staging the very movement of ἀλήθεια—the movement of Heliades also discloses, is a self-disclosing, an unveiling, an apocalypse [ὠσάμεναι κράτων ἄπο χερσί (Parm.1.10)]:

> beings of fire roar out of darkness   an apokalypse
>   from the halls | of night
>   where all paths lead

But their faces, their uncovered heads, never show: here, a silence, a haunting, where the poem speaks an unconcealedness but speaks no further of the unconcealed, so the unconcealed hovers in the span between opening and closing. The unconcealed remains, in a certain fundamental way, concealed.

The subsequent line announces being in and as its ownmost movement and multiplicities: ἔνθα πύλαι Νυκτός τε καὶ Ἤματός εἰσι κελεύθων [*there and then gates of pathways of Night and Day are* (Parm. 1.11)]. This, the poem's initial speaking of *being*, brings out the hinged motion of being in its turnings between the darkness—spoken first, given its primordiality—and light *and* the meaning of being and thinking in their worldliness, being-in-the-world sounded in the *there and then* [ἔνθα], in the belonging together of gates (passages, entries, limits for opening) and pathways [κελεύθων] that open beyond and connect as an intricately wrought already-there and meaning-rich totality, translating or creating opportunities for translation.

---

and the perfect (and more) sense with the transformation of εἶδος from a perfect tense of ὁράω: what one has seen is transformed through the repetition of perfect tense into what one expects to see on return, the vision as a way whose obstacles have already been encountered and take on the character of the familiar, the *known*.

The characteristic movement of disclosure that belongs to the Heliades resounds—*echoes*—in the repetition of their movement of unveiling by Δίκη [typically translated: Justice] as the divine being uncloses the gates [ὤσειε πυλέων ἄπο (Parm. 1.17)], a movement of repetition they bring about through their gently persuasive words [μαλακοῖσι λόγοισιν (Parm. 1.15)]. Further echoing can be heard in the disclosures of Thea, whose address to the traveler introduces the theme as ἀλήθεια, of disclosure, unclosing, the movements of opening-closing and of crossings and permeations, translations. The echoes and voicings of the opening-closing, unveiling-veiling motion of being and-as ἀλήθεια also stress and thematize the opening of thought in its openness, awareness unclosing towards the expansive possibilities energizing, and emanating from, totality. The mutuality of such opening is the meaning of the jointure of thinking and being:

τὸ γὰρ αὐτὸ νοεῖν ἔστιν τε καὶ εἶναι (Parm. 3)

yes—belonging-together-in the jointure moves both open-awareness [νοεῖν] and being

or, as it sounds in *Figures of Motion, Figures of Being*:

since awareness & being open the same on the circle of the same in its turnings its repetitions

As Heidegger has illuminated, this saying speaks of difference or, better, of differing, when the stress falls on the *belonging* more than the *together*, where difference *differing* holds sway in this saying of αὐτό, as in "same on the circle of the same." The event of appropriation in which human openness and being mutually reach each other occurs, or is activated, by and as the *differing* wherethrough the mutuality becomes possible.[316] Such differing likewise constitutes translation, addresses the movements of relation that translation will not collapse, nor mend, nor unify, but rather will enact in its very actions, as Cardozo has unfolded, only however in such a way that the enactment does not allow for a part apart from the acting enacting.[317]

These motions echo a *daimon*, present a moment of the daimonic hauntings in the Song and the Song's openness to such hauntings. As Heidegger puts it, "Wir

---

316 Heidegger, "The Principle of Identity," trans. Joan Stambaugh in *Identity and Difference* (Chicago: University of Chicago Press, 1969), 32-9.
317 Mauricio Mendonça Cardozo, "Notes on Translation, Alterity, and Relationality: From the Regimes of Indistinctness to the Disclosure of Relation," in Spitzer and Oliveira, *Transfiction and Bordering Approaches to Theorizing Translation*, 191-3.

kommen nie zu Gedanken. Sie kommen zu uns" [We never come to thoughts. They come to us].[318] Poetry's language, like thought, opens the poet, disrupting and shifting the sense of agency and self involved in thinking, intervening and undoing the foundational schism of subject-object at the center and as the starting point of epistemology. The poem's narrator is drawn and taken into the halls of the other, the divinity, Thea, and this being-moved (or: being-translated) forms a condition of the exchange, the opening of thinking that follows. Like Athene's appearing-non-appearing [οἴῳ φαινωμένη] to Akhilleus *from behind* [ὄπιθεν (Hom. *Il.* I.194-8)], thinking and the voice of poetry arrive in and as an openness Parmenides names νοεῖν, νοῦς:

> since belonging together is both opening [νοεῖν] and being (Parm. 3)

> behold [λεῦσσε] in the opening [νόῳ] beings arriving doubled in movement [βεβαίως] (Parm. 4.1)

> regulated-involvements [χρή] bind together as being [ἐόν] to gather in speech [λέγειν], to open awareness [νοεῖν], and to manifest [ἔμμεναι] (Parm. 6.1)

The experience of poetry unveils thinking as being-in-the-world, always already an opening as an open expanse of possibility within a turning horizon. As language, poetry, and especially oral poetry, continually emphasizes its shiftings, its motions, its provocations towards new ways of being with things and beings, disclosing substantiality as a having-been-made (*poem, work of poetry-as-making*) that both generates and reinforces *knowing* within the subject-object oppositional structure of epistemology. Relations, manifest in poetic thinking as similes and metaphors, are not the madness of poetry, but the disclosure of being's enmeshment of multiplicities-in-relations, its en- and un-foldingness; in simile and in all its dynamics, poetry is disclosive of being as being-in-the-world, relation. Poetry happens as, and activates, a return to beginning, a *mimesis* or ἀνάμνησις [showing-up of remembering], a reopening or recovery of being that ordinary pathways of thinking—those Thea links to mortals (e.g. Parm. 6)—have closed; like the great *daimon* Eros, poetry's task unfurls as *joining* or, rather, as *calling back into bodied sense and awareness the jointure already-there*.[319] Poetic language, as thinking, bears a sense of haunting, of the *daimonic*.

---

318 Heidegger, *Aus der Erfahrung des Denkens* (Pfullingen: Günther Neske, 1954), 11.
319 This discussion of ἀνάμνησις [recollection] draws on insights in Anne Ashbaugh, "The Philosophy of Flesh and the Flesh of Philosophy," *Research in Phenomenology* 8 (1978): 218-19.

Within the narrated region of the poem, the first-person subject also registers an image of silence. All speech Thea speaks, while the first-person subject remains silent, even as Thea's speech unfurls as narrated, as Memory or returning. This aspect of the narrative seems, too, to comment on the experience of poetry and song in its subversive relation to Aristoteles' formulation of human mastery of language: λόγον δὲ μόνον ἄνθρωπος ἔχει τῶν ζῴων [of living beings human being alone *has logos* (Arist. *Pol.* 1253a.9-10)]. As the first-person subject of the song's early moments opens himself to the moving actions and forces of others—the horses driving the chariot, the divine Heliades-*kourai* guiding the horses—an image of the daimonic emerges, where the subject no longer holds sway over language but *is held* by the forces of poetic speech figured in those entities guiding him:

```
forces draw    the object of primary
                     self to the outer limit of self
    swept   onto a pathway of speech & madness among the din the crush
            pulls       |       for all time
            along the sacred way to ecstasy
                 where human light
                            &
                 vision    end
```

The translation here minimizes the subject through eliminating the first-person pronoun and staging the grammar within the poetic language: an "object of primary self" limns the double-status of a first-person nominative (subject) rendered object within the poem by that subject's being-hurled (*-ject*) both beneath (*sub-*) the powers of others and in the way of or before (*ob-*) those powers, subverting any claims a first-person subject might make to autonomy or independence and a concomitant detached view onto something like an objective reality posed contra the knowing subject for that knowing subject's identification, determination, explication.[320] The first-person self comes forward at once, at the outset, as thrown, *dis*-closed (unclosed, open) and already in advance of itself.[321] An ek-static moment disturbs a self that blurs or disappears

---

320 For another discussion of this approach within translational poetics, see, with connections to the Parmenidean poem, the "Translator's Note" in Spitzer, "Displacements." With reference to the "remainder" in translation and its unpredictabilities, Venuti also articulates ways translation of philosophy can trouble "the stability and authority of the philosophical subject as the autonomous agent of reflection." Venuti, *Scandals of Translation*, 115.

321 The passage might be understood as enacting the being-ahead-of-itself and thrownness Heidegger uncovers of Dasein. Heidegger, *Being and Time*, 329-30.

CHAPTER 4

like a lantern's glow in the radiance of the day's full sun—resonant in the poem's phrase εἰδότα φῶτα,[322] which Lombardo translates "the enlightened,"[323] while in *Figures of Motion, Figures of Being* the phrase says "where human light / & / vision end." Such is the force of song. In *Phaidros*, Platon's Sokrates describes this force as a form of μανία [madness] and κατοκώχη [holding-down, possession] whose action is λαβοῦσα...ψυχήν [grasping...a soul (Pl. *Phdr.* 245a.1-2)].

Just as in the Parmenidean song, poetic speech grips the singer or poet and acts through that person, permeating the self with a foreign entity, a ghost, a *daimon*.[324] But the grip of song is not that between a thinking subject and the object of thought temporarily disrupted by the grip. Rather, the grip of song uncloses the sense of self as an enclosed innerness that can harden in the ordinary transactional encountering of world and others. This very hardening, another grip, presents itself to Herakleitos in the form of forgetfulness or oblivion [λανθάνει] of the wakeful openness that λόγος can bring about, though in a manner contrasted with that oblivion, so that open-awareness has the character of *being-without-experience* [ἀπείρουσιν (Hera. 1)].[325]

Permeation crosses limits and boundaries. The energies of poetic translating language quicken such crossings and again the images of the Parmenidean poem emphasize this dimension. From the outset the poem depicts limits and crossings: the first-person subject narrator reaches his own limits [ὅσον τ'ἐπὶ θυμὸς ἱκάνοι (Parm. 1.1)]; the Heliades leave the halls of Night (Parm. 1. 9); the whole procession crosses the threshold of the gates of the paths of Night and Day (Parm. 1. 11-21); the last of Thea's teaching has to do with crossings and permeations:

...ὡς τὰ δοκοῦντα
χρῆν δοκίμως εἶναι διὰ παντὸς πάντα περῶντα-περ ὄντα[326] (Parm. 1.31-2)

what surfaces on the bright quick slope of going
                    under most of all learn the surfacing the woven shimmering its violence its translation

---

322 On such a resonance with the sun's light, see Gloria Ferrari, *Alcman and the Cosmos of Sparta* (Chicago: University of Chicago Press, 2008), 44-8.
323 Lombardo, *Parmenides and Empedocles*, 11.
324 Thought through an interdisciplinarity weave of philosophy, literature, and psychoanalysis Erdinast-Vulcan writes of an "uncanniness" teeming "at the very core of language and subjectivity," a distancing and haunting in a self. Daphna Erdinast-Vulcan, "Reading Oneself in Quotation Marks: At the Crossing of Disciplines," in Foran, *Translation and Philosophy*, 43.
325 This notion of a hardened enclosed innerness that looks out towards objects and seeks correspondence draws on Heidegger's discussion of correspondence as most the proximal and derivative sense of "truth" that obscures truth as ἀλήθεια. Heidegger, *Being and Time*, 262-8.
326 For a discussion of these terms, supra (pp. 79-80 with notes).

A storm of crossings unsettles the Parmenidean poem. Transgression-translation is thematized from the outset. When read as reflexive statements on music and poetry and thinking as open-awareness, the song discloses a deeply embedded concern for translation in a broad sense of a movement across and through different limits, a movement of "bordering" both involved in the (re-)drawing of limits and in their quickening, a movement of "limiting" in spatial and temporal dimensions that produces "meanings through multiple points of departure" taking place as "textured, layered, spiraled, or otherwise non-linear."[327] The translation of the last passage of the opening scene attempts to foreground the poem's thematics of transgression and translation.

Finally, the poem extends this vision of language as both grasping and permeating the poet to a possible elimination of any others, or any other subjects. Song gathers differences into a sense of unity. Eliot's famous line sings an experience of this sense of unity: "you are the music / While the music lasts."[328] Haunting the singer, the poetic language, the song, moves the voice, moves the body, takes the traveler-narrator to his limits and beyond others in its translational-translating sweep:

		passage of first |		self over the boundary
temple of		thought	& speech	
			i	
entranced		ecstatic	translated	

Yet this identity is not simply attained; a tension persists in the very action of singing an identity or the various disruptions of the self being translated: in this case, the κοῦρος [young man] and the narrator, translated to a self resembling itself yet, in that resemblance, projected into an irreconcilable distance: "entranced ecstatic translated." Translation of the self in the movements of translation forms a passage through which a being with others takes shape, opens as a kind of foreignness haunting the *sameness* of identity. Even as the *daimon* subverts identity by crossing, passing through, translating, and permeating, it does not merely reinforce the very limits there to be crossed; rather, it remakes

---

327 Spitzer, "Bordering Approaches & Trans-Bordering Themes in Dialogue with the Work of Rosemary Arrojo," introduction to Spitzer and Oliveira, *Transfiction and Bordering Approaches to Theorizing Translation*, 7.

328 T. S. Eliot, "The Dry Salvages," *Four Quartets* (New York: Harcourt, 1971), 44 (ll. 210-11).

CHAPTER 4

the limits in such a way that they are dissolved from what Maly has termed the "'where' of the boundary in the traditional metaphysics of substance,"[329] unfurling instead as something like the momentany *forming* and transformation of boundaries in the very movements of φύσις [upsurge].[330]

As a contrast, when Thea turns the direction of her speaking along another pathway, something like the conventional meanings of ordinary human discourse, she draws attention to the composition of her words [κόσμον ἐμῶν ἐπέων ἀπατηλόν (Parm. 8.52)]. Of ordinary human discourse, Thea discloses structuring principles that, however effective for communication, efface the figures of motions and beings and the opening of boundaries, the dissolution of fixed boundaries.[331] These fixed and established [κατέθεντο] principles [μόρφας, γνῶμας-γνώμαις (Parm. 8.53)] as Light and Night compose a dyad of oppositionality [τἀντία-ἄντια (Parm. 8.55)].[332] Deceit does not arise in the latter parts of Thea's teaching, the so-called Doxa, from what Thea says, but from the translation by human thinking of permeable limits and zones of contact and touch—where open-awareness in the movements of its opening (and closing) reconfigure and renegotiate boundaries in a togetherness of speaking-and-hearkening, a togetherness of logos—into stable and fixed identities, especially rendered as oppositions. In the later teachings, Thea showcases the oppositionality characteristic of ordinary, habitual thinking in the catalog of seemingly fixed celestial objects in their regularities (Parm. 11), in the division of cosmic circles or rings into those of fire and those of night (Parm. 12), in the opposition habit takes as governing reproduction (Parm. 12.4-6; 17), and in the fastening of a single "distinctive name" [ἐπίσημον] for each entity (Parm. 19.3).[333] The arrangement of *Figures of Motion, Figures of Being* stages dyadic oppositionality through its formatting throughout the later moments of the poem (fragments 9-19):

shapes gnomic dyad	plural self moves	shapes to name
morph and settled in		unquiet naming

---

329 Maly, "Echoes at the Edge," 124.
330 After Irigaray's thinking of such movements. Luce Irigaray, *In the Beginning, She Was* (London: Bloomsbury, 2013), 57-8.
331 For more on this, see Spitzer, "Being in touch," 7, 11-13. Also see Macé's reading that Thea here discloses the "demiurgical dimension of language" as "a projection of human taste for order onto the whole universe." Arnaud Macé, "Ordering the Universe in Speech: *Kosmos* and *Diakosmos* in Parmenides' Poem," in *Cosmos in the Ancient World*, ed. Phillip Sidney Horky (Cambridge: Cambridge University Press, 2019), 54, 60, respectively.
332 γνῶμας and τἀντία appear in Diels and Kranz, *Die Fragmente der Vorsokratiker*, 239 (28 B8.53, 55, respectively); γνώμαις and ἄντια are in Gallop, *Parmenides of Elea*, 74 (8.53, 55, respectively).
333 Translation is from Gallop, *Parmenides of Elea*, 91.

The regularity of this formatting points back to Thea's statement on giving attention to the ordering of her words (Parm. 8.52) and attempts a subtle reduplication of that ordering. Where it might appear to be structured by pairs of oppositions, the line highlighting Thea's arrangement enacts a crossing in its chiastic form:

μάνθανε κόσμον ἐμῶν ἐπέων ἀπατηλὸν ἀκούων (Parm. 8.52)[334]

Listen to the deceptive order of my words[335]

Similarly, the regular formatting of the poem's later moments in *Figures of Motion, Figures of Being* raises uncertainties through their very form: while these sections do offer something lie a chiastic possibility (read diagonally across the vertical lines), how (else) are these lines to read? Does a reader take each side as a group, reading left-to-right to the edge of the first long gap (in the above example, from "shapes" to "dyad"), then to the lower line (in this example, "morph and settled in")? The language encourages both possibilities and remains open to numerous other approaches to reading these arrangements, so that a mobile, pliable, shifting multiplicity of crossings and re-crossings continually presents itself in the formatting's regularity. The tension quivering within and animating the poem's spoken oppositions manifests in the ceaseless movement of crossing, permeation, translation.

When thought from the perspective of Thea's early-granted lesson of the crossings and permeations of totality, even the limits and boundaries in Thea's later teachings form as moments of saturation, permeation: the Night's darkness and the Day's light (Parm. 1.11), however opposed by naming, also show up along the pathways [κελεύθων] at the place where being announces itself[336]—the site of crossing, translation. Like darkness and light spreading into and enmeshed with one another, the pathways saturate, permeate, spread, they flow expansively as openings, possibilities no longer figured in the language of the boundary of substance-metaphysics. Instead, these fluidities permeate as meaningful-appearings [δοκοῦντα] permeating everything through totality [εἶναι διὰ παντὸς πάντα περῶντα-περ ὄντα (Parm. 1.31-2)], as not shorn into fixed and stable limits scattered and-or joined in array (Parm. 4), as not divisible into discrete units and as bound by similarity (Parm. 8.22), and as self-joining [ξυνεχὲς πᾶν ἐστιν] in the tidal movements of the sea [πελάζει (Parm. 8.25)].

---

334 The chiasmus of the line runs threefold:
    A (μάνθανε) B (κόσμον) C (ἐμῶν) C (ἐπέων) B (ἀπατηλὸν) A (ἀκούων).
335 Translation by Lombardo, *Parmenides and Empedocles*, 17.
336 The first occurrence of a form of εἶναι (εἰσι) sounds in this line describing the gates (Parm. 1.11).

Throughout the opening narrative and the parts of Thea's speech on being, the Parmenidean poem translates its boundaries and limits into *shimmerings*.[337] Resonant of the sea and its ways of manifesting appearing and withdrawal, depths without the hierarchical arrangement of over-under and form-matter of metaphysical thinking, these motions form the ultimate unsaid—the deep silence and pervasive haunting—of the Parmenidean Song of Being: not only as the resonances of a diaspora and its turbulences,[338] but radically as the undulations of being in its movements as-and-within which other motions come to pass. In this way the Parmenidean poem and its many signs course adrift on the absence and haunting that "is *not* there," a "no where" that summons (and perhaps repels) thinking,[339] the tidal swells on which the poem's own *daimon*, at the center [ἐν δὲ μέσῳ], guides all other motions by steering as if a ship [κυβερνᾷ (Parm. 12.3)] on and amidst the silent, unvoiced open expanse. Haunting the totality and unvoiced yet shimmering, being haunts the *daimon* that, first of all plotted, projected [μητίσατο] Eros:

feminine	*centered*
Eros shimmering to guide	*sources-relations*
pairs	*of intimacies distances*

Erotics

"A massive *daimon* [δαίμων μέγας], Sokrates! Truly, he is the whole divine force between divine and mortal."

Then I said, "What power does he hold?"

"He translates and translates [ἑρμηνεῦον καὶ διαπορθμεῦον]: needs and sacrifices from humans to divinities, and, from divinities to humans, arrangements, commands, and exchanges for ritual offerings. Being in the middle of them both, Eros fills them both so that the whole binds itself together with itself (Pl. *Symp.* 202d.13-e.7)

Crossing Platon's ontological boundary of mortal and immortal, Eros the great daimon moves as a central power of translation. As stationed *between* the two zones, Eros' translational action consists in the dual task of joining, or binding, and of preserving the distance and non-identity of the two. A zone Irigaray has articulated as a "between-us" constitutes an originary though unremembered

---

337 These would be transformed—translated—to shimmerings as a name for "the open-ended, unfolding boundary." Maly, "Echoes at the Edge," 125.
338 On the ways the Phokaian diaspora of the mid-sixth century haunts the poem, see Spitzer, "Broken Light on the Ground of Home: Non-Being and Diasporic Trauma in the Parmenidean Poem," *Diacritics: A Review of Contemporary Criticism* 48, no. 1 (2020): 108-26.
339 Maly, "Echoes at the Edge," 124.

mode of relation and being whose very bearing, orientation, and structure as a gendered duality operating as "a source of relations in difference" may come to speech in the Parmenidean poem, though on her reading the poem has already transfigured the fecund possibilities of relation into an exercise in the logic of repetition, of the same.[340] Specifically on translation, Cardozo has articulated the necessity of preserving distances in a range of translational engagements, from translating to reading translations. Translation as relation "does not happen exactly nor exclusively as a connecting force in space," writes Cardozo, "but rather as a kind of *spacing force (écartement, espaçamento)*."[341] Relation does not form a possibility among others; rather, translation (re-)names relation, relation (re-)names translation, and the mode unfolds as a double movement of *joining-parting*. In its movement of joining, relation-as-translation takes place as Cardozo's event of spacing, sustaining difference in its differing-joining.

Forces draw together and keep a distance between translator and text. The Parmenidean poem opens at once into and as this drawing-together-keeping-apart, narrating an event of the jointure of being-drawn and moving in the direction of an other:

> The horses that take me to the ends of my mind
> were taking me now: the drivers had put me
> on the road to the Goddess, the manifest way
> that leads the enlightened through every delusion (Parm. 1.1-3)[342]

or, as *Figures of Motion, Figures of Being* translates:

```
        forces draw           the object of primary
                                  self to the outer limit of self
          swept             onto a pathway of speech & madness among
                                  the din
                  the crush
                                      pulls    |      for all time
                                  along the sacred way to ecstasy
                                         where human light
                                                    &
                                          vision    end
```

---

340 Irigaray, *In the Beginning, She Was*, 53 (quotation), 52-4 (discussion).
341 Cardozo, "Notes on Translation, Alterity, and Relationality," 197.
342 Translation from Lombardo, *Parmenides and Empedocles*, 11.

CHAPTER 4

This joining-parting under the felt need, as if haunted—*daimonologic*—can be thought in the figure of Eros. Writing of Benjamin but also of Hölderlin's translational encounter with Sophokles, Blanchot describes the force of attraction drawing a translator into a center to which the translator is related by "a constant, perilous, admirable intimacy." The center Blanchot thinks as "that unifying power at work in every practical relation as well as in every language" whose power to join always entails the power to separate, the power of "scission." A certain moment of translation—that on the verge of madness, or beyond— resituates the translator within a location between languages where moves "an agreement so deep, a harmony so fundamental that it substitutes itself for meaning, or rather that it manages to make a new meaning originate in the hiatus opened up between the two languages."[343] As if voicing or sourcing an echo, in the future perfect the hiatus that *will have been voiced* by Blanchot, an originary hiatus sounds in the Parmenidean Song of Being as that locus and threshold of translation: the gates of the Paths of Day and Night, after being unlocked in the manner of a disclosure [ὥσειε πυλέων ἄπο (Parm. 1.17)], open so as to enact a poetic event [ποίησαν] of this very hiatus, spoken in near-anaphora as χάσμ' ἀχανές [the chasm unclosing (Parm. 1.18)]. The moment comes to speech in *Figures of Motion, Figures of Being* as:

> beings of fire unclose an emptiness
>
> be-
> yond the gates of day & night
> chasm | tremulous wings of bronze
> echoes spirals of light & sound

The Parmenidean Song of Being lays emphasis on the moment as (if) a poetic translation, *a movement of those seeking—translators—in their approach in-as the jointure-as-scission, the joining-parting: erotics.* This event belongs to and most poignantly reiterates and performs the Song's thematic *crossings* and its call to (from, as) *translation.*

Around this theme, the erotics of translation gathers two figures of-in translation: Parmenides, Empedokles. The translational interaction brings these figures into erotic intimacy through a sequence on or past the edge of μανία [madness]. Lombardo translates Empedoklean thinking:

---

343 Maurice Blanchot, "Translating," trans. Richard Sieburth, *Sulfur* 26 (1990): 86.

as the two gods mingled with each other more
fell together in random collisions
Continuous production of life-forms began.³⁴⁴

Another voicing sounds the passage as:

—when more and more daimon joins
in sex with daimon collapse to-
        -gether struck together
        in a place of no
        place everywhere many others risetranslatedgenerated
[ἐξεγένοντο] (Emp. 59)

Translation—figured in daimonologic joining and generation—churns a cyclics of centripetal and centrifugal forces, Eros at once drawing in intimacy and nearness and casting into distance, dislocating and decentering the work of translation.

Specifically with respect to the Parmenidean poem this figure recommends itself. In the cosmology Thea articulates, a divine feminine being first devised Eros (Parm. 13), while the latter assumes the appearance of a Δαίμων [*Daimon*] and from a central position steers or governs both birth [τόκου] and sexuality [μίξιος (Parm. 12.3-4)].³⁴⁵ Furthermore, the attraction of being to being—where at a moment of translation being transports itself on an oceanic current of self-similarity and its attendant differentiation: *being / always summons be- /-ing / builds waves crashes into being* [ἐὸν γὰρ ἐόντι πελάζει (Parm. 8.25)]—and the repetition through diversity of συν- [*sym-*, together; e.g. συνέχεσθαι (Parm. 8.23), ξυνεχές (Parm. 8.25)] stress the erotics of simile, the dual action of joining and separating embedded in translation.

Turned in one direction, the arrival in the Halls of Night and its darkness deepens the intimacy and erotic charge of the poem: Hesiod sings the upsurge of Φιλότης [sex] from the parthenogenic force of Νύξ [Night (Hes. *Theog.* 224, 213)]. Frequently interpreters take the passage through the gates to involve a

---

344 Lombardo, *Parmenides and Empedocles*, 46.
345 The characterization of τόκου [birth] as στυγεροῖο [hateful] lends a subtle undertone to the poem's governing erotics in which can be heard a profound association of sex and death—Στύξ, *Styx*, Scorned River of the Underworld—anchoring the lines deeply within the realm of emergence and decline, the double-movement of φύσις and the cosmic turnings of fire and night (e.g. Parm. 9, 10).

movement away from senses,³⁴⁶ but Thea's initial gesture re-emphasizes the *haptic* sensibility that has been in play throughout the journey:³⁴⁷

καί με θεὰ πρόφρων ὑπεδέξατο, χεῖρα δὲ χειρί
δεξιτερὴν ἕλεν (Parm. 1.22-3)

	—a self of		primacy drawn under
			by a force of unhuman
			light
			seized handinhand of
	a shimmering	a divine	a glance
the song of being	| suddened	| over the abyss

The resonance of this scene to and from the encounter of Odysseus and Kirke in the *Odyssey* quickens and more fully animates the erotics of the narrator-traveler's entrance to and experience in the halls of Thea.³⁴⁸ In a scene dense with implications for translation because of the whole atmosphere of transformation, Kirke merges μιγέντε [mixing], φιλότητι [sex], and persuasion or trust: verbal echoes take place through the stem -πειθ- [persuade] and its related terms (spoken by Kirke in the *Odyssey* passage as πεποίθομεν [persuade, trust]), while in the Parmenidean poem -πειθ- surfaces repeatedly.³⁴⁹ Given the other resonances across the two poems, one might listen for the erotic hauntings in the silences between the gesture of greeting and the disclosure of the several paths of inquiry (Hom. *Od.* X.334-5). Finally, on Odysseus' return to Aiaia, the

---

346 Some ancient commentators took the journey to be away from the world of the senses and into a world of pure intelligibility (e.g. Eusebios [quoting Pseudo-Plutarkhos]: Parmenides "expels [ἐκβάλλει] senses from truth" [Euseb. *Praep. evang.* I.8.5=DK 28 A22]; Sextos Empirikos similarly claims that Parmenides set aside [ἀπέστη] any firm standing [ἐπιστάσεως] of the senses [Sext. Emp. *Math.* VII.115]). The view persists; Nightingale, for instance, takes the traveler's arrival scene to diminish any reliance on sense perception except the auditory. Andrea Wilson Nightingale, "The philosophers in archaic Greek culture," in *The Cambridge Companion to Archaic Greece*, ed. H. A. Shapiro (Cambridge: Cambridge University Press, 2007), 191. Recently, Mackenzie works with this division, bringing out ways that "visualization" might generate a different perspective on sense experience. Mackenzie, *Poetry and Poetics in the Presocratic Philosophers*, 77-82.
347 For a thorough discussion of touch in the poem, see Spitzer, "Being-in-touch," 1-22.
348 Havelock makes an extensive comparison of the Parmenidean poem and the Kirke-Odysseus scene in the *Odyssey*, but he is silent about the sexual relation of the two. Havelock, *Harvard Studies in Classical Philology* 63 (1958): 137-40. Similarly, Mourelatos reads parallels across the two but lets the erotics of the encounter remain out of view. Mourelatos, *The Route of Parmenides*, 24, 92.
349 Parm. 1.16, 29, 30; 2.4; 8.12, 28, 39, 50.

isle of Kirke, seizing his hand [χειρὸς ἑλοῦσα (Hom. *Od.* XII.33)], the goddess takes Odysseus apart from the crew, unfolds the trials Odysseus will encounter, and gives him instructions for avoiding and-or overcoming those trials (Hom. *Od.* XII.37-141). Here the haptics of the Parmenidean poem may draw on the erotics pulsing in the Kirke-Odysseus scene(s).

Such erotic implicature and undertones suggest an erotics of translation. This approach follows a third way along which a dual action of fusion and fission occurs. One moment of erotics intimately joins those subjects of erotic involvement, generating the pleasure and ek-stasis by which identities are translated, entangled. The narrator's voice of the Parmenidean poem, as it encompasses its distanced self in the first person narrated *kouros* along with the speaking Thea, approaches such a fusing. In a textualized environment, translating the poem as a poem on the page—despite all its internal schisms in the forms of out-of-joint typography, fraying language and syntax, and marked sections of a sequence—still comes to rest in the unity of the presentation. In the language of *Figures of Motion, Figures of Being*, such fusion implicates itself at the edge of Thea's *oratio recta*: "the song of being | suddened | over the abyss." Combined with the suppression of pronouns as the speech "suddens" itself, the translation suggests the fusion or momentary loss of distinct identities surfacing and sounding the narrative.

Through erotics selves are troubled, jarred, shaken. The shaking force of eros Sappho voices:

sex ["Ερος] jolts [ἐτίναξέ] mind self blown as mountain gust tremors oaks (Sappho 47 Campbell)

Yet those involved continue to bear relations one to the other, suspended in positions of non-identity. Here, an erotics of translation gathers in its gestures moments of the archaeologics and daimonologics. By a certain love and affinity for what is to be translated, translation performs a mimetic gesture that vanishes, or ghosts, the ghosted dimensions of "that which was subjugated" in the cognition translation entails. Its archaeologic reconstructions return to fragmentariness by way of an erotics that relinquishes any reconstruction and its attendant risk of installing a fantasy of reconciled wholeness over, and so concealing, the shattered and obliterated, "the marred figure of what we should love, and what the spell, the endogamy of consciousness, does not permit us to love."[350] A mimetics enacted by erotic translation retraces not only that gust of

---

350 Adorno, *Negative Dialectics*, 191.

otherness harbored in the self (and in the poem and the poem's thematic voicings of self-same), but also that which never can be assimilated or located in the self's cognitive reach. Translational erotics marks archaeologic reconstruction of translation by initiating and suspending vacancies in the act and product of translation. As such, the mimesis of translational erotics performs a tragedy, a falling and collapse its own action produced, but its gestures are those of longing and, above all, of great love.[351]

*

* *

What would it mean for translation to reperform the Parmenidean Song of Being? In part, it would involve energizing the dynamics of repetition and variation characteristic of archaic Greek oral poetry and heightening attention towards the nuances generated by that dynamics. In place of assertions of imputed doctrine, this might unfold within an openness to multiple versions characteristic of archaic Greek oralcy. It would mean translating and re-imagining the Parmenidean Song of Being and its performances with attention to what Bernstein has called the "total *meaning* complex" of a poem, all the elements of typography and design that compose the presentation of the work and that suggest ways of reading and vocalizing.[352] Reperforming the Parmenidean poem might call for new techniques that seek, possibly by exploring multi-media presentations, to fire all the senses of the performer(s) and the audience. Two innovative approaches to the Parmenidean Song of Being, or some elements of it, take the forms of digital media, choreography-dance-movement, and videography.[353] Approaching the poem from the apertures of translation and with a renewed focus on oralcy and performance opens the Parmenidean Song of Being, inviting attempts not only to return to the text, but to reimagine the interpretative accesses through which the song is encountered and, perhaps,

---

351 Adorno, *Negative Dialectics*, 45, 17-18.
352 Charles Bernstein, "Artifice of Absorption," in *Artifice & Indeterminacy: An Anthology of New Poetics*, ed. Christopher Beach (Tuscaloosa, Alabama: University of Alabama, 1998), 4.
353 1) a multimedia installation, "Parmenides 1" (2011), produced by visual artist Dev Harlan can be viewed at his website (https://www.devharlan.com/the-astral-flight-hangar/; accessed August 29, 2022).
  2) a movement-based performance by the Ilanio Project, "Deva: Alpha, Full Performance 3: Parmenides," (2014) (https://vimeo.com/178399870; accessed August 29, 2022).

what constitutes the practice of philosophy, or *philosophies*, as translation and oralcy will ever displace a thinking towards *unity*.

Any translation—and not just that presented as *Figures of Motion, Figures of Being*—that re-engages with the text's sayings in ways not determined in advance by the habitual, that is, the traditional interpretations (of philosophy, in the form of *positions* and *doctrines*; of philology, in the form of root, fixed *meanings* and the strictures governing them), even as it passes through and draws energies and insights from such traditions, constitutes an attempt to (re-)awaken the living character of the thinking, to think through its objectified character into more fluid and dynamic movements of surfacing.[354] Translation will then have been a kind of re-enactment or reperformance of Thea's final disclosure in the initial moment of her grasp on the traveler:

most of all learn the surfacing [τὰ δοκοῦντα...πάντα περῶντα-περ ὄντα] *the*
woven shimmering its violence its
translation

(Parm. 1.31-2)

---

354 See, for instance, Cassin's passing vision of a translation of the Parmenidean poem as "arborescence," difficult to present textually with its tangle of "possibilities" and "com-possibilities." Cassin, "The Relativity of Translation and Relativism," 29-30.

CHAPTER 5

Translation as Philosophy

Trans-philosophy Towards Possibilities

...πᾶν ἔστιν ὁμοῖον (Parm. 8.22)
—all *is* similar, differing

Two paths: an archaic Greek poem long situated within the disciplinary bounds of *philosophy*; *translation* as an ample name for manifold events, actions, relations of transformation. Where they cross was where they began and the place to which they return—in this sense, the two paths trace arcs on the same circle, or converge at something like the Parmenidean pathways of the paths of Night and Day, the site of crossings.[355] Throughout *Parmenides & Translation: Figures of Motion, Figures of Being*, those arcs come continually to light, showing themselves in their light of belonging together and in their belonging beyond one another: their belonging together is meaningful and expansive, fluid, not grounded in static definitions, ceaselessly translated and translating. Multiple signs direct thinking to the one path, the shared path circling ever-wider, fragmenting, opening, a path of branching and ever more numerous paths no longer one.

Water to fire, fire to stone, stone again to ice—elementally, the Parmenidean Song of Being in a primary sense *takes place as translation*. Elemental translation re-en-mani-folds translation from its unfolded (flattened) "classical determination" according to which an operation, rooted in—perhaps emblematic of—a metaphysics grounded in the pairs of essence and attribute, form (over) matter, simply reconfigures the material expression, the ontologically inferior or secondary linguistic matter, while retaining the unchanging form (of meaning). Re-en-mani-folding, opening and releasing from the "classical determination" into a more diverse and complex region, translation names relations of being-in-the-world, not only transmission and transportation of thinking, but also the constitutive transformations of transmission and reception, of thinking in the manner of speaking and hearing, λόγος that open a zone for leaning into the

---

355 On those crossings and the shared history of philosophy and translation, see Duncan Large, "The translation of philosophical texts," in *The Routledge Handbook of Translation and Philosophy*, ed. Piers Rawling and Philip Wilson (New York: Routledge, 2018), 307-12; and Spitzer, introduction to *Philosophy's Treason*, v-xviii.

"memory" of what Irigaray has articulated as "an unsaid, of a beyond in which wonder, magic, ecstasy, growth, and poetry mingle, resisting that logical link that is imposed on words, on sentences, on the world."[356] Such translation, motivated by differing as translation's fundamental, might open and expand possibilities for further translations and the embedded interpretations moving them.

The Parmenidean poem activates translation in multiple ways. As a moment along singing's westward journey from Ionia, across the sea dark as wine, reading the poem through translation lets emerge its linkages and belonging in a mode of thinking, *singing*, that keeps the movement of thinking-being alive in its ever-mobile images and figures, the turnings of fire and Night. From within unfolding of doctrinal translation's span, the Song of Being enters into different relations spoken in ways that reduce the shimmering, the *divining* of figures as they enact the play of showing and withdrawing, of ἀλήθεια. Translation's turn becomes epochal in further reduction to doctrine thought as *stone*: the durable, the unmoving, the ὑποκείμενον [underlying thing] in its enduring presence, petrified, neither created nor destroyed but a source [ἀρχή] in the form of a material [ἐν ὕλης εἴδει] that is itself an eternally preserved nature [φύσεως ἀεὶ σωζομένης (Arist. *Metaph.* 983b6-18)]. The epoch makes translation the interlingual expression of a fixed and stable doctrine available to be transported, resaid, repeated in another language while remaining itself the same in the manner of the underlying source and nature that most truly *is*. The epoch of translation becomes the epoch of repetition. The epoch of metaphysics.

Even so, translating, the practice and event in motion, stirs within and agitates that epoch in its reconfiguration of boundaries, in its shimmerings, setting loose the presumed stability of doctrines through (re-)activating tensions in the Parmenidean poem. Opening ways away from the metaphysics determining—indeed, enacted as—translation will not simply be a matter of turning in another direction. As Heidegger suggests, the ways away are also ways *through* the tradition of metaphysics. In this sense, a central task of translation will be what Heidegger calls the "step back" (*Schritt zurück*) into and through that tradition rather than its denial or an attempt to be apart from it.[357] The ways themselves—translational actions and translative gestures that torque from within that tradition and, hopefully from the friction in those twisting motions—produce openings, shimmerings on the edges, some flashes of possibilities that would remain flashing, unstable, unfixed.

---

356 Irigaray, *In the Beginning, She Was*, 2-3.
357 Heidegger, "The Onto-theo-logical Character of Metaphysics," in *Identity and Difference*, trans. Joan Stambaugh, 49-50/115-16 (German).

As a trans-discipline, translation studies and its in-built, constitutive relations with other areas of inquiry, as well as its movement apart from those disciplines,[358] advances as well-suited to the task(s) of activating or releasing the figures of motion pulsing in philosophy's figures of being. So too, as a *trans*-practice translation (translating) bears potencies for plumbing the fissures it is capable of exposing; as Apter has written, such explorations that gauge "deformations, reformulations, and temporal *décalages* of translated works" constitute a way of doing philosophy.[359] Tracing and articulating the continual reconfigurations through different languages of what—through the "effects of an instrumental reduction" that effaces translation— can appear a single unmediated or stable concept sets in motion, by the very coming-into-view of its translated status, and lets emerge in its already-mediated and altered condition, its inalienable *non*- dimension (it is *not* the "original," never [only] itself or a product of a single thinker), its movements-in-translation.[360] In this sense the trans-disciplinarity of translation takes place as its *transformational* force, not merely taking from or entering momentarily into several disciplinary enclosures in the manner of *interdisplinarity*, but through its characteristic task of *altering* as something like *trans-philosophy* or *transphiliation* that works "to relate and relay strata of related/relative meanings, quickened from varied starts towards multiple directions and nodes of relation, entanglements."[361] This would be to work in the direction of a "nonsubstantial ontology" envisioned by Avtonomova that gathers from thinking through translation a sense of the "non-primordiality (translated, transposed, retold, reformulated character)" that unseals the very notion of identity through a broad span of its manifestations.[362]

Along an open circle of translation—open, bearing on its arc numerous possibilities for opening, for interpretation, (re-)beginning—early Greek thinking will (continue to) be transformed. Translations that highlight the discontinuities and even gleaming ruptures on the sites where tradition asserts doctrinal certainty can open the circle, can inspire more numerous and diverse returns and turns to the early Greek thinkers and the mode of singing. Singing is not poetry as it now operates within the rigid determinations of academic compartmentalization.

---

358 Spitzer, "Bordering Approaches & Trans-Bordering Themes," 2-5.
359 Emily Apter, "Kilito's Injunction: Thou Shalt Not Translate Me," in *Against World Literature: On the Politics of Untranslatability* (London: Verso, 2013), 249.
360 Cardozo, "Translation, humanities, and the critique of relational reason," in Spitzer, *Philosophy's Treason*, 127.
361 Spitzer, "Trans-philosophy," 579.
362 Natalia S. Avtonomova, "Philosophy, translation, 'untranslatability:' cultural and conceptual aspects," trans. Tatevik Gukasyan, in Spitzer, *Philosophy's Treason*, 106-7.

Singing is not *only* poetry, but the release of possibilities into further possibilities and thinking's task of re-turning, through a readiness to receive the approach of the Mousa(i)-Memory, to the open already-there un-enclosed by disciplinarity. Singing has the bearing of *trans-philosophy-transphiliation* insofar as its work involves overcoming—and shooting through, *permeating*—disciplines and the mode of disciplinarity. In this direction, Privitello's work rearranging the extant texts according to sonority "as if arranging measures of a musical score, based on pitch, meter, and what, in musical notation, are called 'signs',"[363] configures throughways for renewed possibilities to listen and hear the Parmenidean Song of Being. Privitello began his "apprenticeship" through repeated, meditative recitals of the Greek text; the approach bears much promise for future work that understands the enmeshedness of performance and embodiment—voice, sound, rhythm, feel—alongside interpretation-translation as crucial, vital pathways for engaging not only Parmenides, but the wider region of early Greek thinking, perhaps including the Platonic dramas.

Among other early Greek thinking, Herakleitean sayings beckon to the ear of the listener, call for the fluidities of oral exchange. In his "Fire at Night: A Version of Herakleitos," Hix's translation re-constellates the sayings not according to the traditional ordering found in the edition of Diels and Kranz, but in ways that drive "an interminable search for meaning" that Hix finds characteristic of Herakleitean thinking.[364] The result is a kind of internal reshuffling that disarrays both conventional interpretation and ordinary philosophic compartmentalizations:

> It glows, the dry soul, wisest and best. Best to repress
> one's ignorance, but hard to, unstrung by wine. For the soul
> to get drenched is indulgence *and* death. A drunk man
> leaning on a beardless boy staggers unsteadily, soul-soaked.
> For the soul it is death to turn to water, for water it is death
> to turn to earth. From earth water comes forth, from water
>   the soul.
> Death of fire birth of air, death of air birth of water.[365]

To embed the sayings on the soul's cycle of becoming (Hera. 36) within a paragraph that begins with "It glows, the dry soul, wisest and best" (Hera. 118) and closes with the "deaths" of fire and air (Hera. 76b), suggests thematic interpretation no

---

363 Privitello, "Approaching the Parmenidean Sublime—Part II," 103.
364 Hix, "Fire at Night," 6.
365 Hix, "Fire at Night," 13.

longer determined by philosophical branches such as those structuring Graham's presentation, which sectionalize the presentation of Herakleitean material according to intradisciplinary boundaries: "Human knowledge," "Cosmology," and "Theology and religion."[366] Rather, the paragraphic organization Hix has formulated, propelled by breaking lines in ways that call attention to the ways traditional reception and presentation of Herakleitos bear unnoticed distortions, lets the sayings collide, jar, and grate against one another in ways that enliven some fresh rethinkings of Herakleitos beyond—in excess of—the traditional categories of philosophy.[367]

As a mode of translation that seeks continual openings and re-beginnings— seeking, that is, to unclose the circle of early Greek thinking from the traditional interpretations articulated in the conventional translational protocol and its metaphysics, translation as trans-philosophy or transphiliation looks not only to activate the valences of terms central to a later history of philosophy in a manner that exceeds the encircling appropriation of that history, but also to expand the networks of possibilities as *affiliations of meaning* beyond the ring of philosophy's tradition. In this manner, the term *transphiliation* enacts its own image, resonating with the terms *affiliations* and *filaments* and composing an extension of such *philiations* of meanings through, across, and beyond the cultural borders, in this case into the broader Mediterranean and surrounding imaginaries. Lombardo's translation of Hesiod's *Theogony*, for instance, lets stir and shimmer a moment of the stirrings of these affiliations in a phrase and the accompanying notes. In the opening of the Hesiodic *Theogony*, the Mousai, not yet performing (through Hesiod) the song of divine births, emphasize the threat of violence and exertion of force supporting Zeus' regime. The song sings the Mousai's abundant dance: "and in heaven he reigns-in-rulership [ἐμβασιλεύει], / he himself [αὐτός] holding thunder and shimmering [αἰθαλόεντα] lightning-flash" (Hes. *Theog.* 72-3). Turning towards ancient India and its associations of Indra with thunder and then bringing these into manifest relation with Zeus in *Theogony*,[368] Lombardo translates "He is king in the sky, / He holds the vajra thunder and flashing lightning."[369] Although in the notes given after the translation Lamberton comments on the Vedic provenance of

---

366 Graham, *The Texts of Early Greek Philosophy*, 143, 163, 177, respectively.
367 Hix, "Fire at Night," 6-7.
368 As, for example, the phrase "Who is Indra?...Indra is just the thunder," in Bṛhadāraṇyaka Upaniṣad 3.9.6. Patrick Olivelle, trans., *Upaniṣads* (Oxford: Oxford University Press, 1996), 47.
369 Lombardo, trans., *Hesiod: Works and Days & Theogony* (Indianapolis: Hackett, 1993), 63.

the phrase and that that tradition runs "parallel" to archaic Greek poetry,[370] implying that these are separate and never crossing lines of development, by presenting the phrase *vajra thunder* without italics or other ways of bringing attention to its foreignness within the translation Lombardo discloses the embeddedness of such confluences, that they occur not as something additional, a foreign ornament mounted upon a self-enclosed and contained poetic work, but as teeming as already-there and inextricably infused with the poem's churning flow of multiplicities in relation.

With a transphiliation approach at work, Spitzer offers a translation of Empedokles that seeks to widen further and contemporize the network of relations, affinities, affiliations. Translating two lines of an Empedoklean fragment that run τῶν καὶ ἐγὼ νῦν εἰμι, φυγὰς θεόθεν καὶ ἀλήτης, / νείκεϊ μαινομένῳ πίσυνος (Emp. 11.13-14/115), which Inwood translates as "I too am now one of these, an exile from the gods and a wanderer, / trusting in mad strife,"[371] a transphiliated version spills into new and unexpected affiliations:

—of others I:	I:fugitive
I:departure	
from luminosities	am other from I:
—I:disciple	
to	to
madness	madness
maddened	maddened[372]

From the phrase *madness maddened* the line enters into relation with Herman Melville's sprawling novel *Moby-Dick; or The Whale* (1851 c.e.) that modulates its tone and voice in ways that defy simple categorization. Philiational strands at work as trans-philosophy open a spiralized or helical temporality—the *temps* of the Mousa(i) in their peripheral, helical whirl[373]—that churns multiple times

---

370 Robert Lamberton, "Notes: *Theogony*," in Lombardo, *Hesiod*, 92, n. 73 [72].
371 Translation is from Inwood, *The Poem of Empedocles*, 217.
372 This translation first appeared in Spitzer, "Displacements." The phrase "madness maddened" is from Herman Melville, *Moby-Dick; or The Whale*, ch. 37, "Sunset" (Norwalk, Connecticut: Easton Press, 1977), 178.
373 Their *temps*—the temporality as a storm of foldings and multiplicities—as helical and spiralized describes the movements of the Hesiodic Mousai of *Theogony*, whose dance on Mount Helikon (Spiral Mountain) turns in helical motion *around* [περί] a source of water (Hes. *Theog.* 3). This reading of *temps* as *tempus* (and *tempest*), draws on Jeffrey Jerome Cohen and Lowell Duckert, "Eleven Principles of the Elements," introduction to *Elemental Ecocriticism: Thinking with Earth, Air, Water, and Fire*, ed. Jeffrey Jerome Cohen and Lowell Duckert (Minneapolis: University of Minnesota Press, 2015), 16-17.

together, not homogenous, but textured, differentiated, folded. This specific relation (Melville and Empedokles) only manifests in a slightly voiced, lightly adjacent filamental affiliation—one to be taken up, explored, plumbed by readers, not explained in or by the translation. In this way transphiliation summons close involvement within and beyond its own limits. Differently, both Lombardo's phrase *vajra thunder* in *Theogony* and Spitzer's translation of the passage from Empedokles unspool the imagined containment of *Greek* poetries, opening other and more numerous possibilities for meanings-in-relation, affiliations. So doing, as a trans-philosophy practice, transphiliation (re-)enacts, translates, sets in motion the motions of the Herakleitean saying of expectations: "unless one foresees [ἔλπηται] the unforeseeable [ἀνέλπιστον], one will not disclose [ἐξευρήσει] being [ἐόν]—what refuses disclosure [ἀνεξερεύνητον] and goes nowhere [ἄπορον]" (Hera. 18). Trans-philosophy then might cultivate a readiness for the delights and wonders of surprise, reminders of the foreign turning and gusting in what is most familiar. That would enact, too, a return to a beginning articulated by Aristoteles (Arist. *Metaph.* A 982b11-21), a re-beginning in an experience of wonder as "the outbreak of the extraordinariness of the ordinary."[374] Translating towards unforeseeables offers opportunities, possibilities to those receiving for further engagements and (re-)thinkings, other figures of translation.

*

* *

Voicing the convergence of translation and philosophy and, moreover, the always-already translated-translating aspect of philosophy, trans-philosophy passes through and beyond any one period, thinker, or tradition. Recent volumes, conferences, reading groups witness the spread and widening open circle of philosophy and translation. As Leal and Wilson forecast and articulate five areas in which further attention to the confluence of philosophy and translation or translation studies is due, the first topic they identify has to do with expansion and opening the circle: they observe a need for "Moving beyond the Western canon" because (1) a flattening or homogenization of western philosophy results from the very term *western* (2) the exclusivity, its closed circle, eliminates "voices from other traditions" (3) a domestication of non-western texts manifests as an

---

[374] Sallis "...A Wonder that One Could Never Aspire to Surpass," in Maly, *The Path of Archaic Thinking*, 258

imposition "of Western paradigms and expectations onto source texts."[375] Could trans-philosophy as transphiliation—or other practices sharing its momentary creative-activation of transhistorical, transcultural filaments-affiliations-philiations— enact some of the movement towards other traditions without merely assimilating those traditions (by a reduction or resolution of their foreignness)? That would be to exercise the second of Leal and Wilson's fivefold horizon, an epistemic justice that strives "to open the intersection of translation and philosophy to a plurality of ears and voices, to go beyond Anglophone epistemologies and to showcase different modes of knowledge"[376]—a task richly undertaken in the *Lesekreis* they have organized.

Does philosophy show itself in advance of translation, in advance of a movement towards translating a text? What allows a text its standing in the circle of philosophy? From the first stirrings—perhaps, as or in response to its inauguration among the Greeks[377]—philosophy has turned to poetry, sometimes (as in early Greek thinking) attempting to wrest ideas or concepts from their enigmatic enclosures, sometimes (as with Heidegger's readings of Hölderlin) letting the language of poems open pathways for thinking. In addition to early Greek thinking, how might translation and interpretation that encompasses attention to formal elements, to literariness, to the nuances of texts that, in a diversity of ways and voices and styles, restore-through-translation the field of philosophy as heterogeneous, contoured, richly folded and complex territory?[378] Would such territory, in turn, call for a wider range of participants in the task of translating philosophies, translators beyond the area of "specialized technical knowledge,"[379] whose readings and translations might register and activate dimensions of philosophic texts unheard, unheeded, or overlooked by those within that specialized circle? Playwrights and actors, poets and musicians, visual artists and those whose arts unfurl as dance and movement—philosophic texts and their inextricable literariness might radiate more brightly and engage with more numerous thinkers and thinkings through an increasing diversity of translators and translational involvements.

---

375 Alice Leal and Philip Wilson, "A Tale of Two Disciplines? Philosophy in/on Translation," *Perspectives* 31, no. 1 (2023): 4.
376 Leal and Wilson, "A Tale of Two Disciplines?," 5.
377 As, for instance, Naddaf's insights concerning the entanglements of poetry and allegoresis in philosophy's formation. Gerard Naddaf, "Allegory and the Origins of Philosophy," in *Logos and Muthos: Philosophical Essays in Greek Literature*, ed. William Robert Wians (Albany: SUNY Press, 2009), 99-131.
378 Venuti also makes such an appeal. Venuti, *The Scandals of Translation*, 122-3.
379 Large, "The translation of philosophical texts," 314. Large takes up some examples (including especially Heidegger) in his chapter (315-8).

Might imaginative, creative practices of translation also help to keep open philosophy's boundaries, sustaining and broadening its hospitable orientation? The circle (re-)opening would be altered—translated—by, for instance, not only Campbell and Vidal's critical reflections on their multimodal and collaborative translation(s) of Kurt Schwitter's "An Anna Blume" that involved collage work, film, and performance, but also the translation-translating that takes place as a "deeply embodied process of meaning-making through dynamic transformative processes, which has the capacity to both inform and be informed by philosophical thought."[380] Turning and re-turning on the open circle of mutual informing (re- and multi-)dimensionalizes philosophy: the thinking as the doing, the performing as the translating, the performing-translating as the doing of philosophy, its figures of motion unfurling as gestures of continual transformations.

Philosophy's figures of motion, its figures of translation as *translating*, shape themselves as moments of thinking's continual unfolding and expansion, movements that take place in the plural and in motion. Unfolding: from a commitment to and drive towards unity to an embrace of multiplicity(-ies), from philosophy and translation to philosophies and-as translations-continually-translating; otherwise said, to *trans-philosophy*.

---

[380] Madeleine Campbell and Ricarda Vidal, "On Performing Philosophy through Translation," *Translation Matters* 5, no. 1 (2023): 10-11.

Bibliography

Adorno, Theodor. *Negative Dialectics*. Translated by E. B. Ashton. New York: Continuum, 1973.
Apter, Emily. "Kilito's Injunction: Thou Shalt Not Translate Me." In *Against World Literature: On the Politics of Untranslatability*, 247-61. London: Verso, 2013.
Arrojo, Rosemary. *Fictional Translators: Rethinking Translation through Literature*. London: Routledge, 2018.
---. "Philosophy and translation." In *Handbook of Translation Studies*. Vol. 1, edited by Yves Gambier and Luc van Doorslaer, 247-51. Amsterdam: John Benjamins, 2010.
---. "The Power of Fiction as Theory: Some exemplary lessons on translation from Borges' stories." In Kaindl and Spitzl, *Transfiction*, 37-49.
---. "The Revision of the Traditional Gap Between Theory & Practice & the Empowerment of Translation in Postmodern Times." *The Translator* 4, no. 1 (April 1, 1998): 25–48. DOI: 10.1080/13556509.1998.10799005.
Ashbaugh, Anne Freire. "Consuming Knowledge." In Spitzer, *Studies in Ancient Greek Philosophy*, 130-43.
---. "The Philosophy of Flesh and the Flesh of Philosophy." *Research in Phenomenology* 8 (1978): 217–23. http://www.jstor.org/stable/24654297.
Avtonomova, Natalia S. "Philosophy, translation, 'untranslatability:' cultural and conceptual aspects." Translated by Tatevik Gukasyan. In Spitzer, *Philosophy's Treason*, 87-109.
Bakker, Egbert J. "Activation and Preservation: The Interdependence of Text and Performance in an Oral Tradition." *Oral Tradition* 8, no. 1 (March, 1993): 5-20. http://journal.oraltradition.org/issues/8i/bakker.
Batchelor, Kathryn. "Invisible Untranslatability and Philosophy." *Nottingham French Studies* 49, no. 2 (Summer, 2010): 40-51.
Bekker, Immanuel, ed. *Sextus Empiricus*. Berlin: Reimeri, 1842. https://archive.org/details/bub_gb_j-dEAAAAMAAJ/mode/2up.

Berman, Antoine. "The Project of a 'Productive' Criticism." Chap. 1 in *Toward a Translation Criticism*, translated by Françoise Massardier-Kenney. Kent, Ohio: Kent State University Press, 2009.

---. "Translation and the Trials of the Foreign." Translated by Lawrence Venuti. In Venuti, *The Translation Studies Reader*, 240-53. Originally published as "La traduction comme épreuve de l'étranger," in *Traduction: textualité Text: translatability*, 67-81 (Toronto: Les Éditions Trintexte, 1986).

Bernardakis, Gregorius N. ed. *Plutarch: Moralia*. Vol 5. Leipzig: Teubner, 1893. https://archive.org/details/in.ernet.dli.2015.103630/mode/2up.

Bernasconi, Robert. "Almost Always More Than Philosophy Proper." *Research in Phenomenology* 30, no. 1 (2000): 1–11. https://www.jstor.org/stable/24654793.

Bernstein, Charles. "Artifice of Absorption." In *Artifice & Indeterminacy: An Anthology of New Poetics*, edited by Christopher Beach, 3-23. Tuscaloosa: The University of Alabama, 1998.

Bers, Victor. *Speech in Speech: Studies in Incorporated Oration Recta in Attic Drama and Oratory*. Lanham: Rowman and Littlefield, 1997.

Biers, William. *The Archaeology of Greece*. 2nd ed. Ithaca, NY: Cornell University Press, 1996.

Blanchot, Maurice. "Translating." Translated by Richard Sieburth. *Sulfur* 26 (1990): 82-6.

Bloomfield, Mandy. "Archaeopoetics." Chap. 1 in *Archaeopoetics: Word, Image, History*. Tuscaloosa: The University of Alabama Press, 2016.

Bonitz, Hermann, ed. *Alexandri Aphrodisiensis: Commentarius in libros Metaphysicos Aristoteles*. Berlin: G. Reimer, 1847. https://archive.org/details/commentariusalex00alex/mode/1up.

Boissonade, Jean-François, ed. *Ex Procli Scholiis in Cratylum Platonis Excerpta*. Leipzig: J. A. G. Weigeli, 1820. https://archive.org/details/ektonproklousch000procuoft/mode/2up.

Bowie, Ewen L. "Early Expatriates: Displacement and Exile in Archaic Poetry." In *Writing Exile: The Discourse in Greco-Roman Antiquity and Beyond*, edited by Jan Felix Gaertner, 21-49. Leiden: Brill, 2007. EBSCOhost.

Bradford, Lisa Rose. "Haunted Compositions: *Ventrakl* and the Growth of Georg Trakl." *Translation Review* 95 (2016): 41-54.

Bryan, Jenny. "The Pursuit of Parmenidean Clarity." *Rhizomata* 8, no. 2 (2021): 218–38.

Burch, Robert. "Thinking Between Philosophy and Poetry." General introduction to *Between Philosophy and Poetry: Writing, Rhythm, History*, edited by Robert Burch and Massimo Verdicchio, 1-7. New York: Continuum, 2002.

Burgess, Jonathan. "Achilles' Heel: The Death of Achilles in Ancient Myth." *Classical Antiquity* 14, no. 2 (October, 1995): 217-44. http://www.jstor.org/stable/25011021.

Burkert, Walter. *The Orientalizing Revolution: Near Eastern Influence in the Early Archaic Age.* Translated by Margaret E. Pinder and Walter Burkert. Cambridge, MA: Harvard University Press, 1992.

---. "Prehistory of Presocratic Philosophy in an Orientalizing Context." In *The Oxford Handbook of Presocratic Philosophy*, edited by Patricia Curd and Daniel W. Graham, 55-87. Oxford: Oxford University Press, 2008 [online 2009]. *Oxford Handbooks Online*, 10.1093/oxfordhb/9780195146875.003.0003.

Burnet, John, ed. *Platonis Opera.* Vols. 1-3. Oxford: Oxford University Press, 1900-3.

Bury, R. G., trans. *Sextus Empiricus.* Vol. 2, *Against the Logicians.* Cambridge, MA: Harvard University Press, 1935.

Calame, Claude. "Metaphorical travel and ritual performance in epinician poetry." In *Reading the Victory Ode*, edited by Peter Agócs, Chris Carey, Richard Rawles, 303-20. Cambridge: Cambridge University Press, 2012.

Cambron-Goulet, Mathilde. "The Criticism—and the Practice—of Literacy in the Ancient Philosophical Tradition." In *Orality, Literacy and Performance in the Ancient World*, edited by Elizabeth Minchin, 201-26. Leiden: Brill, 2012.

Campbell, David A., ed and trans. *Greek Lyric I: Sappho and Alcaeus.* Cambridge, MA: Harvard University Press, 1982.

Campbell, Madeleine and Ricarda Vidal. "On Performing Philosophy through Translation." *Translation Matters* 5, no. 1 (2023): 9-28. DOI: 10.21747/21844585/tm5_1a1.

Cardozo, Mauricio Mendonça. "Notes on Translation, Alterity, and Relationality: From the Regimes of Indistinctness to the Disclosure of Relation." In Spitzer and Oliveira, *Transfiction and Bordering Approaches to Theorizing Translation*, 187-99.

---. "Translation, humanities, and the critique of relational reason." In Spitzer, *Philosophy's Treason*, 111-28.

Carratelli, Giovanni Pugliese. "La Θεά di Parmenide." *La parole del passato* 43 (1988): 336-46.

Casanova, Pascale. "Consecration and Accumulation of Literary Capital: Translation as Unequal Exchange." Translated by Siobhan Brownlie. In *Critical Readings in Translation Studies*, edited by Mona Baker, 285-303. New York: Routledge, 2010.

Cassin, Barbara. "Le chant des Sirènes dans le Poème de Parménide: quelques remarques sur le fr. VIII, 26-33." In *Études sur Parménide, vol. 2, Problèmes d'interprétation*, edited by Pierre Aubenque, 163-9. Paris: Librairie philosophique J. Vrin, 1987.

---. *Parménide: Sur la nature ou sur l'étant: La langue de l'être?* Paris: Éditions du Seuil, 1998.

---. "Philosophising in Languages." Translated by Yves Gilonne. *Nottingham French Studies* 49, no. 2 (Summer, 2010): 17-28. DOI: 10.3366/nfs.2010-2.003.

---. "The Relativity of Translation and Relativism." Translated by Roland Vésgő. *CR* 12, no. 2 (2012): 23–45.

Cercel, Larisa and Alice Leal, eds. *The Translator's Visibility New Debates and Epistemologies*. New York: Routledge, 2025.

Cherubin, Rose. "'Mortals Lay Down Trusting to be True'." *Epoché* 21, no. 2 (Spring, 2017): 251-71.

Cohen, Jeffrey Jerome and Lowell Duckert. "Eleven Principles of the Elements." Introduction to *Elemental Ecocriticism: Thinking with Earth, Air, Water, and Fire*, edited by Jeffrey Jerome Cohen and Lowell Duckert, 1-26. Minneapolis: University of Minnesota Press, 2015.

Cordero, Néstor-Luis. "L'histoire du texte de Parménide." In *Études sur Parménide, vol. 2, Problèmes d'interprétation*, edited by Pierre Aubenque, 3-24. Paris: Libraire philosophique J. Vrin, 1987.

Coxon, A. H. "The Text of Parmenides fr. 1.3." *The Classical Quarterly* 18, no. 1 (May, 1968): 69. http://www.jstor.org/stable/637687.

Davis, C. B. "Distant Ventriloquism: Vocal Mimesis, Agency and Identity in Ancient Greek Performance." *Theatre Journal* 55, no. 1 (March, 2003): 45-65. http://www.jstor.org/stable/25069179.

de Campos, Haroldo. "Translation as Creation and Criticism." In *Novas: Selected Writings*, edited by Antonio Sergio Bessa and Odile Cisneros, 312-26. Translated by Diana Gibson and Haroldo de Campos; edited by A. S. Bessa. Evanston, IL: Northwestern University Press, 2007.

de Jong, I. F. J. "Fokalisation und die Homerischen Gleichnisse." *Mnemosyne*, 4th series, 38, no. 3/4 (1985): 257-80. http://www.jstor.org/stable/4431419.

Decker, Jessica Elbert. "I Will Tell a Double Tale: Double-speak in the ancient Poetic Tradition." *Epoché: A Journal for the History of Philosophy* 25, no. 2 (2021): 237-48.

Deleuze, Gilles and Felix Guattari. "Introduction: Rhizome." In *A Thousand Plateaus: Capitalism and Schizophrenia*, translated by Brian Massumi, 3-25. Minneapolis: University of Minnesota Press, 1987.

Derrida, Jacques. *The Ear of the Other: Otobiography, Transference, Translation: Texts and Discussions with Jacques Derrida*. Translated by Christie McDonald. New York: Shocken, 1985.

---. "Structure, Sign, and Play in the Discourse of the Human Sciences." In *Writing and Difference*, translated by Alan Bass, 278-93. Chicago: University of Chicago Press, 1978.

---. "White Mythology: Metaphor in the Text of Philosophy." In *Margins of Philosophy*, translated by Alan Bass, 207-71. University of Chicago Press, 1982.

Diels, Hermann, ed. *Simplicii in Aristotelis Physicorum libros quattuor priores commentaria*. Berlin: G. Reimeri, 1882. https://archive.org/details/inaristotelesphy10simp/mode/2up.

---. *Parmenides Lehrgedicht*. Berlin: Georg Reimer, 1897. HathiTrust.org.

--- and Walther Kranz, eds. *Die Fragmente der Vorsokratiker*. Vol. 1. 6th ed. Berlin: Weidmannsche, 1951.

Dinsdorf, Wilhelm, ed. *Praeparationis Evangelicae*, I-X. Vol. 1 of *Eusebii Caesariensis Opera*. Leipzig: Teubner, 1867. https://archive.org/details/operaeusebius01euseuoft/mode/2up.

Duncker, Ludwig and F. G. Schneidewin, eds. *Hippolyti Refutationis omnium haeresium librorum decem quae supersunt*. Gottingen: Dieterichianis, 1859. https://archive.org/details/shippolytirefuta00hipp/mode/2up.

Ebner, Pietro. "L'errore di Alalia e la colonnizzazione di Velia nel response delfico." *Rassegna Storica Salernitana* 23, no. 1-4 (1962): 3-44.

Eliot, T. S. *Four Quartets*. New York: Harcourt, 1971.

Erdinast-Vulcan, Daphna. "Reading Oneself in Quotation Marks: At the Crossing of Disciplines." In Foran, *Translation and Philosophy*, 41-52.

Fabricius, Albertus ed. *Sexti Empirici Opera Graece et Latine*. Leipzig: Kuehn Library, 1841. https://archive.org/details/bub_gb_6Qwh5Nu2AOEC/mode/2up.

Faraone, Christopher A. "Taking the 'Nestor's Cup Inscription' Seriously: Erotic Magic and Conditional Curses in the Earliest Inscribed Hexameters." *Classical Antiquity* 15, no. 1 (1996): 77–112. https://doi.org/10.2307/25011032.

Ferrari, Gloria. *Alcman and the Cosmos of Sparta*. Chicago: University of Chicago Press, 2008.

Figal, Günter. "Tautophasis: Heidegger et Parménide." Translated [into French] by Anne Merker. *Les Cahiers philosophiques de Strasbourg*, no. 36 (2014): 45–58.

Foran, Lisa. "Translation as a Path to the Other: Derrida and Ricouer." In Foran, *Translation and Philosophy*, 75-87.

---, ed. *Translation and Philosophy*. Bern: Peter Lang, 2012.

--- "What is the Relation between Translation and Philosophy?" Introduction to Foran, *Translation and Philosophy*, 1-11.

Ford, Andrew. "From Letters to Literature: Reading the 'Song Culture' of Classical Greece." In *Written Texts and the Rise of Literate Culture in Ancient*

Greece, edited by Harvey Yunis, 15-37. Cambridge: Cambridge University Press, 2003.

Forte, Alexander S. W., and Caley C. Smith. "New Riders, Old Chariots: Poetics and Comparative Philosophy." In *Universe and Inner Self in Early Indian and Early Greek Thought*, edited by Richard Seaford, 186-203. Edinburgh: Edinburgh University Press, 2016.

Freiert, Will. "The End of Athens." Lecture, University of Arkansas, Fayetteville, Arkansas, February, 2004.

Gadamer, Hans-Georg. *Der Anfang der Philosophie*. Translated into German by Joachim Schulte. Stuttgart: Philipp Reclam, 1996.

Gallop, David, ed. and trans. *Parmenides of Elea: Fragments: A Text and Translation with an Introduction*. Toronto: University of Toronto Press, 1984.

Gerber, Douglas E., trans. and ed. *Greek Elegiac Poetry from the Seventh to the Fifth Centuries BC*. Cambridge, MA: Harvard University Press, 1999.

Graham, Daniel, ed. and trans. *The Texts of Early Greek Philosophy: The Complete Fragments and Selected Testimonies of the Major Presocratics*. Vol. 1. Cambridge: Cambridge University Press, 2010.

Greenwood, Emily. *Afro-Greeks*. Oxford: Oxford University Press, 2010.

Hägg, Robin, ed. *The Greek Renaissance of the Eighth Century B. C.: Tradition and Innovation*. Proceedings of the Second International Symposium at the Swedish Institute in Athens, 1-5 June, 1981. Stockholm: Swedish Institute in Athens, 1983.

Hardwick, Lorna. "Singing Across the Faultlines: Cultural Shifts in Twentieth Century Receptions of Homer." In *Homer in the Twentieth Century: Between World Literature and the Western Canon*, edited by Barbara Graziosi and Emily Greenwood, 47-71. Oxford: Oxford University Press, 2007.

Harlan, Dev. "Parmenides I." Aluminum and video projection, 8 x 8 x 8. https://www.devharlan.com/the-astral-flight-hangar/. Last accessed August 29, 2022.

Havelock, Eric A. "Parmenides and Odysseus." *Harvard Studies in Classical Philology* 63 (1958): 133-43. http://www.jstor.org/stable/310850.

---. "Pre-Literacy and the Pre-Socratics." In *The Literate Revolution in Greece and Its Cultural Consequences*, 220-60. Princeton: Princeton University Press, 1982.

Hegel, G. W. F. "Die Eleaten." In *Vorlesungen über die Geschichte der Philosophie*, Teil 2: *Griechische Philosophie I. Thales bis Kyniker*, edited by Pierre Garniron and Walter Jaeschke, 49-69. Hamburg: Felix Meiner Verlag, 1989.

Heidegger, Martin. "ALETHEIA: (Heraklit, Fragment 16)." In *Vorträge und Aufsätze*, 249-74.

---. *Aus der Erfahrung des Denkens*. Pfullingen: Günther Neske, 1954.

---. *Basic Problems of Phenomenology*. Translated by Albert Hofstadter. Bloomington: University of Indiana Press, 1982.

---. *Being and Time*. Translated by John Macquarrie and Edward Robinson. New York: Harper and Row, 1962.
---. "...Dichterisch wohnet der Mensch...." In *Vorträge und Aufsätze*, 181-98.
---. *Early Greek Thinking: The Dawn of Western Philosophy*. Translated by David Farrell Krell. San Francisco: Harper & Row, 1984.
---. *Identity and Difference*. Translated by Joan Stambaugh. Chicago: University of Chicago Press, 1969.
---. *Parmenides*. Translated by André Schuwer and Richard Rojcewicz. Bloomington: Indiana University Press, 1992. Originally published as *Parmenides* (Frankfurt am Main: Vittorio Klostermann, 1982).
---. "Der Spruch des Anaximander." In *Holzwege*, 321-73. Rote Reihe edition. Frankfurt am Main: Klostermann, 1950.
---. *Vorträge und Aufsätze*. Stuttgart: Klett-Cotta, 1954.
Hejinian, Lyn. "The Rejection of Closure." In *The Language of Inquiry*, 40-58. Berkeley: University of California Press, 2000.
Hermans, Theo. "The Translator's Voice in Translated Narrative." *Target* 8, no. 1 (1996): 23-48.
Hicks, R. D., trans. *Diogenes Laertius: Lives of the Eminent Philosophers*. Vol. 2. Cambridge, MA: Harvard University Press, 1950.
Hix, H. L. "Fire at Night: A Version of Herakleitos." *The Yale Review* 103, no. 2 (April, 2015): 1-15. DOI: 10.1111/yrev.12242.
Hude, Charles, ed. *Herodoti Historiae*. Vol. 1. 3rd ed. Oxford: Oxford University Press, 1927.
Hutchinson, G. O. "Parmenides, *On Nature*." Chap. 6 in *Motion in Classical Literature: Homer, Parmenides, Sophocles, Ovid, Seneca, Tacitus, Art*. Oxford: Oxford University Press, 2020. https://doi.org/10.1093/oso/9780198855620.003.0007.
Hunter, Richard and Ian Rutherford. Introduction to *Wandering Poets in Archaic Greek Culture: Travel, Locality and Pan-Hellenism*, edited by Richard Hunter and Ian Rutherford, 1-22. Cambridge: Cambridge University Press, 2009.
Ilanio Project. "Deva: Alpha, Full Performance 3: Parmenides." 2014. https://vimeo.com/178399870. Last accessed August 29, 2022.
Inwood, Brad, ed. and trans. *The Poem of Empedocles: A Text and Translation with an Introduction*. Rev. ed. Toronto: University of Toronto Press, 2001.
Irigaray, Luce. *In the Beginning, She Was*. London: Bloomsbury, 2013.
Jacobs, David C. "The Ontological Education of Parmenides." In *The Presocratics after Heidegger*, edited by David C. Jacobs, 185-202. Albany: SUNY Press, 1999.
Jaeger, Werner, ed. *Aristotelis Metaphysica*. Oxford: Oxford University Press, 1957.
---. *The Theology of the Early Greek Philosophers*. Translated by Edward S. Robinson. Oxford: Clarendon Press, 1947.

Jaitner, Sabina Folnovic. "Philosophical untranslatables and the concept of equivalence." In Spitzer, *Philosophy's Treason*, 73-86.

Jakobson, Roman. "On Linguistic Aspects of Translation." In Venuti, *The Translation Studies Reader*, 126-31.

Johnson, Barbara. "Taking Fidelity Philosophically." In *Difference in Translation*, edited by Joseph Graham, 142-48. Ithaca, NY: Cornell University Press, 1985.

Kahn, Charles H. *Anaximander and the Origins of Greek Cosmology*. Indianapolis: Hackett, 1985.

---. "The Thesis of Parmenides." *The Review of Metaphysics* 22, no. 4 (June, 1969): 700-24. http://www.jstor.org/stable/20124945.

Keane, Niall. "The Silence of the Origin: Philosophy in Transition and the Essence of Thinking." *Research in Phenomenology* 43, no. 1 (2013): 27-48. http://www.jstor.org/stable/24659787.

King, J. E., ed. and trans. *Cicero: Tusculan Disputations*. Cambridge, MA: Harvard University Press, 1927.

Kingsley, Peter. *In the Dark Places of Wisdom*. Inverness, California: The Golden Sufi Center, 1999.

Kirk, G. S. and J. E. Raven, eds. *The Presocratic Philosophers: A Critical History with a Selection of Texts*. Cambridge: Cambridge University Press, 1957.

--- and M. Schofield, eds. *The Presocratic Philosophers: A Critical History with a Selection of Texts*, 2nd ed. Cambridge: Cambridge University Press, 1983.

Kirkland, Sean D. "Nietzsche and Drawing Near to the Personalities of the Pre-Platonic Greeks." *Continental Philosophy Review* 44, no. 4 (2011): 417–37. DOI: 10.1007/s11007-011-9199-0.

Kraut, Richard. "Plato." In *The Stanford Encyclopedia of Philosophy* (Spring 2022 Edition), edited by Edward N. Zalta, https://plato.stanford.edu/archives/spr2022/entries/plato/.

Krell, David Farrell. "Nietzsche Hölderlin Empedocles." *Graduate Faculty Philosophy Journal* 15, no. 2 (1991): 31-48.

Kurfess, Christopher John. "Restoring Parmenides' Poem: Essays Toward a New Arrangement of the Fragments Based on a Reassessment of the Original Sources." PhD. diss., University of Pittsburgh, 2012. ProQuest. http://search.proquest.com/docview/1328158897?accountid=14168.

Laks, André and Glenn W. Most, eds. *Beginnings and early Ionian Thinkers*. Vol. II, part 1, of *Early Greek Philosophy*. Cambridge, MA: Harvard University Press, 2016.

---. *Western Greek Thinkers*. Vol. V, part 2, of *Early Greek Philosophy*. Cambridge, MA: Harvard University Press, 2016.

Lamberton, Robert. "Notes: *Theogony*." In *Hesiod: Works and Days & Theogony*, translated by Stanley Lombardo. Indianapolis: Hackett, 1993.

Large, Duncan. ""The translation of philosophical texts." In *The Routledge Handbook of Translation and Philosophy*, edited by Piers Rawling and Philip Wilson, 307-23. New York: Routledge, 2018. DOI: 10.4324/9781315678481.

Leal, Alice and Philip Wilson. "A Tale of Two Disciplines? Philosophy in/on Translation." *Perspectives* 31, no. 1 (2023): 1–15. DOIi:10.1080/0907676X.2023.2148984

Lee, Kyoo. *Reading Descartes Otherwise: Blind, Mad, Dreamy, and Bad*. New York: Fordham University Press, 2012.

Lefevere, André. "Mother Courage's Cucumbers: Text, System and Refraction in a Theory of Literature." *Modern Language Studies* 12, no. 4 (Autumn, 1982): 3-20. http://www.jstor.org/stable/3194526.

Lentz, Tony. *Orality and Literacy in Hellenic Greece*. Carbondale: Southern Illinois University Press, 1989.

Lesher, J. H., ed. and trans. *Xenophanes of Colophon: Fragments: A Text and Translation and Introduction*. Toronto: University of Toronto Press, 1992.

Lloyd-Jones, Kenneth. "The Tension of Philology and Philosophy in the Translations of Henri Estienne." *International Journal of the Classical Tradition* 1, no. 1 (Summer, 1994): 36-51. DOI: 10.1007/BF02679078.

Lombardo, Stanley, trans. *Hesiod: Works and Days & Theogony*. Indianapolis: Hackett, 1993.

---. *Homer: Odyssey*. Indianapolis: Hackett, 2000.

---. *Parmenides and Empedocles: The Fragments in Verse Translation*. San Francisco: Grey Fox Press, 1982.

Long, A. A. "Parmenides on Thinking Being." In *Proceedings of the Boston Area Colloquium in Ancient Philosophy*, vol. 3, edited by John J. Cleary and William Wians, 125-51. Lanham: University Press of America, 1998.

Lord, Albert B. *The Singer of Tales*. Cambridge, MA: Harvard University Press, 1960. Reprint, New York: Atheneum, 1973.

Macé, Arnaud. "Ordering the Universe in Speech: *Kosmos* and *Diakosmos* in Parmenides' Poem." In *Cosmos in the Ancient World*, edited by Phillip Sidney Horky, 42-61. Cambridge: Cambridge University Press, 2019.

Mackenzie, Tom. *Poetry and Poetics in the Presocratic Philosophers: Reading Xenophanes, Parmenides and Empedocles as Literature*. Cambridge: Cambridge University Press, 2021.

Malkin, Irad. *The Returns of Odysseus: Colonization and Ethnicity*. Berkeley: University of California Press, 1998.

Maly, Kenneth. "Echoes at the Edge: Shimmering Images in *Delimitations*." In Maly, *The Path of Archaic Thinking*, 121-32.

---. "Parmenides: Circle of Disclosure, Circle of Possibility." *Heidegger Studies* 1 (1985): 5-23.

---, ed. *The Path of Archaic Thinking: Unfolding the Work of John Sallis*. Albany: SUNY Press, 1995. EBSCOhost.

Mansfeld, Jaap. "Aristotle, Plato, and the Preplatonic Doxography and Chronography." In *Studies in the Historiography of Greek Philosophy*, 22-83. Assen/Maastricht, The Netherlands: Van Gorcum, 1990.

---. "Insight by Hindsight: Intentional Unclarity in Presocratic Proems." *Bulletin of the Institute of Classical Studies* 40 (January 1, 1995): 225–32.

Marciano, M. Laura Gemelli. "East and West." In *Ancient Philosophy: Textual Pathways and Historical Explorations*, edited by Lorenzo Perilli and Daniela P. Taormina, 1-40. London: Routledge, 2018.

---. "Images and Experience: At the Roots of Parmenides' *Aletheia*." *Ancient Philosophy* 28, no. 1 (2008): 21-48.

Melville, Herman. *Moby-Dick; or The Whale*. Norwalk, Connecticut: Easton Press, 1977. Originally published 1851.

Mikalson, Jon D. "Erechtheus and the Panathenaia." *American Journal of Philology* 97, no. 2 (Summer, 1976): 141-53. http://www.jstor.org/stable/294404.

Miranda, Elena. "Nuove iscrizioni sacre di Velia." *Mélanges de l'Ecole française de Rome, Antiquité* 94, no. 1 (1982): 163-74. DOI: 10.3406/mefr.1982.1319.

Mourelatos, Alexander D. P. *The Route of Parmenides: A Study of Word, Image, and Argument in the Fragments*. New Haven: Yale University Press, 1970.

Murray, Oswyn. "The Symposion as Social Organization." In Hägg, *The Greek Renaissance*, 195-9.

Mutschmann, Hermannus, ed. *Sexti Empirici opera*. Vol. II. Leipzig: Teubner, 1914. https://archive.org/details/sexti-empirici/mode/2up.

Naddaf, Gerard. "Allegory and the Origins of Philosophy." In *Logos and Muthos: Philosophical Essays in Greek Literature*, edited by William Robert Wians, 99-131. Albany: SUNY Press, 2009.

Nagy, Gregory. "Homer and The Evolution of a Homeric Text." Chap. 3 in *Homeric Questions*, 78-125. Austin: University of Texas Press, 1996.

---. "Oral traditions, texts, and authorship." In *The Greek Epic Cycle and Its Ancient Reception*, edited by Marco Fantuzzi and Christos Tsagalis, 59-77. Cambridge: Cambridge University Press, 2015.

---. *Poetry as Performance: Homer and Beyond*. Cambridge: Cambridge University Press, 1996.

Neils, Jennifer. "The Panathenaia: An Introduction." In *Goddess and Polis: The Panathenaic Festival in Ancient Athens*, edited by Jenifer Neils, 13-27. Hanover, NH: Hood Museum, Dartmouth College, 1992.

Nietzsche, Friedrich. *Die Philosophie im tragischen Zeitalter der Griechen*. In *Die Geburt der Tragödie und weitere Schriften zur griechischen Literatur und Philosophie*, edited by Bernhard Greiner, 152-224. Berlin: Alfred Kröner Verlag,

2014. Translated by Marianne Cowan as *Philosophy in the Tragic Age of the Greeks* (Washington, D. C.: Regnery, 1962).

Nightingale, Andrea Wilson. *Genres in Dialogue: Plato and the Construct of Philosophy.* Cambridge: Cambridge University Press, 1995. EBSCOhost.

---. "The philosophers in archaic Greek culture." In *The Cambridge Companion to Archaic Greece,* edited by H. A. Shapiro, 169-98. Cambridge: Cambridge University Press, 2007.rsity Press, 2000.

le Nourry, Nicolai, ed. *Clement of Alexandria, Stromata.* 2 vols. Paris: J.-P. Migne, 1857. https://books.google.de/books?id=QAgRAAAAYAAJ&hl=de&pg=PA1#v=onepage&q&f=false.

Olivelle, Patrick, trans. *Upaniṣads.* Oxford: Oxford University Press, 1996.

Palladino, Chiara, ed. The Text of *The Sketch of Geography* [Agathemeros]. http://www.digitalagathemerus.org/text.html. Last accessed March 6, 2023.

Pedley, John Griffiths. *Paestum: Greeks and Romans in Southern Italy.* London: Thames & Hudson, 1990.

Pelliccia, Hayden. "The Text of Parmenides B1.3 (D-K)." *The American Journal of Philology* 109, no. 4 (Winter, 1988): 507-12. http://www.jstor.org/stable/295076.

Privitello, Lucio Angelo. "Approaching the Parmenidean Sublime: A New Translation and Resequencing of the Fragments of Parmenides." *Epoché* 23, no. 1 (2018): 1-18.

---. "Approaching the Parmenidean Sublime—Part II." *Epoché* 25, no. 1 (2020): 101-34.

Rée, Jonathan. "The Translation of Philosophy." *New Literary History,* vol. 32 (2001): 223-57.

Robb, Kevin. *Literacy and Paideia in Ancient Greece.* New York: Oxford University Press, 1994.

Robinson, T. M., ed. and trans. *Heraclitus: Fragments: A Text and Translation with a Commentary.* Toronto: University of Toronto Press, 1987.

Sachs, Joe, trans. *Plato's Theaetetus.* Newburyport, MA: Focus, R. Pullins, 2004.

Sallis, John. "…A Wonder that One Could Never Aspire to Surpass." In Maly, *The Path of Archaic Thinking,* 243-74.

---. "Image and Phenomenon." *Research in Phenomenology* 5, no. 1 (1975): 61–75. https://www.jstor.org/stable/24654275.

---. *On Translation.* Bloomington: Indiana University Press, 2002.

Schleiermacher, Friedrich. "On the Different Methods of Translating." Translated by Douglas Robinson. In *Western Translation Theory: From Herodotus to Nietzsche,* edited by Douglas Robinson, 225-38. Manchester: St. Jerome, 2002.

Sedley, David. "Parmenides and Melissus." In *The Cambridge Companion to Early Greek Philosophy,* edited by A. A. Long, 113-33. Cambridge: Cambridge University Press, 1999.

Segal, Charles. "Spectator and Listener." In *The Greeks*, edited by Jean-Pierre Vernant, 184-217. Chicago: University of Chicago Press, 1995.

Shapiro, H. A. "Hipparchos and the Rhapsodes." In *Cultural Poetics in Archaic Greece: Cult, Performance, Politics*, edited by Carol Dougherty and Leslie Kurke, 92-107. Cambridge: Cambridge University Press, 1993.

Shaw, Michael M. "Aither and the Four Roots in Empedocles." *Research in Phenomenology* 44, no. 2 (2014): 170-93. www.jstor.org/stable/24659881.

Smith, P. Christopher. "Parmenides and Poetry: Taking Gadamer's Reading One Step Further." *Journal of the British Society for Phenomenology* 34, no. 3 (October, 2003): 265-80.

Snell, Bruno. "Die Nachrichten über die Lehren des Thales und die Anfänge der griechischen Philosophie- und Literaturgeschichte." *Philologus* 96 (1944): 170-82.

Solmsen, Friedrich, R. Merkelbach, M. L. West, eds. *Hesiodi Theogonia Opera et Dies Scutum Fragmenta Selecta*. 3rd ed. Oxford: Oxford University Press, 1970.

Sourvinou-Inwood, Christiane. "A trauma in flux: Death in the 8th century and after." In Hägg, *The Greek Renaissance*, 33-48.

Spitzer, D. M. "Archaic Images of Totality." In Spitzer, *Studies in Ancient Greek Philosophy*, 37-55.

---. "Being-in-touch: Touch, Contact, and Bodies in the Poem of Parmenides." *Epoché: A Journal for the History of Philosophy*, 29, no. 1 (2024): 1-22.

---. "Bordering Approaches & Trans-Bordering Themes in Dialogue with the Work of Rosemary Arrojo." Introduction to Spitzer and Oliveira, *Transfiction and Bordering Approaches to Theorizing Translation*, 1-17.

---. "Broken Light on the Ground of Home: Non-Being and Diasporic Trauma in the Parmenidean Poem." *Diacritics: A Review of Contemporary Criticism* 48, no. 1 (2020): 108-26. DOI: https://doi.org/10.1353/dia.2020.0004.

---. "Detours of Babel." In Spitzer and Oliveira, *Transfiction and Bordering Approaches to Theorizing Translation*, 79-93.

---. "Displacements: Poems of Trauma & Migration from Ancient Greek." *Ancient Exchanges* 1, no. 1 (2020). https://exchanges.uiowa.edu/ancient/issues/departures/displacements/.

---. "Divining: ΥΔΩΡ, Opacity, and Thalean Considerations." *Research in Phenomenology* 51, no. 3 (2021): 426-47. DOI: 10.1163/15691640-12341483.

---. "Figures of Motion, Figures of Being: On the Textualization of the Parmenidean Poem." *Ancient Philosophy* 40, no. 1 (2020): 1-18.

---. "Ghost in the kerameikos: Parmenides, Translation, and the Construction of Doctrine." *Labyrinth: An International Journal for Philosophy, Value Theory, and Cultural Hermeneutics* 21, no. 2 (Winter, 2019): 61-87. DOI: 10.25180/lj.v21i2.193.

---. "Images in Archaic Thinking." *Epoché: A Journal for the History of Philosophy* 26, no. 1 (fall, 2021): 1-19. DOI: 10.5840/epoche2021816198.
---. "Introduction: philosophy's treason." In Spitzer, *Philosophy's Treason*, v-xxix.
---. "Past the Fire's Edge: Figures of Translation from Herodotos 1.86." *Translation Review* 99, no. 1 (November, 2017): 15-25.
---. "SAGP: Studies and Society." Introduction to Spitzer, *Studies in Ancient Greek Philosophy*, 1-17.
---. "Trans-philosophy: Translating philosophy on & beyond the boundaries." *The Journal of Speculative Philosophy* 37, no. 3 (2023): 564-83. DOI: 10.5325/jspecphil.37.4.0564.
---, ed. *Philosophy's Treason: Studies in Philosophy and Translation*. Wilmington, DE: Vernon Press, 2020.
---, ed. *Studies in Ancient Greek Philosophy in Honor of Professor Anthony Preus*. New York: Routledge, 2023.
--- and Paulo Oliveira, eds. *Transfiction and Bordering Approaches to Theorizing Translation: Essays in Translation Studies in Dialogue with the Work of Rosemary Arrojo*. New York: Routledge, 2023.
Stehle, Eva. *Performance and Gender in Ancient Greece*. Princeton: Princeton University Press, 1997.
Stephanus, Henricus, ed. *ΠΟΙΗΣΙΣ ΦΙΛΟΣΟΦΟΣ: Poesis Philosophica*. np. 1573. https://archive.org/details/bub_gb_2FubCxGs7jMC/page/n223/mode/2up.
--- and Gentianus Hervetus Aurelius, eds. and trans. *Sexti Empirici: Opera quae extant*. Geneva: Petrus and Jacob Chouët, 1621. https://archive.org/details/bub_gb_duVWlm_RcoIC/mode/1up.
Stuhr, John J. "Lost, Looking Around, and Looking Ahead." *The Journal of Speculative Philosophy* 32, no. 1 (2018): 35–49. 10.5325/jspecphil.32.1.0035.
Tarán, Leonardo, ed. and trans. *Parmenides: A Text with Translation, Commentary, and Critical Essays*. Princeton: Princeton University Press, 1965.
Tell, Håkan. "Sages at the Games: Intellectual Displays and Dissemination of Wisdom in Ancient Greece." *Classical antiquity* 26, no. 2 (2007): 249–75. https://www.jstor.org/stable/10.1525/ca.2007.26.2.249.
Thomas, Rosalind. *Literacy and Orality in Ancient Greece*. Cambridge: Cambridge University Press, 1992.
Valentine, Joanna. "The Archaeology of Parmenides: Philosophy, Poetry and Ritual in Fifth-Century Campania." PhD. diss., University of Southern California, 2011. ProQuest.
Venuti, Lawrence. *The Scandals of Translation: Towards an Ethics of Difference*. New York: Routledge, 1998.
---, ed. *The Translation Studies Reader*. 3rd ed. New York: Routledge, 2012.

---. "Invisibility." Chap. 1 in *The Translator's Invisibility*. New York: Routledge, 1995.
Verdenius, W. J. *Parmenides: Some Comments on his Poem*. Amsterdam: Adolf M. Hakkert, 1964.
West, M. L. *Early Greek Philosophy and the Orient*. Oxford: Oxford University Press, 1971.
---, ed. *Iambi et Elegi Graeci: ante Alexandrum Cantati: Vol. 1: Archilochus, Hipponax, Theognidea*. Oxford: Oxford University Press, 1971.
Whitaker, Albert Keith, trans. *Plato's Parmenides*. Newburysport, MA: Focus, 1996.
Wians, William. "From *Logos* and *Muthos* to…" Introduction to *Logoi and Muthoi: Further Essays in Greek Philosophy and Literature*, ed. William Robert Wians, 10-17. Albany: SUNY Press, 2019. EBSCOhost.
Wilamowitz-Möllendorff, Ulrich. "Lesefrüchte." *Hermes* 34, H 2 (1899): 203-30. http://www.jstor.org/stable/4472686.
Wilkinson, Lisa Atwood. *Parmenides and To Eon Reconsidering Muthos and Logos*. New York: Continuum, 2009.
Wright, M. R. *The Presocratics: The Main Fragments in Greek*. London: Bristol Classical Press, 1985.
Wyke, Ben Van. "Imitating Bodies and Clothes: Refashioning the Western Conception of Translation." In *Thinking Through Translation with Metaphors*, edited by James St. André, 17-46. Manchester: St. Jerome, 2010.

Index

A
ἀήρ [*aer*] 23, 28-29
αἰθήρ [*aither*] 28-29
Akhilleus 32-33, 51, 112
ἀλήθεια [*aletheia*] 5, 21 with notes, 22-23, 53, 110-111, 128
already-there 13, 18, 25, 28, 59, 107-108, 110, 112, 130, 132
ἀνάγκη [*ananke*] 33-34, 36-37, 42, 48-49
Anaximandros 1, 16-18, 26
Anaximenes 16-18
ἄπειρον [*apeiron*: translated as open-expanse] 18-19, 35
   in Anaximandros 23, 26, 33, 35
   in Melissos 34-37
   in Zenon 33-34
Apollo 1-2, 16
ἀρχή [*arkhe*] 18, 36, 47-48, 128
Athene 41 with n106, 62n175, 73-74, 112
Athens 38, 40-42
   kerameikos 40-41
   Panathenaia 41
Aristoteles 113
   Parmenidean poem 47-48, 50
   translational action 2, 47-52, 59-60, 66n195
   Zenoan paradoxes 50-51
αὐτό [*auto*] 2-3, 27, 34, 44-45, 111

B
beginning 6-7, 16-19, 32-33, 37-38, 51n141, 61-63, 112, 129-130, 133
being [τὸ ἐόν] 12
   as differing 37
   as emerging 36 with n89, 69, 74-75, 78
   intralingual translation 75-78
   Parmenidean doctrine of 53-54
   and touch 48
   as untranslatable 36-37
   in Zenoan thinking 32-34
boundaries *see* limits

C
chaos *see* Khaos [τὸ Χάος]
chariot 25-26, 28, 42, 62-63 with n180, 71-72, 79, 110, 113
composition 61, 63, 69-72, 78-79, 84-85
   see also performance, writing
content 54, 57-58, 67, 68
   see also form, translation
crossings 111, 114-115, 118-119, 120, 127
   see also transgression, translation
Cup of Nestor 64

D
daimon [δαίμων] 27, 80-82, 109-112, 114, 115-116, 118-121
dialectics 18, 40, 42-43, 54-56

see also Hegel, G. W. F.
diaspora 2, 42, 61-62, 64, 98, 118 with n338
Diels, Hermann 66-67, 80-81, 83, 130
Δίκη [Dike] 76-77, 111
doctrine *see* Parmenides
δόξα [doxa] 23n64, 52-53 with n147, 56-57, 66-67, 116
see also meaning

E
echoes 19, 40-41, 43, 60, 62-63, 67, 90, 111, 122
editing 65-66, 80-84
ek-stasis 72-73, 78, 113-116, 123-124
elements 13, 23-29, 31, 51, 52
see also Milesians, translation
Empedokles 10, 27-31, 38, 120-121, 132-133
Ἔρος [Eros] 27, 42, 118-119, 120, 121, 123-124
Estienne, Henri *see* Stephanus
experience 18-19, 23, 35, 76-78, 114

F
figures
  characters 3 n4, 26, 38-44, 51, 62, 120
  poetic 10-11, 14, 16, 26, 32, 47-48, 51, 54, 57, 59, 69-70, 75, 78-79, 91, 97, 105, 110, 116, 128-129, 135
  of translation 133, 135
  see also images
fire 17, 26, 27-32, 37-38, 51-53, 59, 90, 94, 98, 100, 128, 130-131, *see also* Night [Νύξ]
foreign 7, 14 with n33, 27, 39-40, 48-49, 76, 114, 131-132, 133
form
  εἶδος-ἰδέα [eidos-idea] 43n109, 46, 72, 118, 127-128
  poetic 15, 23n62, 57-58, 66-68, 107-108 (sequence), 117 (chiastic)

verbal 75, 80-81, 109-110 n315, 117 n336
see also content, textualization, translation
fragmentation 107-109

G
gates 10, 26, 40-41, 78-79, 89-90, 110-111, 114, 120, 121-122
Gorgias *see* Sophist compendia

H
haptics 121-123
Hegel, G. W. F. 54-56
Heliades [Ἡλιάδες] 3, 26, 28, 63, 81, 110-111, 113, 114
Helios 62-63
Hephaistos 31, 38-39
Herakleitos 5-6, 39, 44n112, 114, 130-131, 133
Hesiod *Theogony* 16, 19-21, 22, 25, 32, 47-48 and n126, 62, 121-122, 131-132 with n373
hexameter 23n62, 24 and n65, 44n113, 50
  tradition 23-31, 32-33, 37-38, 61-64,
  Milesians 15-16, 19-20
  movement 69-70
  performance 70-76, 87
  and philosophy 54-55, 58, 67
  see also Hesiod, Homer, singing, writing
Hippias *see* sophist compendia
Homer
  Iliad 16, 20, 38n95, 62, 63, 72, 112
  Odyssey 62n175, 122-123
horses 26n72, 41-43, 62-63, 72-73, 113, 119-120
ὕδωρ [hydor, water] 16, 18, 23-24, 26, 28-29 and nn.78-79, 33, 51-52, 102, 127, 130-131, 132n73

I

Ibykos 41-43
identity 20-21, 23, 29, 31, 68, 95-97, 123, 129
  first-person 72-73, 113-116
  fixed 16-17, 36-37, 69
  repetition (Cassin) 27, 34
  same 46-47
  see also αὐτό [auto], Ἔρος [Eros]
images 14, 16-18, 32-34, 40-44, 50-51, 54, 55, 59, 69-72, 87-88, 91, 114-115, 128-129
interpretation see editing, translation

K

Kalliopeia 28-29
kerameikos see Athens
Khaos [τὸ Χάος] 16-17, 22, 62
Khronos-Kronos 22n59, 36
  see also temporality
kouros [κοῦρος] 3, 25, 83, 115, 123

L

language 35, 111-113, 115
light 16-17, 89-93, 97
  disclosure 21-22 and n56
  κλέος 20n51,
  Parmenides 10-11, 26-27, 62, 110, 113-114, 116-117
  speaking 23, 28
  see also upsurge
limits 33-34, 36
  disciplinary 6-7, 8, 9-10, 38 with n96, 88, 130-131, 134-135
  theme in Parmenidean poem 10, 95, 114-119
  and memory 19-21
  and translation 128
  see also crossings
listening 7, 20-23, 30, 68, 74-78

literacy see reading
logos [λόγος, λέγειν] 77-78, 113-114, 116, 127-128

M

meaning 18-19, 51-52, 116-117, 120
  see also δόξα
  see also translation
Melissos 32, 34-37, 39, 55
metaphysics 36-38, 46, 72, 116-118, 127-128, 131
  see also translation
Milesians 15-19, 23
mimesis 49, 112, 123-124
Mimnermos 22, 62-63
Mnemosyne [Μνημοσύνη] 19-25, 35, 48, 51, 61, 64, 130
  see also already-there
motion 51, 70, 74-75, 76, 114-115, 118
Mousa(i) 19-22, 25, 28, 59, 130, 131, 132
multiplicity 26, 29-30, 33-34, 35, 38, 84-85, 86-87, 107, 117, 135
  see also ἄπειρον

N

nature see upsurge-withdrawal [φύσις]
Nietzsche, Friedrich 19, 23, 56-57
Night [Νύξ] 16, 26-27, 40-41, 62 with notes, 89-90, 98-100, 110, 116-117, 120-122, 127
νοῦς/νοεῖν [nous/noein] 25 with n67, 35-36, 62n179, 75-78, 110-112
number 26, 33-36
  see also ἄπειρον, multiplicity

O

object 55-56, 86, 89-90, 111-114
opacity 23, 27, 33-34, 98-99
oralcy 12-13, 61, 63, 67-68, 70-73, 75-76, 84-86, 88, 109, 124-125

153

P

Parmenides 1-7, 39-40, 56, 66-67
   doctrine 43-44, 47-48, 52-59, 68-69, 80-84
   tensions 50, 52-53, 60, 69-70, 71-72, 74-79, 85-86, 88, 117
   text of 65-68
   totality in 53, 79-80, 117-118
   see also being [τὸ ἐόν], hexameter, singing
pathways 91
   habitual 18-19
   κελεύθος 26, 110-112, 117-118
   multiple 1, 7-12, 14, 61-64, 87-88, 106-107, 129-135
   two 38-39, 53, 127
perception 24-25 with notes, 97, 121-123 with notes
   see also νοῦς/νοεῖν
performance 72-79, 84-88
   contexts 70-71
   see also hexameter, symposion, variants
Pherekydes 22n59, 36
philosophy
   formation 17-18, 38, 38n96, 43, 52
   translational protocol 15, 43, 45-49, 51-59, 124-125
Phokylides 62
φύσις [physis] see upsurge-withdrawal
Platon 38
   Ion 73-74
   Parmenides 39-44
   Phaidros 114
   Symposion 118-119
   Theaitetos 44-46
   and translation 39-47, 50-51, 59-60
plurality 23, 34-36, 87, 133-134
   see also identity, multiplicity, unity
poetry 16, 32, 43, 67, 85-86, 88, 112

prose 32-34, 37, 43-45, 61, 67
Protagoras see sophist compendia
Pythagoras 5-6, 25-26, 31n84

R

reading 10-13, 20, 40, 64, 69, 72-80, 117, 124
repetition 9, 18-19, 27, 30-31 with n85, 33-34, 37-38, 47-51, 52, 75-76, 84-86, 111, 119, 121, 124-125, 128
   see also translation
rhizomes 11-12, 28-31, 106-107

S

same see αὐτό
Sextos Empirikos 2, 4-5, 54, 76n241, 81, 82n266, 83, 122n346
silence 25-26, 44, 62n177, 94, 109-110, 113, 118
simile 5, 16-18, 27, 32, 37, 62, 79, 94, 112, 121
Simplikios 2, 16, 29n79, 34, 51, 54, 65, 67
singing 1, 12-13, 16, 23-24, 31-33, 38-39, 45, 50, 52-53, 59, 61-64, 79, 109, 128-130
Sokrates 2-3, 38, 43n109, 45-47, 50-51, 74, 114, 118
   see also Platon
Solon 22
sophist compendia 39, 47
stasis 53, 56, 68-75, 78-79
Stephanus (aka Henri Estienne) 54, 65-66, 81, 82n266
subject 56, 72-73
symposion 63-64

T

temporality 20-21, 36, 93-95, 115, 132-133
textualization 65-66, 68-69, 72
Thales 16-18, 23, 26n73, 32-33, 57

INDEX

Thea [Θεά] 14, 25-26, 32-34, 41n106, 48-49, 57-58, 72-78, 82-87, 111-113, 116, 121-123
Theognidea 63
Thestorides 62
thinking 2-3, 6-7, 10-11, 13, 18-20, 22-23, 37-38, 110-115, 129-130, 134-135, *see also* hexameter, simile, singing, translation
touch *see* haptics
transfiction 9-10
translational actions 9, 13, 16-18, 20-21, 25, 35-38, 43-52, 56-57, 59-60, 118-119
translative gestures 9-10, 24-25, 26, 28, 39-43, 128
translation
    archaeologics 11-12, 106-109, 123
    classical determination (Sallis) 18, 37, 44, 47, 50, 59, 127
    daimonologics 109-118
    differing 33, 35-36, 38, 49-50, 111, 119
    elemental 15, 24-25, 27, 28-29, 31, 37-38, 50-52, 127
    erotics 118-124
    essentialism 46-47
    experience 18-19, 23, 35, 38, 111-112
    interlingual 8-9, 18, 128
    intralingual 9, 18 with n44, 49, 78
    mimesis 123-124, 125
    reductive 47, 48, 50, 57-59, 68
    relation 35, 106, 119, 127-128
    trans-discipline 129
    violence 36n90, 39-40, 91, 131

transmission 2, 15, 29n79, 31n84, 32, 52-53, 65, 127
    see also hexameter
transmodal 18 with n44, 124-125
transphiliation 129-134
trans-philosophy 6-7, 128-135

U

unity 33-35, 50-53, 57, 60, 66, 79-80, 84, 86, 124-125
untranslatability 28-29, 35-36
upsurge-withdrawal [φύσις] 16-17 with n36, 24, 47, 53, 62-63 with n179, 66n195, 78, 115-116, 121n345

V

variation 19, 31n85, 45 and n115, 88, 124-125
    see also repetition
variants 79n252, 80-85
vox universalis 65-66

W

writing 12-13, 17, 64, 67-68, 70-74, 84

X

Xenophanes 1, 4, 6, 19, 23-25, 26, 31-33, 48, 54-55, 70

Z

Zenon 2-3, 7, 15, 32-34, 39-40, 55-56
Zeus 16, 22, 28 with n78, 41n106, 131-132